KENNETH WILLIAMS on PLEASURE BENT

D1186580

* KENNETH WILLI...

* * CABARET

KENNETH WILLIAMS Starring

KENNETH WILLIAMS
****

With His Regular Guests

CANTABILE
****

And His Special Guests

LOIS LANE
****

PETER GOODWRIGHT
****

And With Music Provided By

THE BURT RHODES ORCHESTRA
****

Produced By

JONATHAN JAMES-MOORE

Saturday, 11th December 1982, The Part...
Kenneth Williams, 1430; Cantabile, 1...
Lois Lane, 1630; Peter Godbwright, 17...

Saturday, 11th December, The Paris Stu...

(SLN50)LLG366M799

RECORDING:

R.P.REF.NO.:

TRANSMISSION

Kenneth Williams Unseen

WES BUTTERS &
RUSSELL DAVIES

Kenneth Williams Unseen

THE PRIVATE NOTES, SCRIPTS AND PHOTOGRAPHS

HarperCollins*Publishers*

HarperCollins*Publishers*
77–85 Fulham Palace Road,
Hammersmith, London W6 8JB

www.harpercollins.co.uk

First published by HarperCollins*Publishers* 2008

10 9 8 7 6 5 4 3 2 1

With thanks also to the Written Archives Centre at Caversham

ISBN-13 978-0-00-728085-8
ISBN-10 0-00-728085-8

Printed and bound in China
by Leo Paper Products Ltd

Contents

Acknowledgements

For two decades Kenneth's circle of friends have remembered their mutual friend in private, respectfully recognizing that that's the way Kenneth would have wanted it. Why then should they confess all to me? 'Because Kenneth would have liked you,' Michael Whittaker tells me. And it is Michael whom I must acknowledge first. I can see why Kenneth viewed him as 'best of people and best of my friends.' Indeed, the other three beneficiaries of Kenneth's will, Michael Anderson, Robert Chidell and Paul Richardson, have been exceptionally helpful in revealing the untold story.

So have Stanley Baxter, Gyles Brandreth, Richard Bryan, Angela and Isabel Chidell, Norman Hudis and Dr Christopher Pease.

For more unseen images, my thanks go to Nick Lewis, Peter Cadley, Helen Craig, Howard Imber Vivienne Roberts and Robert Ross.

I am grateful to the contributions given by Janet Brown, Fenella Fielding, Sarah Greene, John Harding, Ted Robbins, Mike Walsh and Barbara Windsor. Thanks also to their agents and assistants: Alison Brown, Dianne Edwards, Kevin Francis, Will Francis, Polly Imber and Scott Mitchell.

As this is my first book I would like to pay tribute to the expert guidance of my editor Natalie Jerome, designer Colin Hall and agent Nick Canham.

I dedicate this to my daughter Maisie, whose infectious fun and laughter are comparable to any of the *Carry On* films.

Wes Butters

It's a well-known fact of broadcasting life that only a fraction of what is collected in interviews ever meets the ear of a listener or viewer. The voluminous offcuts are either filed away in the vaults, or junked immediately. This was emphatically the case with Radio 4's 1994 profile of Kenneth Williams, 'I Am Your Actual Quality', which I wrote and compiled with the help of producer Simon Elmes, now Creative Director, Features and Documentaries. I thank Simon for his encouragement, both then and now. I am also very grateful to Vicky Mitchell of the BBC Commercial Agency for clearance to use words collected for a BBC copyright transmission. I believe I hold the only complete set of raw interview tapes, which I have now offered to the BBC Sound Archive for their safe keeping. In the case of Pat Williams, Kenneth's sister, the tape represents a unique record of her memories. Most of the participants in our programme are now sadly deceased, but to the happy survivors – Sir Clement Freud, Peter Rogers, Richard Pearson, Bill Pertwee and Jeremy Swan – I offer thanks for permission to perpetuate their insights.

The BBC's Written Archive at Caversham is an invaluable resource and a haven of academic calm, and not for the first time I thank Jeff Walden, the redoubtable Archives Researcher, for his guidance there. It's my belief that the role of BBC work in sustaining Kenneth Williams's long freelance career has been under-appreciated, and I hope that a peek into his dealings with producers and Heads of Department will help to emphasize that point. As far as I know, the BBC staff members quoted are no longer alive, the last to leave us being the admirable producer and network Controller, Sir David Hatch. I'm indebted to two living veterans of the Light Entertainment Department (alias 'Comedy Corridor'), Pete Atkin and Richard Edis, for their impressions of Kenneth at work, and similarly to two departed stalwarts of the same unit, Richard Willcox and (former Head of Light Entertainment) Jonathan James-Moore.

I wish I could say that the e-mail revolution has transformed me, a typical procrastinator, into a paragon of promptitude, but it hasn't. Special thanks are therefore due to Natalie Jerome, our editor at HarperCollins, and to Kate Latham. It's also a pleasure to salute my agent and old friend Pat Kavanagh.

At home, meanwhile, I must apologize to my three small sons, Joe, Matt and Olly, for the somewhat truncated bedtime stories they have suffered of late. To their mother, Emma, my thanks for everything else.

Russell Davies

Cast of Characters

Michael Anderson (b. 1929) One of the four beneficiaries of Kenneth Williams's will, Michael became Kenneth's agent (at ICM) in 1980, shortly after the death of his initial representative, Peter Eade.

Gyles Brandreth (b. 1948) The prolific author and former Conservative MP for Chester (1992–7) worked closely with Kenneth on his literary productions. Uniquely among Kenneth's friends, he has blamed himself publicly for 'giving up' on Ken, deterred by his difficult behaviour in the last years.

Peter Cadley (b. 1965) He was a young employee of Michael Whittaker's when a casual remark, mentioning his admiration for the *Carry On* films, led to a surprise dinner for him to meet his hero. He maintained close friendships with both Pat and Louie after Kenneth's death.

Angela Chidell (b. 1941) The mother of Robert Chidell was a piano teacher in North London. She suggested Kenneth Williams as her son's godfather because of their long-standing family connection.

Isabel Chidell (b. 1918) The paternal grandmother of Robert Chidell is the sister of the actor John Vere, the man who, Kenneth said, 'taught me all I know about comedy'.

Robert Chidell (b. 1975) Kenneth's godson became front-page news at the age of 12 after inheriting 50 per cent of Kenneth's belongings plus £30,000. An aspiring musician, he lives in the West Country with his wife and baby son.

Isabel Dean (1918–97) A dignified and beautiful actress, very popular in her profession, she was snubbed by the major West End manager-producer of her day, and never enjoyed the career she deserved. She was one of several women invited to consider the possibility of living with Kenneth Williams.

Sir Clement Freud (b. 1924) Grandson of Sigmund Freud, the former Liberal MP for the Isle of Ely (1973–87) was a fellow panellist on Radio 4's *Just a Minute* throughout Kenneth's involvement in the show.

John Harding (b. 1948) After reading glowing press accounts of his play, *For Sylvia*, in Edinburgh, Michael Codron cast him in *My Fat Friend*. It was his first West End engagement and was mired by another of Kenneth's insecure walk-outs that, at the time, he cited as 'health reasons'.

Sir David Hatch (1939–2007) Successful as a Cambridge Footlights revue member in the Cleese generation, he became a radio comedy producer, originating *Just a Minute*, then successively Head of Light Entertainment (Radio), Controller of Radio 2 and Controller of Radio 4. He took over as Managing Director (Radio) but was out of place in the John Birt era. He ended his career as Chairman of the National Consumer Council, then finally Chairman of the Parole Board.

Norman Hudis (b. 1923) The forgotten man of the *Carry On* tradition wrote the first six films in the series. Moving to America, he wrote for *Cannon*, *Hawaii Five-O* and *The Man from U.N.C.L.E.*

Nick Lewis (b. 1966) As a Warwick University undergraduate, he struck up a correspondence with Kenneth Williams in the late 1980s. They met just once: at Joe Allen, eight weeks before Kenneth's death.

Betty Marsden (1919–98) The ripe-voiced actress shared both the microphone and the stage with Kenneth in *Round the Horne*, *Beyond Our Ken* and *Cinderella*. She also appeared in two of the *Carry On* films. She lived in an elegant houseboat in Isleworth.

Eric Merriman (1924–2003) The prolific scriptwriter created *Beyond Our Ken* with Barry Took, and after Took's departure wrote it alone. He went into television and co-wrote, for example, several series of the celebrated sitcom *Terry and June*.

Derek Nimmo (1930–99) Chiefly famous for his comic-cleric roles on TV, he was a long-term fellow panellist on *Just a Minute*, and most active late in life as a theatrical impresario, organizing worldwide tours. He died after a fall downstairs at his home.

Richard Pearson (b. 1918) A character actor with a wonderful career in meek and understated roles, he shared with Kenneth and Maggie Smith the success of *The Private Ear* and *The Public Eye*. His family became a domestic refuge for KW.

Bill Pertwee (b. 1926) The surviving doyen of *Dad's Army* (as Warden Hodges), he had been the bits-and-pieces man in the casts of *Round the Horne* and *Beyond Our Ken*. He also participated in three *Carry On* films.

Paul Richardson (b. 1944) Kenneth's friend and neighbour at Marlborough House for sixteen years, he was left 50 per cent of KW's belongings, including his diaries and letters. He is currently Technical Director of Sadler's Wells.

Peter Rogers (b. 1914) The producer of the *Carry On* films, who entered the film industry as a writer of religious subjects for the Rank Organisation, still works at the Pinewood Studios.

Jeremy Swan His vast list of credits in children's programming include *Jackanory* and *Rentaghost*, of which Christopher Biggins has said: 'It was all due to the most brilliant director-producer – a mad Irishman called Jeremy Swan, and it was he who instigated all the completely insane stuff like the pantomime horse. We used to cry with laughter.'

Barry Took (1928–2002) Best known to the public as a quiz chairman and TV presenter, Took had collaborated with Merriman on the first seasons of *Beyond Our Ken*, and then co-wrote *Round the Horne* with Marty Feldman. He later employed Kenneth as a voice-over artist.

Michael Whittaker (b. 1938) A businessman – unusually in Kenneth's circle – he is acknowledged in the diaries as 'best of people and best of my friends' because of his unfaltering loyalty and kindness in caring for Kenneth and Louie.

Louie Williams (1901–91) Kenneth's mother and greatest fan was seemingly ever-present at his recordings, particularly in radio. She had given birth to Ken at 11 Bingfield Street, Islington, off the Caledonian Road, close to what is now the 'Cally' swimming pool.

Pat Williams (d. 1994) Kenneth's sister – the full circumstances of her birth, could not be revealed during her lifetime. The allusion Kenneth made to the matter in his diaries did not appear in the published version.

Dennis Main Wilson (1924–97) The *screenonline* website, developed by the British Film Institute, describes the producer of *Hancock's Half Hour* as 'arguably the most important and influential of all comedy producers/directors in British radio and television'. He was responsible for getting *The Goon Show* on the air.

Barbara Windsor MBE (b. 1937) Even though it feels like it should be more, she appeared in only nine *Carry On* films, most notably in *Carry On Camping* where her defective bra and Kenneth's immortal line 'Matron, take them away!' has proved the most used clip of the entire series.

Introduction
by Russell Davies

❛ On boarding the plane I was stuck next to this woman who asked: "They all call you Mister Williams … are you famous? Should I know you?" I told her "No – I'm nobody dear … just got a yard and a half in Who's Who, that's all" ❜

Diary, 13 April 1983

Kenneth, 1986.

It is possible that we already know, or think we know, more about Kenneth Williams than we've ever learned about any previous British actor, classical or comical. Yet there is much more to be known, as this book will show. The public appetite for intimate details of his life, which has not diminished in the twenty years since his death, was created by him. Williams knew that his was a most unusual, possibly unique, personality type, and the glimpses he publicly offered of himself – those half-hinted confessions and protestations of celibacy – were not simply made as teases to keep his public interested. He himself wanted to know, I think, how people would regard him if they came to know more of the truth of who he was. To that end he would sneak out fragments of his authentic self. An opportunity was lost in his autobiography, *Just Williams*, the kind of carefully judged performance that could have been read on Radio 4 without expurgation. A franker book might have helped him, and us.

As Kenneth was aware, the world from which he disappeared in 1988 was already changing quickly. But he had never been ashamed of his own retro tastes – the Victorian poetry, the music from Buxtehude to Fauré but not much further – and with his health restored he might have found the energy to convince an increasingly shallow public of the worth of his ruminative pursuits. As an 82 year old in 2008, he could have held his place in the media firmament alongside surviving contemporaries like Sir David Attenborough and David Jacobs, his fellow-broadcasters, and his old friend Stanley Baxter, all born in 1926. (Indeed, Kenneth was almost exactly two months older than Her Majesty the Queen.)

Parts of his comedy world ought by now to be in ruins. The *Carry On* tradition was insular even in its own day, laden with funny foreigners and semi-inflatable, perpetually shocked, seaside-postcard women. But we've heard so much about the cast members and their off-screen interactions (which have even been dramatized in a National Theatre play, Terry Johnson's *Cleo, Camping, Emmanuelle and*

'I didn't like the King's Cross world: it was grimy and dirty and I always envisioned myself in much more romantic and grand surroundings. I thought I was somebody posh. I never really thought that I belonged to the working-class area at all.'
(Kenneth, **Comic Roots**, 1983)

Kenneth, early 1930s, Manchester Street Infants School, first row, second from left.

Dick) that we now read the on-screen narrative twice as it goes along: once in its own silly terms, and once in terms of the ways the actors are surviving the material, and in some cases one another. By contrast, the campery of the Kenneth Horne radio performances seems almost uncorroded, and has lately become a mainstay of BBC7, the digital-radio archival network. And though the parlour game *Just a Minute* has now been running longer without Williams than with him, one can still hear younger panellists putting into practice the lessons he taught, under the guidance of David Hatch, about playing the game 'outrageously'. The extent to which his career relied on the continuity of BBC work has perhaps been underestimated before, but it is thoroughly explored in these pages.

This book began, in a sense, at the end, with the death of Kenneth Williams, so it's with that topic that we do begin. In my view, his death itself is not very mysterious – for debatability it's not in the class of, say, Robert Maxwell's demise – yet it does continue to be debated. Kenneth was much loved, in both a show business and a personal sense. Many of his friends and fans will forever argue hotly against the notion of his suicide, and in favour of misadventure. Meanwhile the open verdict which the Coroner actually returned stands as a perpetual invitation to reconsider the case.

But some important opinions have never been heard. Neither in 1988, nor in 1993 when my selection from his diaries was published, was any comment made by the friends named in Kenneth's will: his agent, Michael Anderson; his companion on cultural travels, the businessman Michael Whittaker; his neighbour, Paul Richardson; or his godson, Robert Chidell. The world knew nothing of these gentlemen at the time, and they very reasonably preferred to keep it that way. Now, thanks to the persuasion of Wes Butters, they have spoken, enabling us to present the fullest picture of the circumstances of Kenneth's death that posterity can hope for. It seemed unlikely that the pathologist employed on the case would add much detail to that picture, especially as he now works in New Zealand; but again, Wes's initiative prevailed, and Dr Pease has contributed a remarkably vivid account of his involvement.

To understand the participation of the Chidell family in Kenneth's life, it's necessary to know something of the history of the actor John Vere, a friend of his from the 1950s and a fellow cast-member of Tony Hancock's TV show. Robert Chidell is John Vere's great-nephew, though John had been dead fifteen years

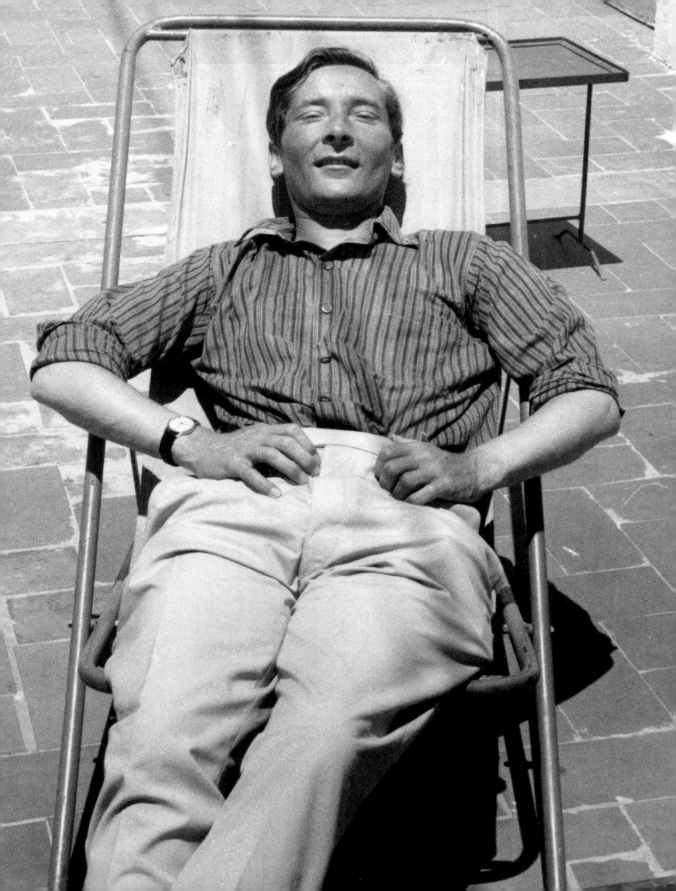

by the time Robert was born. Vere committed suicide in 1961, at the age of only 45 (he 'played older', as they say in the profession). Although Kenneth found him cranky and annoying towards the end, in kinder times he'd been fond of Vere's gentle presence. Isobel Chidell, Vere's sister, tells his story, which runs as a kind of forecast of Kenneth's; though Vere enjoyed a much more aristocratic professional grounding. Vere's story stands for several others that were played out on the borders of Kenneth's life: actors, directors and writers who started out with the same bright hopes, and gradually settled (or not) for something well short of stardom.

One family figure in the story who has remained seriously under-illuminated has been Kenneth's sister, Pat. She, like Ken, was regarded with some wonderment by those who met her socially, chiefly on account of her unforgettable voice, a growling cigarette-fuelled basso that was very nearly male. At the time of the diaries' publication Pat was still alive, and it would not have been fair to tell her full story, as revealed in one of the early diary volumes. The fact that Charlie Williams was not her real father explained much of the tension between daughter and Dad, and indeed between Pat and Kenneth. For the same reasons of tact, the subject was not raised, either, when Pat's only sound interview was recorded, in 1995, for my Radio 4 programme *I Am Your Actual Quality*, in the series *Radio Lives*.

Even so, the interview, which was conducted by the BBC producer Simon Elmes, proved to be of the greatest possible interest, both as a portrait of the otherwise unknown Pat and as an evocation of the Williams family's home life. By some mischance the BBC Sound Archive had lost their copy of this unique testimony, but I was relieved to find that my own archive had retained it, and I have since taken the opportunity to restore to the Archive's shelves one of the more amazing voices to be found there. Pat Williams was already enduring her final illness when she gave her interview, and several others who recorded their impressions at that time have also left us: Isabel Dean, Betty Marsden, Derek Nimmo, Dennis Main Wilson, Barry Took and Eric Merriman. Only fragments of their testimony appeared in the original programme, and I am grateful to the BBC for allowing them to speak now at length, if only on the printed page. A brief outline of their careers and preoccupations is given in the 'Cast of Characters' listing.

Kenneth Williams kept his memorabilia neatly filed and classified. Had he put together his own scrapbook of his life, much of it would have looked very like the book you are holding. Taken together with the sound of his voice, which is still so readily and multifariously available, these pages bring him as nearly back to life as we can manage. We hope he would have understood our desire – even need – to do so.

'Went to Liverpool St where I met Johnny Morris. At the Swan Hotel at Southwold, we met Percy Edwards and Roger (sound) and Vanessa (producer) and we were told that we would all meet at 4 o'c. tomorrow morning to drive to a spot where we'd hear the dawn chorus. It's absurd to journey all this way to ad lib a few daft comments, eat a lot of unnecessary food, get constipation and tongue ulcers ... for what? About fifty quid, at the end of the day! And probably 25 after tax.' **(Diary, 20 May 1982)**

...ch and lonely voice

KENNETH Williams has
died at the age of 62.
With his nasal, quickfire
voice which swooped
articulated emphases
words, those flared
and eyebrows rising
to mark another of
double entendres, he
of the most distin-
st-war British come-
ough he graduated
revues with a
nley Baxter to a
ar of 22 Carry On
st End stage and
liams essentially
eries of elegant
n a single comic

s the personifi-
of homosexual
lised in suave
e verbal leer
now be termed

orn into the
ut never, he
felt himself
cuts above
le his Lon-
ly in Peter
eth Tynan
nd young

Kenneth Williams . . . variations on a single comic theme

reaching its last phase of popu-
larity. Although he act
tably in straight

fearful of going abroad and of
inviting friends home for fear
that they would have need to
put their bottoms upon his lava-
tory seats. Sexual contact was,
he believed, the sure route to
germs and disease.

Joe Orton, the playwright, a
close friend of Williams, observed his loneliness and commented in his diaries: "His only
outlet is exhibiting his extremely funny personality in
front of an audience and when
he isn't doing this he's a very
sad man indeed."

Nicholas de Jongh

*Kenneth Williams, born
February 22 1926. Died April 15.*

Kenneth Williams: image of a somewhat soiled garden pixie

By Hugh Montgomery-Massingberd

Jennie Linden in My Fat Friend   In Christmas show   In Carry On, Cleo   In Carry On, Dick   With co-star in Follow...

KENNETH WILLIAMS, the
who has died aged 62,
an extraordinarily origi-
and inventive enter-
er, whose range of hilar-
ly exaggerated voices
expressive face, with its
ous flared nostrils, gave
mense pleasure to
llions.

Although best known for his
tstraged double-takes and the
bawdy double entendres in the
Carry On films and his contributions to such radio series as

had managed a hairdressing
shop. Kenneth Williams was
born in the Caledonian Road,
North London in 1926 and edu-

English experience of Feydeau
at the Winter Garden in 1956,
with Alec Guinness and Irene
Worth romping about.

Here Williams's repertoire of
accents was given full rein,
from the agricultural burr of
"The answer lies in the soil" to
the strangulated tones of cho-

Honest Ken true to self

Dear Pink Postbag,

I was also very sad at the death of
Kenneth Williams. He was a one off, a
lovely man, capable of being brilliantly
funny, as anyone who was lucky
enough to see the clutch of revues he
appeared in twenty odd years ago, or
heard him on radio, will confirm.

But Howard Barker has got it wrong.
He wasn't in the closet, that wasn't his
style. He was [ ] to the point of
absurdity. He [ ]
school, a bit [ ]
climate and [ ]
himself. He [ ]
his own in [ ]
us have p [ ]
mirror ar [ ]
would li [ ]

You cov [ ]
but no [ ]
they c [ ]
come [ ]
from [ ]
unu [ ]

In laughing memory of Ken Williams

By RICHARD WALLACE

WITH a string of risque jokes, poems and
world of showbusiness yesterday said fa
Kenneth Williams.
There was no solemnity at the memorial service to the
Carry On star, who died earlier this year.

Instead there was lau
applause as such cele
Stanley Baxter, Gordon
Derek Nimmo and Barbar
sor celebrated his career.
They were among 200 p
St Paul's, the actors' chu
Covent Garden.
Many wept tears of laught
Lance Percival mimicked son
Williams's catchphrases. He
later, "Kenneth has stopped "n
sin' about" but his characters n
linger with us for years.
Ned Sherrin told the congrega
tion that Williams was 'one of the
most vividly theatrical figures of
our time'. And actresses Sheila

Kenneth Williams is found dead

By Jane Thynne, Media Correspondent

KENNETH WILLIAMS, star of the Carry On films
and Round The Horne and a superlative performer on
BBC's Just a Minute, died yesterday in his sleep. He
was 62.

He was found in his central London flat, where he lived
alone, by his 87-year-old mother, Mrs Louisa Williams, who
lives with his sister in the same block.

He had been undergoing
treatment for stomach ulcers.
According to friends, Williams,
who had often said that he did
not want to live beyond 65, had
recently lost weight.

Kenneth Williams had made
22 Carry On films and had been
due to start shooting the next
film in the series later this year.
More recently he had hosted
the Terry Wogan Show and in
1980 directed Loot by his friend

Kenneth Williams, prince of comedy, dies

John Ezard

THE actor Kenneth Williams,
who based his art on the
postcard
raptures
bawdy an
once said
tion" wa
London
age of 62
His 8
Louisa W
the sa
Park,
raised
no o
ing
the
na
w

British funny bone was located
and tickled it at will for 40 years
or more," the BBC's managing
director network radio, Mr
David Hatch, said last night.
A friend, the ventriloquist
Ray Alan, said Mr Williams had
said him on Thursday of his
facing a gastric ul-
seemed

liams than anyone
of. He just made me
Kenneth Willia
the son of a str
hairdresser near
London. "But I d
long in the Ca
with the whelk
later. "I always
was the uncl
prince,"

Happy farewell to st...

Farewell smiles . . . Carry On co-stars Barbara Windsor and Liz Fras...

Kenneth Williams . . . extrovert

CARRY O LAUGHIN

CARRY ON comedy stars paid
their final tribute to Kenneth
Williams yesterday . . . and they
were determined to make it a
happy farewell.

Among them was Barbara
Windsor, a lifelong friend of the
actor who died in April at the age
of 62, after taking an overdose of
sleeping pills.

As she went into St Paul's
Church in London's Covent
Garden, she said: "Today is a
celebration day—there will be no
tears.

"We will have a nice' time
thinking about Kenneth and
we will have a good
laugh.

"It's what he would
have wanted.

About 200 people—
many from the world of
films, TV and radio—
packed the church.

They included
comedians Stanley
Baxter and Kenneth Con-
nor, actresses Sheila
Hancock and Liz Fraser.

Also there was
Williams' 87-year-old
mother Louisa. The
congregation was told
that the bachelor actor
'adored her above all
others."

The youngest mourner
was [ ]

'It
K
w
w

The death of Kenneth Williams

‘ I don't think he had any class aspirations. He was proud to be a Cockney. And he always said that when he died, and if there was a wreath, it had to be "Gates of Heaven Ajar" which, apparently, is a London tradition ’

Michael Whittaker

Whenever a comedy entertainer dies an unnatural death there's an odd feeling in the air. It seems wrong. We all know it happens, and it can even feel understandable when there's a long decline, a wasting-away of the beloved talent, to warn us that a sudden plunge might come. Such was the case with Kenneth Williams's old colleague Tony Hancock, whose professional disintegration had been in progress for some time when he ended his life in 1968, on the other side of the world. Even if Hancock had left no suicide note there would have been little doubt that his exit was deliberate. Nobody needed to ask why.

Kenneth Williams left us twenty years after Hancock, and in the twenty more years since it happened few conversations about him can have failed to include the question, 'Do you think he killed himself?' The coroner at his inquest recorded an open verdict, and that naturally encourages speculation, since the 'openness' refers to the technical possibility that the case could be brought back to court and re-examined. That's not going to happen, but the re-examination still goes on, informally, wherever Ken's fans are gathered together.

Many factors are involved in the discussion, including the state of Kenneth's career. He was still earning acceptably, and registered occasional astonishment when, say, an advertisement for dairy products brought him a cheque larger than the one he'd been accustomed to getting for a *Carry On* film. But in general his working life had begun to consist of spin-offs and guest appearances; the central column of his career was inert, without its theatrical and cinematic inputs, and with little serious drama even on radio. Probably the first sure symptom of a decline was his trip to Australia in 1981, to do two Michael Parkinson shows in

'Kenneth spent a week on The Mike Walsh Show in Australia, which meant five appearances of about twenty minutes. He was very amusing and, after a few appearances, won over the studio audience who were at first a bit wary of such an exotic creature! He was even more amusing at a boardroom dinner we threw for him, but even that, I thought, was just another 'performance' to him. Personally, I found him a polite and rather shy man. Happy memories.' **(Mike Walsh)**

Kenneth on **The Mike Walsh Show**, April 1983. (Photographs courtesy of Hayden Productions)

'It is marvellous! I look good, the house looks good and the direction is superb! It's the first time in my life I've been presented so beautifully.' **(Diary, 12 October 1983)**

An Audience with Kenneth Williams. © LWT

the style he'd already refined at home. 'I don't seem to have anything else to do,' he confessed to his diary, where the Australian visit was later characterized as 'like an insane nightmare. At my age, the truth begins to dawn: look in the mirror and see an old face and the grey hair & know that you're no longer dreaming of adventure . . . just desperately trying to provide for the old-age pension.'

Kenneth knew he wasn't the only one to show his age, but the sight of his own generation at work wasn't encouraging either ('Benny Hill looks more and more like a desperate adipose decrepit'). Early 1983 found him 'thinking that it would be far better to snuff it', and at that point his physical pains amounted only to a stubborn cough. There came a high point later in the year with the television recording of *An Audience with Kenneth Williams*, his one-man entertainment in front of an all-star gathering of friends, but it wasn't long before he was lamenting again the marks of age on his televisual image. His mother's health scares begin to disrupt life at home. 'I am now uninterested in work,' he recorded in November 1984, the first time this particular form of negativity had afflicted him. His book *Back Drops* was remaindered the following year, and then, on 2 January 1986, 'I noticed awful pain behind the ribs — seemed the alimentary tract was afire.'

That marked the beginning of the end, and the end came a little over two years later. Broadly speaking, there are two views on the matter, both very sincerely held. Among his friends, the feeling remains widespread that Kenneth simply couldn't or wouldn't have committed suicide, because of the family responsibilities he bore. His neighbour Paul Richardson feels that strongly, even though the subject of suicide had arisen between them.

Paul Richardson: 'He once said to me on Warren Street, "Oh, I'm going to do away with all this. I'm going to commit suicide." I said, "No, you're not.""No," he said. "It takes guts, doesn't it?" I don't believe he did intentionally commit suicide. I do not believe that at all. I think with him taking Gaviscon and all kinds

Back Drops, a collection of Kenneth's diary entries for 1982, failed to repeat the success of his first book, **Acid Drops**. 'I have not tampered with the originals in any way,' he said in its Foreword. 'Back Drops is quite simply edited highlights from a year in the life of yours truly.'

'Back Drops was a spoof – with only fragments based on the real diaries. The rest we cobbled together from old material and Kenneth's wild imaginings!' (Gyles Brandreth)

of pills to stop the pulsating pain, he did take an accidental overdose. I firmly believe that, because in no way would he have left behind Louie on her own. And I really think it was an accidental death.'

Derek Nimmo: 'I remember once I ran his mother home after a recording "he'd gone off" and then I got a really lovely letter from Kenny a few days later because I'd taken his mother home. Something which he didn't do, of course. And then on another occasion I gave her a silk scarf at Christmas, and I got a great long letter from Kenny saying how touched he was that I'd given it to his mother – I mean he deeply loved his mother, that's why I always thought the whole suicide business seemed to be so unlikely, I know Freud also agrees with me. When the Coroner was asked whether he could have taken sleeping pills accidentally, "possible but not probable" I think were the words he used. I just can't imagine that he would have killed himself, knowing his mother was going to be left behind, especially as he hadn't really provided for her in his will. His mother was the most important person to him in the world, I think.'

Below Left:
Daily Star,
17 June 1988.

Below Right:
Daily Mirror,
17 June 1988.

Kenneth's agent, Michael Anderson, feels that a form of professional pride would have got in the way, too.

Michael Anderson: 'I personally don't think that he did commit suicide for the rather curious reason because he had a commercial to do that day. Kenneth was far too professional not to do that. I just don't think he meant to do it. I think it was a mistake. I wasn't asked to go to the Coroner's inquest. I would have said that if anybody had asked me. He had a job to do. I think it was a mistake.'

Louisa Williams.

Kenneth's mother and sister held to the same belief, quoting not a professional engagement on the timetable but a domestic one. Ken and Lou had an appointment together at the chiropodist's the following morning.

Pat Williams: 'He wouldn't have done it to Mum. He would have known she would be ready at 10.30 the next morning for the chiropodist, that she would come in and find him there. He'd never talked about suicide, he'd never thought about doing anything like that. Nothing will convince me he took his own life.'

In contrast, outside the family he had talked a good deal about the subject, starting as early as his Combined Services entertainment days in post-war Singapore, where he recalled discussing suicide with Stanley Baxter. In a 1947 diary entry he identifies himself as 'a suicidalist', and the best part of a year later he is 'seriously thinking about taking my own life'. This can of course be read as the rhetorical desperation of a young man without a defined path through life, but the feelings never quite go away. The summer of 1963 finds him 'thinking all the while of death in some shape or another'. By 1972 he finds he has started 'envisaging suicide and letters to friends and coroners' – this, interestingly, in the middle of a bout of severe neck pain. Nothing disoriented Kenneth so much as physical suffering.

There is much more evidence of suicidal feeling in the diaries, but it all looks rather notional when laid alongside the harder evidence which Kenneth actually displayed to a couple of his friends. He evidently regarded the revelation as a kind of test.

Michael Whittaker: 'Years before his suicide he showed me some pills, they were in his kitchen. He said, "Do you know what these are?" Well of course I didn't, so I asked him what they were for. "For exiting this life," he said. "You mean they're suicide pills?" "Yes," and he'd been collecting them for sixteen years or more. I didn't quite know what to say so I said, "Surely if they've been collected for that long, then you can't count on them, and would you like to be half dead? Take them and then find yourself half-alive and half-dead?" He said, "No, I've got enough to kill sixteen people. Thanks for nothing." He was annoyed.'

It would seem that Kenneth had drawn attention to his store of pills as a gesture of intimidation, much as he kept his diaries on display, threatening visitors with inclusion within the blue-black binding of the current volume. But on this occasion his friend had failed to respond with the appropriate signs of fear and dismay, so the dramatic gesture misfired. The incident of the pills ended there, but not without leaving a profound impression on Michael Whittaker.

❛ I asked him what they were for. "For exiting this life," he said. "You mean they're suicide pills?" ❜

Michael Whittaker: 'I got such a shock. They were all different colours. I'd seen them there before but I didn't know what they were. Then for him to say he'd been collecting them specifically to end his life, I was at a loss for words.

Lou and Charlie arriving at Dublin airport, July 1959.

I didn't know what the proper response was. It was a weak response but he didn't like it. Knowing his strong character, nothing I would have said would have stopped him. He did just what he liked to do.'

Gyles Brandreth had collaborated with Kenneth on the editing of his tactful autobiography, *Just Williams*. During that process, too, the subject of suicide had arisen – necessarily, since Kenneth's own father, Charlie, had died a somewhat mysterious death in 1962. The Hammersmith Coroner's Court had returned a verdict of 'Death by Misadventure, due to corrosive poisoning by carbon tetrachloride'. The causes were restated on the death certificate as 'Bronchial Pneumonia, and Carbon Tetrachloride poisoning, self-administered, by accident', according to Kenneth's diary note. He himself did not attend the inquest, on the grounds that his presence would attract a degree of publicity upsetting to his mother. He continued to perform nightly in the theatre throughout this period, with no signs of distress. Nor are there any expressions of regret in the diaries. Indeed, rumours of uncertain origin circulated at the time to the effect that the police were examining the possibility that Kenneth was somehow connected with his father's death, at least to the extent of putting Charlie 'in harm's way' by exchanging bottles, substituting carbon tetrachloride for some more palatable drink the old man expected. But if any theories of that kind were tested, nothing came of them.

❛ … in a sense he was almost licensed to commit suicide because of the way his father had gone ❜

Gyles Brandreth: 'It was when we were doing the autobiography that he told me that his father had committed suicide and I said to him that he must put that in the book. He said, "I can't put that in the book while Louie's alive because she doesn't believe it and won't believe it. But it is the case." It is because he knew his father had committed suicide that when Kenneth took his own life I was not totally surprised. It is a well-established phenomenon that people who commit suicide sometimes come from families where suicide is part of the heritage. That almost, as it were, your forebears and family have given you permission: this is one of the ways this family does. So in a sense he was almost licensed to commit suicide because of the way his father had gone.'

But why in mid-April 1988? There was indeed work to be done, none of it the most congenial he'd ever been offered, but healthy enough. Kenneth had never been rich, but poverty had not threatened for many years. Certainly the multiple pains were a factor; back pain and ulcerations in the digestive system. The diary records his sufferings exhaustively. Peter Cadley, a new friend from Michael Whittaker's circle, was unlucky enough to catch the rising tide of complaint.

Peter Cadley: 'The health was always an issue. He talked about it constantly. He talked about health constantly and he talked about sex constantly. The two seemed to combine, but there was also a very puritan streak to him. If we were out for dinner and perhaps drank too much he'd go home and sometimes use an enema to purge himself of the decadence of the evening. There were

'At 9 o'c. the bell rang. It was a nun asking for money. I refused smilingly and closed the door. It's the impertinence I object to.' (Diary, 6 October 1967)

definite times where you could see he was in a great deal of pain with his ulcers, and either he'd talk about it or be very stoic about it and not mention it at all. There was a lot of medication being taken, a lot of pills, a lot of kaolin and morphine. It was a constant battle at the end to keep the pain at bay. And I was always surprised, I have to admit, that nobody could seem to do anything about it. You would think with the advances in medical science that having an ulcer isn't completely incurable. Before he died there were plans to go into hospital and have something done, which frightened him quite a lot. I could see there was a great deal of fear in having to go into hospital to have major surgery.'

❛ He ended his life not quite running down a hospital corridor but wheeled down one, pursued by demons ❜

Gyles Brandreth: 'I didn't think about it too much because he was a self-dramatizing person. It's funny to think of the man who had so much fun in hospitals, being pursued down corridors by Hattie Jacques, actually having an irrational fear of them. He ended his life not quite running down a hospital corridor but wheeled down one, pursued by demons. He was very frightened of the idea of going into hospital, frightened of the idea of more operations, and I think he thought, "Where is my life going?"'

Michael Anderson: 'I did think there was something very wrong with his health. He was fairly explicit to me with descriptions of his terrible pains in his gut. It did worry me. I think Kenneth thought he had cancer. We didn't talk about it specifically but I sensed that he wasn't going to grow old gracefully; he wanted to fight it off.'

Gyles Brandreth: 'Kenneth Williams was a hypochondriac. I would say from the moment I met him in the early seventies till the end he was talking about his bowels. We would have dinner parties and he'd come and sit there, with the great and the good, and the first thing he'd talk about would be piles! After a few drinks he'd be dropping his trousers to show you his "bum hanging down in pleats". It's an awful thing to say, but people who become depressed become bores. It's a self-fulfilling thing: the more depressed you get the more boring you are. It's the same with hypochondria: the more you bang on about it, the less interested people are. So whom did Kenneth have? Frankly, he had his mother who had her own concerns, he had his sister, a handful of wonderful friends like Michael Whittaker, who were people of infinite patience, sweetness and kindness, who tolerated him and went along with him. But a lot of his show-business friends and colleagues had their own lives to run and didn't have the time for any of this. I saw him less and less towards the end because he became more and more demanding. The last communication I had from him, shortly before he died, was a postcard of him looking into a periscope, and it simply said, "Is there still life in SW13? Are you there?" '

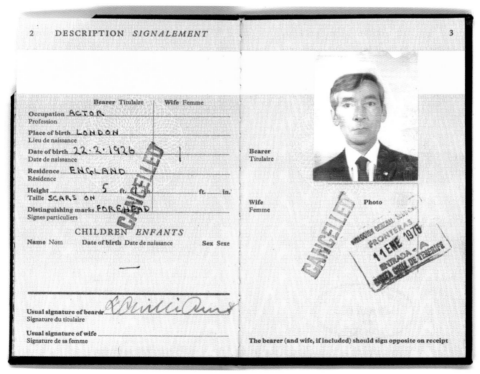

'The new passport arrived. The photograph certainly makes me look awful: and old. What a going-off was here! It is obvious from the ruinous nature of the face, that the qualities in one do affect the looks of one. In my younger photographs, the lips are generous and the eyes wide with hope: now the lips are thin and pursed with the ungenerous nature showing thro' them, and the eyes are narrow with distrust and scepticism and the lines round them show the tired ennui with which it's all viewed.' (Diary, 8 March 1975)

'Ken used to get up very early in the morning; he'd be up at six o'clock in the morning, across the road to Great Portland Street to get the **Telegraph** and have the crossword done by seven.' (Paul Richardson)

It wouldn't be surprising if, by 1988, a kind of general fatigue had crept into Kenneth's friendships and acquaintanceships, on both sides. Ill-health, previously thought of as an amusing sub-current in his conversation, had loomed much more boringly large, and it's quite possible that he had begun to bore himself. Yet nobody felt actually alarmed by the deterioration in his morale. Only afterwards did little psychological signposts, like this one, point the way to what might have been seen coming.

Michael Whittaker : 'What made me think twice in 1988 was that every time I would go on holiday with my other friends I would telephone him and say, "I can't be with you and Louie on Sunday, Kenneth, because I'm going away." His answer was always the same, I don't think he meant it: "I hope the car breaks down, I hope it rains. Lou and I left behind!" and bang would go the telephone. After a time this was the standard response. But in 1988 I knew he'd got ulcers, had given up cigarettes and was pretty low-spirited, and I telephoned him and said, "You know I'm away next Wednesday, Kenneth?" I thought, Here we go. He'll say the usual and bang the receiver down. But he actually said, "Yes, I'll be thinking of you. Think of me, won't you?" I said, "What? What about the car breaking down? And what about it raining?" "No, no, you just think of me. I'll be thinking of you." All the way to Italy I was thinking, Why after eight years has he been so untypically concerned and polite?'

Paul Richardson: 'He died on the Thursday and I last saw him on the Tuesday, very briefly. He seemed fine. He looked slightly drawn but he was his usual chirpy self. "I'm just going into her!" he said, which meant Louie's for his tea. "Don't forget about Friday." So I said that I'd see him then. "Do I need to ring you up and remind you?" he said, but I said no, I'd be there. And of course it never happened.'

The scene in Louie's flat, the night he died, was very much as usual, except that the TV session with his mum ended early for Kenneth. Lou herself recalled it starkly for readers of *Woman's Own*:

Louie Williams: 'We were watching television and he said to me, "I've got a rotten pain. I think I'll have an early night." I think it was only quarter to nine. I said, "Ta-ta. Hope you feel better in the morning," because we were having our feet done at the chiropodist the next morning. And he said to me, "Don't forget. Be ready for half past ten." '

Paul Richardson: 'I'm not a religious person but on the night of the 14th I was lying in my bed and I suddenly looked up and – this is absolutely true – I saw this figure. All I could see was the head and down to the stomach. And I looked. And it was someone grinning at me. And I pushed at it and said, "Go away, go away!" And it just disappeared. The next morning I had to go and get something at John Lewis's, and I came out of the flat about half past eight and I always looked up at Kenny's window, and I thought, That's strange. His curtains are closed. Now that is odd … '

Experiencing the same puzzlement as the breakfast hour passed without communication, Kenneth's mother went into his flat.

Louie Williams: 'He was still in bed. I touched his hand and it was cold. I said, "Ken, Ken, you all right?" And there was no answer. Then I called the porter. I was trying to keep calm. I didn't realize what had happened. The porter said, "He's dead." But I didn't believe it. I thought he was just asleep. But then Pat came and she told me he was dead.'

Paul Richardson: 'And I walked to John Lewis's, and I was going to go from John Lewis on to Sadler's Wells to do something at the theatre, and then come back and meet Ken for lunch at one o'clock. Something told me to turn back. It was as though I was being pushed. So I went to John Lewis's after about an hour and half, and as I came back and crossed Euston Road from Great Portland Street all I could see outside were cameras, police, people milling around. I said to myself, "That's Ken. He's dead." When I got to the block the porter, old Mr Dunthorpe,

Daily Mirror, 16 April 1988.

said to one of the press, "That's his mate there," and then turned to me and said, "Ken's gone." I just got into my flat and wept.'

Michael Whittaker: 'When I eventually got to the house in Italy the hostess said would I go upstairs because there was a message for me from London, and it was that Kenneth had been found dead. When Louie had found him dead she'd telephoned my office. Luckily my colleague Joan comforted her and I think, in retrospect, a woman offering sympathy to another woman was probably the best thing.'

Michael Anderson: 'The porter from Marlborough House rang me and said, "I'm the porter where Kenneth Williams lives and I've got very bad news. I'm afraid he's dead." Well, that was a terrible shock; I had no idea that this might happen.'

'Gordon came to tea. Burned my curtains with a cigarette! Outrageous. He is very charming though and laughed it off with aristocratic indifference.' **(Diary, 2 April 1957)**

Gordon Jackson (1923–1990) whom Kenneth first met in Orson Welles' stage production of **Moby Dick**, June 1955.

Angela Chidell: 'At the time Robert was at a friend's house, and I first heard about it on the evening news so I collected him, I didn't want him to hear the news on his own. I brought him home and we were all shocked and very surprised. We all shed tears because we all loved him very much.'

Gyles Brandreth: 'There is no doubt in my mind that Kenneth committed suicide. There is the end of the diary – "Oh, what's the bloody point?" – but there's also my knowledge: the moment I'd heard he was dead I assumed it was suicide. My mind went straight back to us sitting in my dining room and us getting to the point in his book where he wrote about his father's death. Kenneth talked about suicide. He referred to his stash of poison to me more than once.'

In due course these matters would be considered by the Coroner. Those public proceedings would be hard to bear, but they were for another day. The struggle to maintain daily life had to begin at once.

Paul Richardson: 'Pat had arrived and she had taken Lou back to the flat in Camden. I saw her the following Sunday and she was remarkably composed, it was quite extraordinary. We talked and the vicar was there, and we did a blessing with Lou and Pat. Stanley Baxter and Gordon Jackson turned up and we all had to introduce ourselves because Ken used to pigeonhole everybody so you never met anyone at all.'

Michael Whittaker: 'A BBC producer named David Bell, who was a friend of Kenneth's oldest friend Stanley Baxter, organized the funeral and held the lunch at his house afterwards. Stanley's wife Moira did the catering.'

❛ When we arrived there was a choir and about a dozen people, close friends. It was a moving service ❜

The press was taken by surprise. 'Secret Funeral for Carry On Ken', reported the *Sun*. 'The 30-minute service, held on Thursday, was so hush-hush that many of the staff at London's St Marylebone Crematorium did not know it was taking place.' This article appeared on the Saturday, so the secrecy had indeed worked. Not even those who attended the service were quite sure what was happening.

Pat Williams: 'All we knew was that the car was going to pick us up at 4 o'clock. We'd said no flowers, because Ken hated flowers. We only had one wreath from the two of us and it looked so bare.'

Paul Richardson: 'It was a blustery day and nobody knew where we were going. Pat, Lou, Barbara [Windsor] and I got into this car. We drove and drove and I thought, "I know where we're going, we're going to Marylebone Crematorium!" Pat said, "How do you know?" So I said, "We're going that way!" Sure enough,

Page 27 Mother and son, c.1980, photographed by Terence Donovan (1936–1996), paid for by Michael Whittaker to celebrate Lou's long service in the WRVS.

when we arrived there was a choir and about a dozen people, close friends. It was a moving service. He was cremated and his ashes were spread over the lawns.'

Michael Whittaker: 'I came back from Italy for the funeral. Many of his close friends were there. It was all rather secret. We had a lunch afterwards and that's where I met Dame Maggie Smith, whom Kenneth was always very proud of and how she, more than once, credited Kenneth with a lot of her acting ability. He thought the world of her. I do remember asking about another famous actress, a very well-known person, what he thought of her. "Oh, very rep!" he replied.'

Paul Richardson: 'Pat was in bits, and in actual fact, at the funeral at Marylebone Crematorium, she was to my left and as the coffin was leaving, Pat let out this yelp. Louie turned to me and said, "What's wrong with that silly bitch?" '

Michael Anderson: 'His sister was a bit of a drama queen, I think. She put on quite a performance during the funeral. Her attitude was like being at an Italian funeral almost, she did make quite a fuss showing she cared. His mother bore up very well.'

Pat Williams: 'When we first came back here, Lou saw the photo of her with Ken and started crying, but I said, "You mustn't be like that. We're not going to take it down. We must talk about him and keep him in the open." '

The clearing of Kenneth's flat was a particularly wrenching experience. His intimates knew how spartan his living conditions had looked, so they were prepared for a cheerless spectacle; but at least there had been, during their visits, the bracing presence of Kenneth himself to offset the bleakness of the ambience. Now only the bleakness was left.

Paul Richardson: 'It was terrible to go into Ken's flat so soon after his death with a Mr Spanton, the executor of the will, and have to go through his personal belongings. In fact it was very upsetting. Angela Chidell went with a friend of hers to clear the flat because I couldn't face it.'

Angela Chidell: 'Going into Kenneth's flat one last time was difficult. I believe his sister was asked if she would like to clear the flat and she didn't want to, and Paul [Richardson] didn't want to, so for some reason it fell upon me to do it. So over two days my best friend Jenny Copsey [daughter of Lord Healey] and I, with our cars, ferried things back and forth, odds and ends. Most of the furniture had already gone, things that Kenneth's sister wanted. It was just a question of cleaning up. Most of the things I put in black bags and I simply got rid of. Some of the clothes went to the Salvation Army because his sister had said he was very fond of them and we had a good place at Wood Green so a lot of them went there.'

Robert Chidell: 'We went round to his flat and walked around, picking things up and taking things. It was all a bit strange. Paperweights, lots of pens that I've still got. I was just taken to this old flat, it looked like an old person's flat to be honest. It was tiny, tiny. A very simple place. It felt quite dark, it felt as though it hadn't been decorated for a long time. It felt quite sad in a way … One of his suits fitted me perfectly when I was a teenager for a short while, because he was super slight. It was a tiny fitted suit. I loved it and remember being gutted when I grew out of it.'

Angela Chidell: 'As I walked around the flat I saw photographs and personal things of ours which brought home yet again that the closeness I felt to him was real, and wasn't imaginary or a celebrity thing. It's so easy to think you can attach yourself to people just because they're famous. It was very sad. All these records of wonderful music of Albinoni, Schumann, Beethoven, Bach, organ recitals, Albert Schweitzer, all the great pianists and autographed copies of Jorge Bolet, programmes of Liszt. But that was the other side of Kenneth. He was an entertainer but he was a quiet man, which is so true of entertainers, isn't it?

'The second day, clearing up, I don't know … I just travelled through it doing what I had to do and then closed the door. And that was that.'

The **Sun**, 21 September 1988.

Ex 1.

Bookster hoopers prelude + fugue in G minor
played by FIN VEEDERO which we used in
Constituence played in ST. JOAN — Curiously
it was thro' this, that I got into my first
stage musical! I went into a production of MOBY DICK
— which Orson Welles adapted for the stage around 1954.
+ the movement was all done by Billy Chappel
+ one day during rehearsals I was singing
+ he said 'you've a v. good voice' I said
that's very perspicacious of you 'because
modesty forbad open overt agreement + about
3 months later he asked me to audition for
Sandy Wilsons musical play THE BUCCANEER
+ I got the job! I played an awful boy in short
trousers who edited a boys paper + was something
between Kingsley Martin & Lytton Strachey. Pity
I didn't have the high voice to match. It was
during this period that I saw THE BOY FRIEND
+ the number which I've chosen from that
is IT'S NEVER TOO LATE

"music, it's saying something profoundly
that is find. Broad maxims are dreary at
any rate misleading. Rolling Stones do gather
moss, watched kettles do boil baths made beds
don't have to be laid upon - you can get out + re make
them. It's never too late to start again. Windows that
have been nailed shut can be prised open, letting
light in, letting air in + letting love in — It's never too
late to have a thing for autumn just as nice as spring —

Man of Action, a BBC Radio 3 show which showcased his record collection, produced by
Patrick Lambert, 21 December 1976: 'This week the actor Kenneth Williams introduces
his personal choice of records.'

Ex 3.

When I mentioned (farther) the Moby Dick production, I should have say it was a musical landmark too — for it was during this (play) that I met my great chum Gordon Jackson who did so much to enlarge my experience of music. One of the most precious gifts he ever gave me (and goodness knows he's given me (hundreds)) was this recording of the Brahms Requiem conducted by Rudolph Kemper. I love the musical setting of the passage "How amiable are thy dwellings O Lord of Hosts — my soul hath a desire and a longing to enter into the courts of the Lord" (those) would could be written on my tombstone but for the fact that I shall be cremated. Gravestone up too much space in the modern world. But if there is any kind of service I'd like this played —

§ ~~#.~~ BRAHM Vee lieblich sint diner Wohnungen (Vonungen)
B   from Brahms GERMAN REQUEM
               Sung by the Choir of St. Hedvigs Cathedral
               with the Berlin Philharmonic Orchestra
               conducted by Rudolph Kemper

Well of course she played — go to other script

There remained the unpleasant matter of the inquest. It was held in mid-June, two months after Kenneth's death. Startlingly, his GP, Dr Carlos Clarke, testified that during the previous November he had given his patient 100 sleeping tablets, but not the kind that had killed him. But the most important testimony came from the London Hospital pathologist, Dr Christopher Pease, whose initial, inconclusive findings led to a second battery of tests, some of which had a bearing on Kenneth's general state of health. Dr Pease now resides in New Zealand, but remembers the case with impressive clarity:

Dr Christopher Pease: 'I was fully aware of Kenneth's fame and had watched all of the *Carry On* series. As a doctor and pathologist, however, we are trained from a very early stage not to allow our own emotions to interfere with the task at hand. On that day Kenneth was one of fifteen autopsies I performed in several different areas in and around London, so my examination needed to be precise and comprehensive for future reference. I was particularly aware of the contention around Kenneth's sexuality and made a specific decision not to examine parts of Kenneth's anatomy which were not relevant to his death, choosing to perpetuate his privacy in that area.

'The pills he took were Mandrax; these are a mixture of amphetamine and barbiturate. I have no idea how many pills he took. Kenneth was known to have a large collection of various medicaments and drugs, all of which were labelled and available for him to self-medicate when he chose to do so. I think he was known to be rather hypochondriacal. The bottle containing the remaining

Daily Express, 17 June 1988.

INQUEST'S OPEN VERDICT AS BARBARA LEAVES IN TEARS SAYING: IT MUST HAVE BEEN AN ACCIDENT

Carry On star Ken died from overdose

By Express Reporter KIM WILLSHER

COMEDY star Kenneth Williams left a mystery yesterday after an inquest heard that he had died from an overdose of sleeping pills.

It was not certain whether the overdose was deliberate or accidental, and an open verdict was recorded.

But after the hearing pathologist Dr Christopher Pease said: "It is possible he could have accidentally overdosed but probably not likely."

Kenneth, 62, was found dead in bed at his flat in Regent's Park, London, by his 87-year-old mother Louisa in April. An empty pill bottle was in the kitchen.

St Pancras coroner's court heard Kenneth had been in extreme pain for 18 months because of a stomach ulcer and had been due to have an operation.

He died from an overdose of a barbiturate called sodium amylobaritone.

The Carry On star's GP Dr Carlos Clarke, told the hearing he prescribed tablets for the ulcer and sleeping pills—but not those from which he had died.

Coroner Dr John Elliott said: "Where Mr Williams would have got these from we won't be able to establish and there is no indication as to why he should have taken this overdose and therefore I record an open verdict."

Later Dr Pease said: "He was in a great deal of pain with his ulcer. It is possible he could have accidently overdosed but probably not likely.

"It's unlikely anyone takes a sizeable amount of tablets accidentally if they are compos mentis. Then again if you

are in a large amount of pain you have a different perception of what is right."

Carry On star Barbara Windsor left the inquest in tears. She said: "There is absolutely no question of him doing it deliberately. That is stupid. It was an accident, I am 100 per cent sure of that."

She said she saw Kenneth a week before his death and he was looking forward to his operation and to having a holiday.

Barbara, who sat through the hearing with the star's sister, Pat, and Paul Richardson, a close friend of the actor, added: "He was just wonderful and we loved him so much. I still miss him and I'm still grieving for him."

Williams: Ulcer

Barbara: Friend

32

Mandrax tabs was unlabelled, in stark contrast to all of his other bottles. The levels of amphetamine and barbiturate in his blood were not a fatal dose of either compound, but in combination were lethal.

'After the inquest I was besieged with reporters, almost all of whom mis-quoted me (apart from the *Sun*, as far as I remember). When asked if I thought that he had killed himself, as the Coroner had left an open verdict, my reply was, "It is most unlikely that an adult, if compos mentis, would take an acciden-tal overdose." There had been no evidence that he wasn't, despite his fear of sur-gery for his gastric ulcer in the next week or two.'

As for the general state of Kenneth's body, Dr Pease recorded a strikingly favourable general impression, blighted by one fairly horrific condition.

Dr Christopher Pease: 'There was no mention of changes related to smoking or drinking in my autopsy report. There was no sign that he had damaged his body with either habit. In fact, Kenneth was in extremely good health for his age. In particular, he had a totally healthy heart. I have performed over 2,000 autopsies, and Kenneth's coronary arteries were the most pristine of them all in the same age group, as healthy as a 20-year-old's, in fact! There was no evi-dence of liver disease, and all other organs appeared healthy.

'He did, however, have a very large (35 mm), deeply penetrating posterior (at the back of the stomach) gastric ulcer, and this was adherent to his pan-creas. The stomach wall was intensely congested and inflamed. These findings were likely to be a combination of true inflammation of the stomach and bar-biturate effect. Undoubtedly this ulcer would have been extremely painful and would have produced intense upper abdominal and back pain. There was no evidence to suggest the ulcer was malignant.'

From this it is distressingly clear that Kenneth had in no way exaggerated the intensity of his bodily sufferings. The pains he'd endured were every bit as severe as he said they were. In the event, the Coroner, Dr John Elliott, clung to the letter of the law, insisting, in the words of the *Daily Mail*'s report, that 'there was no evidence to show why he took the lethal dose of sleeping pills'. No sui-cide note, in other words, or equivalent message of intent. How much weight was attached to Kenneth's diary entries cannot now be known. Only the last volume, for the early months of 1988, had been examined in any case. So the Coroner cannot have seen the diary entry for 30 August 1987, which reads in part: 'All that is in my mind now is the way to commit suicide …', or indeed for 5 October 1987: 'Counted my capsules of poison and I have got over 30 so there should be enough to kill me.' On the other hand, the entry for 22 March 1988 (only three weeks or so before the death) was available to be seen and interpreted: 'Came back to flat & got out the Sodium Amytal & then had cold feet. Took 2.'

Michael Whittaker: 'I think he did commit suicide. Paul Richardson doesn't think so, and obviously the Coroner didn't, so we have to accept the Coroner's verdict. But he always said he would. The idea of ageing or losing faculties didn't appeal to him at all.'

One factor that seems to complicate the argument is Kenneth's will, in which he shocked the world by distributing his goods around a small circle of male friends, leaving nothing to the 87-year-old mother who had been, in one way or another, his companion through life. If he had intended to kill himself, the argument runs, then he would have made some formal provision for Lou. But again, his diary indicates that he had considered the matter less than a month before the fatal night: 'Thought of making an end of it tonight & then wondered whether things were left in proper order. Should I write a letter to Michael? best of people & best of my friends. Would it be fair to ask him to tell all the others?' It would seem that the problem of Lou was already settled in his mind, and Michael now confirms that it was so.

Michael Whittaker: 'He hadn't left Louie any money because he thought that she would go into a home and the home would take her money. He thought she would never ever live with her daughter, which she subsequently did. He said to me, because I was being left some of his money, "Anyway, if she's in the home I know you'll keep your eye on her." I thought all this was academic anyway, that she'd die before Kenneth. To find that she was living with her daughter, sleeping on her sofa in a one-bedroom flat in Camden, I thought if Kenneth was alive

This is the last Will

of me KENNETH CHARLES WILLIAMS of 8 Marlborough House Osnaburgh
Street London NW1 3LY --

1.   I REVOKE all former wills and testamentary dispositions made
by me ---

2.   I APPOINT MIDLAND BANK TRUST COMPANY LIMITED (hereinafter
called "the Company") to be Executor and Trustee of this my will upon
its published Standard Conditions as now in force (as if the same were
here set out) with remuneration as provided by those Conditions and the
Company's Standard Scale of Fees in force at my death and with power to
charge remuneration in accordance with any later Standard Scale of Fees
of the Company for the time being in force --------------------------

3.   I DEVISE free of capital transfer tax my leasehold property
8 Marlborough House Osnaburgh Street London NW1 3LY with all my
household goods and personal effects to such of PAUL RICHARDSON of 29
Marlborough House aforesaid and my god son ROBERT CHIDDELL of 66
Redston Road London as shall survive me in equal shares absolutely ---

4.   I GIVE all royalties and residual fees whether performing or
literary to MICHAEL ANDERSON of ICM 388-396 Oxford Street London ---

5.   I DEVISE AND BEQUEATH the whole of my estate both real and
personal subject to the payment of my debts funeral and testamentary
expenses and capital transfer tax and any legacies bequeathed by this
my will or any codicil hereto (hereinafter called "my residuary
estate") to MICHAEL WHITTAKER c/o Reed Executive plc 114 Peascod
Street Windsor Berkshire absolutely with the request that he retains
my stocks and shares as invested and only realises them should the need
arise ---

6.   I GIVE my body for the purposes of medical education or
research in accordance with the Anatomy Acts 1832-1871 as re-enacted by

The infamous last Will and Testament that seemingly left no provision for his beloved
87-year-old mother.

the Anatomy Act 1984 plus but if not so required I desire that my body

be cremated ---

7.   IF FOR ANY REASON the aforesaid gifts to the said MICHAEL

ANDERSON or MICHAEL WHITTAKER shall fail to take effect I DIRECT

that the bequest which he or they would have received shall pass to my

said godson ROBERT CHIDDELL absolutely on attaining the age of 21

years --

IN WITNESS whereof I have hereunto set my hand this *eighteenth*

day of *July*   One Thousand Nine Hundred and Eighty Five

SIGNED by the testator   )
KENNETH CHARLES WILLIAMS)
in our presence and   )
attested by us in his   )
presence and in the   )
presence of each other:)

A R JARDINE   D HANNON.

DRAFT PRESS RELEASE

In the recently published will of KW, no provision is made for his mother, Mrs Louisa Williams.

KW was devoted to his 87 year old mother, who until his death lived next door to him in the flat he had provided for her.

He must have expected to outlive his mother or otherwise have thought that she would be looked after, if he died first.

During his lifetime he had provided for his mother and was very closely involved with her day to day existence.

In his will, he left his London flat, household goods and personal effects to a neighbour/friend and his godson. He left all performing and literary royalties to his agent. He left the residue of his estate to a good friend of both himself and his mother MW, a businessman who KW probably thought would be the best person to deal with his affairs and ensure that his mother was looked after.

Mr W is helping to purchase a larger flat where Mrs Williams and her daughter can live together. He has also made proper arrangements to ensure that KW's mother has sufficient income for the rest of her life.

'It never went off. Some of the papers, usual stuff, they said "Kenneth Williams leaves his mother nothing", "Poor woman out on the street", all this drama! That's why I was going to make a statement but it wasn't necessary in the end. It was drawn up by my lawyers to say that she hadn't been completely abandoned and I did, indeed, look after her.' (**Michael Whittaker**)

Draft press release to address the questions Kenneth's will had raised.

now to see his ageing mother like this! So I arranged for her to get an annuity and also to buy the flat upstairs which had two bedrooms and two bathrooms.'

Leaving the welfare of his closest relatives in the hands of Michael Whittaker proved a safe policy, though at first Lou and Pat Williams saw only the slight in it and not the wisdom. When they talked to *Woman's Own*, Michael's arrangements had yet to be made.

Pat Williams: 'One of Ken's beneficiaries came round, and he said, "I've been left half of Ken's flat." I rang the solicitor and said, "At least you might have had the common decency to have advised my mother first." He said, "Why should I tell you? Neither you nor your mother are mentioned in the will." I said to him, "I'm not interested for myself but my mother's very upset," and he said he'd send us a copy of the will.

'It wasn't a shock that I hadn't been left anything, but the only thing that niggles me is that as Mother devoted so much time and affection on him, the least he could have done was make a proviso when he made out his will. He should have said, "I leave everything to Joe Bloggs, providing he looks after my mother for the rest of her life." '

Effectively that's what did happen, once Michael Whittaker had realized that Pat and Lou were living together under cramped and stressful circumstances.

Michael Whittaker: 'He always thought Louie would go into a home and she would never live with her daughter, because her relationship with Pat had been rocky, to say the least. But she did indeed live with her daughter, and after things were sorted out she lived quite a few more years. She had that great London vitality. She was a real Cockney sparrow. She went dancing at the Irish Club in Camden.

'Pat found it quite stressful. Fundamentally she liked having Louie there, but it was stressful. One day the doctor said to Pat, "Look, you need a rest. I'll think up some excuses for Louie to have tests at the hospital, she'll go in for a few days and give you rest." Well, Louie went in to University College Hospital, then got a bug and died. Pat felt terrible.'

KENNETH WILLIAMS

I.C.M.
388/396 Oxford Street
London W1N 9HE

4 January '87

My dear Michael
It was particularly kind + thoughtful of you to give me the OBSERVER piece on Maggie. Read it when I came home + thought it well put together. These profiles are not easy things to do + in Mag's Case maybe more difficult 'cos she hates publicity. My life as a sort of mentor jailer + male nurse is restricting. Even if it came to a HOME, Lou would still be on my mind – visiting etc – but I am finding it more + more of a BORE. The thanks of the old are fulsome as the time, but gutter as quick as a candle. But whenever you are there, it's different again. She thinks you're wonderful. I will always be grateful for your patience

Love
Kenneth

Even in the later years of his life, Kenneth was torn between putting Lou into a care home and continuing to look after her himself, as he revealed in a letter to Michael Whittaker.

Paul Richardson: 'He changed his will about two or three years before he died because I was actually with him. After seeing his bank manager, we walked down the road with him tearing up the old will and putting it into each of the bins we passed. "You're in it!" he said. When he died, his flat was left to myself and his godson along with all the contents of it which included the diaries and letters. Michael Whittaker was left the flats and the bulk of the money, and Michael Anderson was left the royalties.'

Michael Anderson: ' "I've been to see my lawyer," he said, pointing at me. "You can keep the royalties, and I don't want to hear any more about it!" I'd forgotten all about it, and then his lawyer rang me up and said, "Mr Anderson, Kenneth Williams has left you his royalties." Then it all came back to me. An unusual thing to happen, that an agent be left somebody's royalties. My colleagues could-n't believe it! I did ask them – because they represented some pretty important people – and not one of them had ever been left anything by their clients! I think he thought it was tidy. He did say to me, "Because it's easy, you don't want to start sending them to other people. You may as well keep them yourself. It's tidier that way." It was a very practical solution for him. His royalties included sales of tapes of *Round the Horne*, sales of *Acid Drops* and the other books. No *Carry Ons*, obviously, because they were buy-outs.'

Many of Kenneth's friends complained in his lifetime that they were allowed to dwell only in one zone of his life, and never glimpsed the totality of his acquain-tanceship. Their one chance to do so came in the autumn of 1988.

Nick Lewis: 'Michael Whittaker rang and invited me to the memorial service, which was very generous of him to remember me, because I'd only met Kenneth once. So on the 29th of September, a Thursday, I went down to St Paul's Church in Covent Garden, and pushed passed the photographers on the steps to get in. It was, as the vicar said at the beginning, a very happy service, we were there to celebrate Kenneth's life, not to mourn him. It was more like a variety show per-formed by Kenneth's old friends: Gordon Jackson playing the piano while Kenneth Connor did that wonderful pidgin French song, various poetry readings, and my favourite – and this has stayed with me ever since – was Barbara Windsor singing an old music-hall song called "The Boy I Love is up in the Gallery". First of all I was stunned by what a good singing voice she had, and the way she was singing it to the back of the church, it was just full of meaning as though he was up there watching us and enjoying it all. It was truly, really touching.'

Angela Chidell: 'That was very, very moving. Her voice never once wavered and she sang unaccompanied. I was carried away by the perfectionism of the woman. Being something of a performer myself I appreciate those moments when something is so right that it's a *rare* moment. She shone like a star from above. Everything just stood still and there was a beam of light across the whole congregation. It was a moment of time that you can't forget, like a teardrop.'

INTRODUCTION

THE REVEREND MICHAEL HURST – BANNISTER
Senior Chaplain – Actors' Church Union

REMEMBERING KENNETH

HYMN

All things bright and beautiful,
All creatures great and small,
All things wise and wonderful
The Lord God made them all.

Each little flower that opens,
Each little bird that sings,
He made their glowing colours,
He made their tiny wings.

The cold wind in the winter,
The pleasant summer sun,
The ripe fruits in the garden,
He made them every one.

He gave us eyes to see them,
And lips that we might tell
How great is God Almighty,
Who has made all things well.

EILEEN ATKINS

KENNETH CONNOR

SHEILA HANCOCK

GORDON JACKSON

DEREK NIMMO

LANCE PERCIVAL

NED SHERRIN

BARBARA WINDSOR

HYMN

And did those feet in ancient time
Walk upon England's mountains green?
And was the holy Lamb of God
On England's pleasant pastures seen?
And did the Countenance Divine
Shine forth upon our clouded hills?
And was Jerusalem builded here
Among those dark Satanic Mills?

Bring me my Bow of burning gold!
Bring me my Arrows of desire!
Bring me my Spear! O clouds, unfold!
Bring me my chariot of fire!
I will not cease from Mental Fight,
Nor shall my Sword sleep in my hand,
Till we have built Jerusalem
In England's green and pleasant land.

PRAYERS AND BLESSING

ORGANIST
RALPH ELSTON

PIANIST
RICHARD HOLMES

The collection at the end of this Service will be for
The Combined Theatrical Charities Appeals Council

KENNETH WILLIAMS

THE ACTORS' CHURCH
ST PAUL'S BEDFORD STREET COVENT GARDEN LONDON WC2
THURSDAY 29 SEPTEMBER 1988 AT 12 NOON

The memorial service running order, which featured 'All Things Bright and Beautiful' – a song Kenneth would often recite in German! (Even though the Actor's Church has hundreds of commemorative plaques, a lack of wall space prevents any further tributes to deceased artists, including Kenneth.)

KW

Honi soit qui mal y pense
Fait vos jeux, reconnaissance
'ammersmith 'Palais de danse
Badinage ma crepe suzette.

Double entendre, restaurante
Jacques Cousteau, Yves Saint Laurente
ou est la plume de ma tante
c'est la vie ma crepe suzette.

Corsage, massage, frere Jacques
Salon, par avion, Petula Clarke

Fiancee, ensemble, lorgnette,
lingerie, eau de toilette,
Gauloises cigarette
Entourage ma crepe suzette.

Citron, mirage, caravelle
Hors d'oeuvre, Brut and Chanele
Chaise longue, Sacha Distele
Fuselage, ma crepe suzette.

Pince nez, bidet, commissionaire
Mon repos, Brigitte Bardot, Jeux sans frontieres.

Faux pas, grand prix, espionage
Gruyere, Camembert, fromage
Mayonnaise, all night garage
RSVP, ma crepe suzette.

'On one occasion when we worked with Kenneth he performed "Ma Crepe Suzette" and, of course, it brought the house down. We completely adored it and, rather nervously afterwards, asked him if we could use it. He was delighted and said, "I nicked it off someone else so you might as well nick it off me!" When he sang it, he sang it to the tune of Auld Lang Syne. Collyer had given it to him and said that he should do it to the tune of Sorrento and, because Kenneth didn't know what Sorrento was, he worked it around Auld Lang Syne. So he gave us his blessing that we should take it and perform it, and we did. He said that he'd get the lyrics to us and, because we'd established a closeness, one evening there was a ring at the door bell and there, at the bottom of the stairs, was Kenneth! He was huge at that time so I was well impressed that he hadn't sent a minion round with it or put it in the post: he had bothered to walk round. I invited him up and he said, "Oh no, no, wouldn't dream of it", then just disappeared into the night.' **(Richard Bryan, Cantabile)**

Kenneth's infamous pidgin French song, 'Ma Crepe Suzette', his party-piece of many a chat-show, written by Derek Collyer and performed by Kenneth Connor at the memorial service.

Nick Lewis: 'At the end, in the closing prayer, the vicar came out with the words "Comfort us in our loneliness", which really gave me a pang. It was just the most beautiful service and we all felt enormously happy afterwards.'

Peter Cadley: 'When we left the memorial service there were hundreds of cameras there because John Thaw and Sheila Hancock had split up the day before and she was doing something at the service. Click, click, click, went the cameras for Sheila. Meanwhile I had Lou on one side and Pat on the other, arm in arm, and all the photographers had no idea who they were. I thought, "You're missing one of the shots of the day!" But they were far more interested in bags under Sheila Hancock's eyes or Barbara Windsor's bosoms. The lunch afterwards was far more fun because it was a tighter group of people. It was in a very interesting Greek restaurant in Camden that Pat had chosen. We had the whole of the downstairs. I was sat opposite Maggie Smith and next to Gordon and Rona Jackson. Lou and Edie were sitting at the head of the table.'

And those two had much to talk about, ranging back to 1926, and the beginnings of Kenneth's story.

Daily Mirror,
30 September 1988.

Marchmont Street

'Two rooms, kitchen and a bathroom. The walls were white, there were no pictures, he had a bookcase with all his books, a record player and a Roberts radio which would always sit on the floor next to his Parker Knoll chair'

Paul Richardson

'All my life is an act and a hollow sham, the concrete things like my belongings and my privacy and my books and things are NECESSARY – they're the only things I have.' **(Diary, 22 September 1972)**

Kenneth Williams in his final home, 8 Marlborough House, Osnaburgh Street, London NW1.

In his later years, the home life of Kenneth Williams became the subject of some discussion and even wonderment, at least within the acting profession. Everyone in the business seemed to know, though few at first hand, that he lived on a small scale, in a barely furnished ambience that offered very little to a visitor and not much more to the occupant himself. Derek Nimmo, for example, never visited Kenneth's flat, yet he had worked up in his mind an elaborate image to account for what he knew to be the monastic rigour prevailing there.

Derek Nimmo: 'Stanley Baxter made him put some pictures up once, but I think he took them down again quite soon. I remember once in the Escorial in Spain I went to Philip of Spain's cell, and I use the word advisedly because it was a bedroom really, but just beside this great baroque altar. And Philip of Spain had a little window which he could open and see this extraordinary opulent, rococo-baroque world outside the great high altar. But he lived in a kind of white, spartan room. And I think that was Kenny's way. He liked to look out on this extraordinary world he'd created or would observe, but he didn't want to be part of it, he went back to his little whitewashed cell.'

Paul Richardson: 'Two rooms, kitchen and a bathroom. The walls were white, there were no pictures, he had a bookcase with all his books, a record player and a Roberts radio which would always sit on the floor next to his Parker Knoll chair. And that was it in the room. It was a galley kitchen, nothing in there. It's true there was cellophane on the oven stove. All the cupboards were full of medicines, no food at all. In his bedroom was one single bed, with his desk – where he'd write all his diaries – and a small wardrobe, and that was it.'

'I do love Louie. She's the only person I've ever loved. By love I mean caring so much that it's altruistic, and feeling her presence when she's physically not there, and missing her.' (Diary, 22 September 1973)

Louisa Williams, 1935.

'My father and I didn't get on. He was football and cricket mad and wanted a son who enjoyed that. I loathe anything like outdoor or competitive sports. He also liked to go to the pub for a pint of bitter. When I asked for a sweet sherry, he would be shocked. He would say, "You namby-pamby sod."'
(Kenneth, interview, 1984)

Charlie Williams, 1936.

Yet Kenneth wasn't quite alone in his little flat. There were times when he could have wished to be more solitary than he was, according to his older sister, Pat.

Pat Williams: 'He'd come up here sometimes, and he'd drink cup after cup of tea. "Oh put the kettle on again, make some more tea." And he said, "You know what, Pat, honestly and truly, I can't fart without she hears me." I had to sit here and laugh. "It's all very well for you to sit up here in your grandeur of Camden Town. I'm the star! I ought to be livin' here, and you ought to be livin' in that flat down in Osnaburgh Street, next to Mum. You'll have a bash of her." I said, "But she doesn't want me, she only wants you." "Yes, aren't you lucky. You don't care about me." I said, "I do, Ken, I do, honestly I do." "What are you laughing at then?" "Well, you make me laugh." And I just couldn't help laughing.'

The presence of his mother, Louie Williams, across the landing offered him some kind of companionship, most of all in the evenings. But it must also have constantly refreshed his memories of a fretful inner-city childhood, not many streets away. There was an anger in those memories that couldn't always be kept down. And it was shared by his sister, who gave her only extended interview to the BBC in 1994. Fragments of it were broadcast in a Radio 4 programme called *I Am Your Actual Quality*, part of the *Radio Lives* series, where listeners were quite startled by the basso growl of Pat Williams. She sounded at moments like one's idea of the father she had so roundly detested.

❛ Nobody got on with Charlie Williams. He was a real old-fashioned Victorian bully ❜

Pat Williams: 'Nobody got on with Charlie Williams. He was a real old-fashioned Victorian bully. You know the Charlie Chaplin walking stick? He had one of them. Canes. He used to hang it on the side of the mantelpiece. In the flat where we lived we had an old-fashioned range, you know, the fire one side and the oven the other. And as he came in for his meals he'd take the cane down from there and hook it on the side of the table, near where he sat. And we weren't allowed to speak, and we were only allowed to eat whatever was on our plate. Weren't allowed to move until it had all gone. Well, Ken loathed cabbage, spinach, sprouts, anything that was green he hated. And of course me, I'd eat anything, I was the dustbin of the four of us ... And Dad used to have the sauce bottle, you know, the Daddie's sauce. And he'd have his paper folded so that he could lean up and see what the day's racing was, and he'd be so intent on watching his racing tips or working it out, I'd slide over the left, Ken would slide over to the right, and when I thought the old man wasn't looking, as quick as you like I'd pop the fist out, grab a fistful of sprouts and eat it. And do you know, that old bugger used to see me every time. I got to think, well, he can see through paper. He wouldn't say a word. Just pick up the cane, whish! And under the table he'd give me a whack across both legs. And I used to think, Ooh you rotten swine, one of these days I'll get the better o' you.'

Pat Williams had the habit of relating a particular incident and making it sound like a regular occurrence. It was just her way of narrating things. But from what she said, you do get the sense that these individual scenes could indeed have stood for many more of the same type. How many times, for example, did Charlie Williams favour his son like this, in hopes of making a conventional man's man of him?

Pat Williams: 'And Dad would come home with his present, you see. "Present for you, son, 'ere yar, mate." "Ooh good. Where's mine?" "You ain't got no present. It's for the boy." And Ken would open this parcel, see a pair of boxing gloves. And he'd hold 'em out in each hand. "What am I supposed to do with these?" "Put 'em on yer bleedin' fists and have a fight! Get in and fight yer own battles. Don't rely on yer sister." "No, thank you." And he'd just drop them in father's lap and walk out the room. And the old man would go mad.'

Other vignettes seem to have exactly the same flavour, without the pugilistic props.

Kenneth, early 1930s, Manchester Street Infants School, third row, fourth from left.

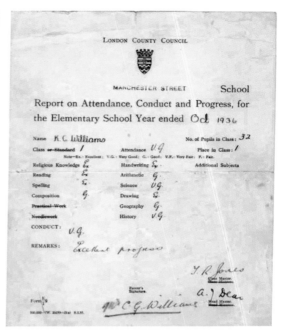

Pat Williams: 'Well, he would talk to Ken. "How'd you get on at school today?" "Why?" Ken gave as good as he got. I would stand and argue with the old man, defy him if you like, and Ken used to just look at him with utter contempt. I knew he was going to be an actor. Dad would say, "I wanna know how you're gettin' on at school, mate." "I fail to see why you're interested in me. I'm not in the least interested in you." And he walked out of the room! I'd die laughing, and the old man would go mad.'

Within the family there was a particular reason why Kenneth seemed to be spared the worst retribution, in spite of his disdain for traditional norms like male aggression. The fact was that he and Pat Williams were not full brother and sister. Louie, unmarried then, had been 'knocked up', as the saying went. In the Williams diaries (though not the published version) there is a glancingly sour allusion to the conception, which apparently took place in the hallway of a tenement. The honourably old-fashioned role of Charlie Williams in this crisis was to step in and 'make an honest woman' of Louie, to use another phrase that has mercifully expired. So all through life it was Pat Williams's bad luck to remind her mother of a painful indiscretion, her father of his entitlement to self-righteousness, and Kenneth of

Lou and
Charlie,
centre.

his status as the one true child of the union and the household. It was a difficult
selection of prejudices to confront, and taken together they left Pat's life — and
her views of her brother — uneasily poised between humour and bitterness. The
semi-siblings were at their closest in infancy, where Kenny was already the dom-
inating spirit. He it was who organized the children's remarkably effective escape
fantasy, which they called 'Our Game'.

Pat Williams: 'Ken and I used to share a bedroom. Mind you, we were only little. I should have known then what I know now, oh dear! I'd run a mile. And we
had little iron beds, you know those little iron beds? We used to have to be in
bed early, gotta get your sleep, you must have ten hours' sleep, or whatever.
And then on Saturday night we got to have our bath, wash our hair, in the zinc
bath in the scullery, as it was. And we had to be in bed by five. My mum used to
go and meet my dad from work, and they'd go out to the pub and have a Guinness
and a gin. So we used to sit up in bed and Mum used to read 'Little Nell' to us,
and all these little stories. Then she'd go, you see, now we gotta be good children, don't let anybody in, don't get out of bed . . . So we used to play Our Game,
and Ken was every other voice, I was only ever me. And if I said the wrong thing

'About the age of 11 I came to the Lyulph Stanley Central School. I seem to remember I spent most of the time, rather aimlessly, staring out of the window. But the one thing I did enjoy were the German lessons, and we were made to sing German songs. A whole group of us were sent, as part of a great London choir, to County Hall where we sang Beethoven's Die Himmel Ruhmen Die Ehre Gottes Aus Der Natur [Opus 48 No. 4] and Die Lore Lei. We were all dressed up in lederhosen, we all had to make our own costumes, little shorts and braces and funny hats with a feather in them. Of course I enjoyed it, it was all part of performing. I think it was that period that sowed the seeds of a lasting love for the German Romantic Movement, both in music and literature.' **(Kenneth, Comic Roots, 1983)**

Kenneth, first row, fourth from left, 1937.

'When I did [impersonations] at school, the other boys would recognise the character. When I did the headmaster, they said, "Cor, that's just like him."' **(Kenneth, Just Williams, 1985)**

Kenneth, mid-1930s, Manchester Street Junior School, first row, first from left.

I got bawled out, "You're supposed to say" and then he'd give me the next thing. "Oh, sorry." "Right, you ready then?" And these stories he'd cook up. He would make them up. And they could be anything. "Today we're going for a picnic." "Oh, are we?" "You can use the red MG today, the little two-seater red MG." "Oh, thank you very much." And he would describe exactly where we were going, what we were going to have to eat, how long it was going to take to get there, who the other people at the picnic were, and home again. And he'd say, "That was good, wasn't it?" "Yeah, I enjoyed that day out in the country." And I really felt as if I'd been in the country! Ridiculous! Ridiculous. Because we'd be somewhere, you see, bored out of our minds, and he'd go "O G", and he'd just mouth it, not say the words. And we'd nod and wink, and just gradually sneak out, and if it was anybody's house that had a garden we'd go and sit in the garden, if it was another room we'd go and sit in the other room, and they invariably came and found us. And they'd say, "What are you doing in here? Come on

'Taken on the roof of my Junior School in Manchester Street – now called the Argyle Street Junior School. It shows me in the school production of the play **The Rose and the Ring**: first time I was ever in drag.' **(Diary, 11 January 1968)**

'Kenneth Williams with his mincing step and comical demeanour, as Princess Angelica, was a firm favourite with the audience to whom his snobbishness and pert vivacity made great appeal.' **(St Pancras Gazette, c.1935)**

out in the sunshine!" "We are quite happy here, aren't we, Pat?" "Yes, thank you, Ken." I'd do anything the boy said. I mean if he said go and lay down in the middle of Piccadilly Circus for a half-hour, I would.'

But that was Saturday. It was typical of this mercurial and outspoken family that Sunday brought different feelings altogether.

❛ You rotten stinker. I gave you my penny, you bought the sweeties, you've eaten all the sweeties, you didn't even give me one ❜

Pat Williams: 'I'll tell you what the little bugger used to do. We used to go to Sunday school every afternoon. Mum used to give us a penny for the collection. And we'd get round the corner, you see, out of sight, and I would say to Ken, "I'll give you my penny so you can buy sweeties, and I'll meet you here at four o'clock, and you can tell me what the story was, and then we go home." And he said, "All right." So I'd part up with my penny, go and play football with the boys, and then I'd meet him at four o'clock and he'd tell me whatever it was, all about Noah and the Ark or whatever. And as soon as we got home, Mum used to say, "Right, come and sit down, tell me what it was about. Did you get a text this week?" Sometimes they'd give us a little text. And Ken would say, "No, I didn't get one, but she got one, didn't you, Pat?" I'd say, "Yes, thank you, Ken." And she'd say, "Right, now you can get the tea ready," and we always had to get the afternoon tea ready. And wash up afterwards. And he'd say, "Pat'll wash up." And I'd say, "You've got to do your share." "If you don't wash up, I'll tell Mum you didn't go to Sunday school." And he would hold it over my head all the bloody week, true as I'm sitting here.

Pages 56–60 'Feel in a strangely reflective and autumnal mood this afternoon – Dvorak on the radio, the October fog coming down – at 5 o'c. it is too dark to see without electricity – and I am thinking wonderful possibilities – I could write a play, I could be a mad success.' (Diary, 29 October 1958)

Turning memories of family life at 57 Marchmont Street into drama. Note the use of Lou's favourite saying – 'Gawd help us' – and the revision at the top of page two: 'He'll be up in a minute', corrected to 'down in a minute' for his father's barbershop was below the living quarters.

1

Louie –
(laying the table etc)
Why don't you eat something, it will do you good – I've got a nice bit of best end, there's plenty to go round

Gran :
I can't eat anything, it'll only start me off again, I've had terrible wind all over the week end – I think it was them skates eye balls – and my legs have been playing me up again

Louie:
You should see the Doctor

Gran
What's the good of doctors? – anyway I don't like that Chinese woman that comes round I don't know why they put me on her panel. What do the Chinese know about our illnesses?

Louie
Illness is Illness all the world over, the Chinese are the same as us –

Gran
Course they aint. All they know about is rice. That's all I need! Rice is the worst thing for me, rice makes wind and that's a fact – all these national health people are no good – half of 'em are black and the other half Chinese – I don't know why they started the national health. We was all right before – I used to like that Mary O'Donell in Copenhagen street. I could talk to her, and she never asked you to take your clothes off – just looked at your eyes and your tongue. She could tell by your eyes, she had the knack

Louie
Miss Nagasi's been very good to you – come round to see you at all hours. She got you through pneumonia didn't she.

Gran :
My bones
makes you all your clothes off, horrible cold hands on your body – I don't like it its not decent. And she told me to bath! – bath at my age! Gawd help us, that would put me in me grave all right I've never got into one of them things in me life

Louie
You should do. Everyone should have a bath – all the doctors say so – in hospital they make you –

Gran
Oh Mary O'Donell never made me. I've always washed meself down with a flannel in the basin. She said it was all right – and she used to say to me "you have a glass of stout" she said a glass of stout every day did you more good than all your medicines put together

Louie
Well I haven't got any stout here

Gran
Its all right, I've brought me own. You can give me a glass though

Louie:
Yes all right – though I don't know how you can drink that stuff in the daytime I think its a terrible smell on your breath

Gran:
I should worry. Nobody's kissing me

56

Lou: If you're for wind, that stuff won't help — why don't you eat something — you could have it with Charlie - he'll be down in a minute

Gran: I don't want anything to eat. Don't want to eat with him either

Lou: He's your own son.

Gran: He may be my son but you've been more good to me than any of my sons — or my daughters for that matter. They aint worth a farthing - Charlie's no better than the rest of them

Lou: Its wicked to talk like that. He's my husband. He's been good to you, he gives you the five shillings every week doesn't he?

Gran: Only because you made him.

Lou: The others give you five bob

Gran: Only Jack does. Lylie gives me half a crown

Lou: Well she don't have much, poor bitch

Gran: She has plenty of fancy men

Lou: I thought she was going steady with that Sid who drives the lorry.

Gran: That Mrs. Houth lives on the first floor and she sees 'em come and go....

Lou: Oh! that's a disgrace

Gran: That Mrs. Houth told me in the gardens. She's always in them gardens— I see her in there with a load of bread for the birds — I go through for the short cut to the Richmond of an evening

Lou: I don't like that Mrs Houth, I think she's a dirty bitch. She's got no right to talk about Lylie, you could spit in her eye and it wouldn't choke her —

Gran: She makes you laugh - she opened her handbag and showed me the other day — you should have seen the money she had — she goes in the back of the cinema and holds their dicks for 'em and they give 'er a bob —
      (Holds it for 'em)

Lou: It's a disgrace —

3

Fran: She said you have to be careful when the usherette comes along shining the torch, or they can see — she made me laugh —

Lou: She don't make me laugh. I think it's disgusting. A woman of her age — fancy her talking to you like that - wonder she didn't ask you to go with her to the pictures, so you could meet some of her dirty old men.

Fran: I don't want no dirty old men thankyou. I never touched no men since my Henry died — thirteen children I had + I don't want no more

Lou: It isn't likely don't worry yourself — no men (there's no men) are knocking on your door

Fran: Every night I go in the Richmond, that Mister Plume always calls out 'allo Ma!' and he always buys me a glass of stout — he'd have offered to marry me only he's got a wooden leg

Lou: You know what he'd have done into that don't you?

Fran: Oh! oow— you dirty cow — what a thing to say —

Enter.

Charlie: Hallo, (to Gran) you still here?

Gran: Don't worry I'm not staying. I'm on me way to Cousin Soph's

Charlie: Whats she giving away?

Gran: Nothing. She's got these interlock bloomers + I need a couple of pairs + she's got them cheap. Only six and eleven. — they're a bargain

Charlie: Whats she asking ~~you~~ for them?

Gran: Six and eleven.

Charlie: Then they're no bleeding bargain.

Gran: You're always nasty about Cousin Soph

Charlie: 'Cos she's a crafty conniving mare thats why —

4

Fran   You don't like her because of mister Whittiker —

Char   Bugger mister Whittaker — I don't care what she does with her spare time
        and I told her so, outside Kings Cross Station

Fran: That was terrible. You pulled her valour hat right down over her eyes —
        she couldn't see where she was going — she was crying —

Lou: I'd better go down to the shop Charlie, 'cos of the money —

Char.   Yes — theres old mother Howard under the drier — she only wants
        combing out, + Bill's got one man in the chair — don't let him
        go near the till — Mother Howard's just perm ends — thats all —
        she's economising — take her down a cup of tea will you ?

Lou: Oh! I can't stand her —

Char: Neither can I, but she brings in custom — her daughter has her hair done
        and she's brought in Mrs Beatty — the one that has the henna

Louie   I can't stand her either

                                                        its important in hairdressing
Char   Its all business. Give her a cup of tea — they like all that ∧ — its a little
        gesture and it costs nothing —

Louie   It costs milk + tea + sugar —   (exit

Char   (after her) Who gives you the housekeepings ? — (to gran) always moaning about
        money —

Fran: So would you be if you had to go to the shops - I go half over London trying to
        get a bit of meat cheaper. Its not easy to make ends meet — I've only got me
        pension and I know —

Char: You get the extra from me

                        don't
Fran: yes I know but it doesn't amount to much, after food and coal — coal is
        a terrible price, it's wicked it really is   (smokeless fuel)
                                                        And this smokeless stuff they make
                                                        you 'ave don't heat the room at all.
                                                        It only glows - thats all it does

5

Char: Well there's Jack — he gives you something — and Kylie —

Gran: Don't talk to me about Kylie — I could be dead for all she cares — I haven't seen her for weeks — she sent the kid round with the half crown — I was wondering if you could let me have a bit more — I can't manage like this —

Char: You know bloody well I can't lay out any more — I've been forking out right and left haven't I ? — and now this bloody WEDDING — you got any idea what weddings cost ?

Gran: Its your own daughter — you've only got the one.

Char: Thank god for that.

Gran: You want to see your own daughter married in style don't you ?

Char: Yes — only I wish she was paying for it.

Gran: She'll have a lovely life out there with him — his people are very comfortable I should think — she'll have a lovely time —

Char: Doreen ? — out there ? — she'll hate it.   And I've told her so.

Gran: You shouldn't have done that. That's driving a wedge.

Char: She's used to this country — she's been born + brought up here, all her life — her nature is not adaptable — she can't adapt — she'll hate it out there —

Gran: I wish someone would give me the chance to go to Australia — I'd like a bit of sun for a change —

Char: You'd hate it yourself — women are not allowed in the pubs —

Gran: Gawd 'elp us —

And I used to say, "You rotten stinker. I gave you my penny, you bought the sweeties, you've eaten all the sweeties, you didn't even give me one." And all the week
he'd threaten. He thought that was very clever.'

Life was at least less cramped when the family moved on, to live both under
and over Charlie Williams's barber-shop in Marchmont Street, at the non-
literary end of Bloomsbury, nudging towards St Pancras.

Pat Williams: 'You see, we moved out of this flat when Dad had the opportunity to buy the shop. The only thing he didn't have was the money … So uncle
loaned him the money to buy the business, but it meant that money was very
tight, and although there were three storeys above, at the top was a three-roomed
flat, then the next floor down was two rooms, a very big one and a smaller one,
down below there was another big room and a smaller one, then it was street
level, where the shop was, and then the two rooms downstairs. And we all had
to go from the flat every Sunday and wash walls and hang paper and everything
until it was all clean. We all had to do it, whether we liked it or not.'

❛ "Gawd, he's got some guts, that kid." You know, 'cos he was only a youngster after all ❜

Marchmont Street was the scene of the most significant confrontations between
Kenneth and his father. Fortunately for the boy, the layout of the place lent itself
to nimble escapes from the site of the battle.

Pat Williams: 'Especially during the war, when we lived in Marchmont Street,
'cos our dining-room and the room we lived in was underground. And Kenneth's
bedroom, my bedroom, all bedrooms were two and three storeys up. So we had
to go up three dirty great flights of stairs. And Ken would go charging up the stairs
– of course he'd lick the old man, he'd got no chance of getting up there – and
he'd get in his room and lock it. And the old man would be bangin' on the door,
and Ken would suddenly turn on Gilbert and Sullivan that he was raving about
in those days. The old man would be bangin', and he'd just make the music go

'My parents spent many happy hours at The Boot with their friends Alf and Edie Palmer. The Palmers lived on the other side of Cromer Street in Clucas Place and they used to trundle their piano across for an evening in the pub. Edie Palmer was always very outgoing, she always loved numbers, numbers like "I'm A Lady Policeman". Then she'd do all kinds of very suggestive things with her truncheon!'
(Kenneth, Comic Roots, 1983)

Edie Palmer, Charlie and Lou, Margate, 1935.

louder and louder. And I used to laugh, "Gawd, he's got some guts, that kid." You know, 'cos he was only a youngster after all, he was only thirteen, fourteen.'

In quieter moments the family lived an utterly standard inner-London life, even down to their rare exits from the city.

Pat Williams: 'We used to go to Southend every year for our holiday. And Dad and I used to get up at some unearthly hour in the morning, go down to the beach and have an early-morning swim, then we called in the butcher's for Ramsgate sausages. And we'd buy a pound of Ramsgate sausages, bring them back to the boarding house, to this one room, where Mum used to cook 'em. And if ever we saw speckled sausages, even as recently as my mother dying, four years ago, I'd say, "Oh Mum, look, Ramsgate sausages." "Oh yes, just like them, aren't they?" It became a standing joke. But Ken nearly drowned, and he was a

LONDON COUNTY COUNCIL.

L.C.C. SCHOOL OF PHOTO-ENGRAVING & LITHOGRAPHY,
6, Bolt Court, Fleet Street, E.C.4.

DAY TECHNICAL SCHOOL.—TERMINAL REPORT.

Name _Kenneth. Chas. Williams_   Term _Christmas_ 19 _41_.

Place in Form _2 nd._   Number of Boys in Form _13_   Year _2 nd_

Subject.	Work of Term Max. 100	Exam. Max 100	Work of Term Max 200		Remarks.
Trade:—		100			
(a) Studio.		75			(
(b) Etching.	70				
(c) Litho Drawing	93				
(d) Photo-Litho.					
English.	200	95			
Chemistry.	98	85			
Mathematics.	92	54			
Light.					
Art.	92				
Physical Training					
Metal Printing		70			
Retouching	65				

Conduct during term _Very good._   No. of times absent _5_

School reopens on _6 th January_ 19 _42_.

The enclosed certificate of health, to be signed by the parent or guardian, will be required on the first day of the new term.

General remarks ~~of Principal~~ _Has made very good progress and deserves to make a success of his future_

Date _19 th. December_ 19 _41_   _B. O'Shaughnessy._

Signature of Principal.
Headmaster.

63

bit scared of water after that. He didn't like games of any description, but I was in the athletic team. King's Cross.'

Young as Ken was, he needed to learn a trade, according to his father, so his general education ceased in 1940, when he was 14 years of age. His early interest in calligraphy, and his all-round neatness with a pen, seemed to suit him for an apprenticeship somewhere in the printing trade.

Pat Williams: 'And then he went away to Bolt Court School of Lithography and Lithographic Printing. I thought it was just dreadful, to send my little brother away. And when I came home from work and saw him with his label on, oh God, it broke me in two. They all had labels on them, with their name and where they were for.'

Bolt Court had been sited off Fleet Street, but the worsening air-raids on London meant that the school juniors, like most other young folk, were scheduled for evacuation to more tranquil parts of the country. So young Kenneth's label must have carried the name of Bicester, in Oxfordshire, where part of the Bolt Court enterprise was now operating. Although by the end of 1941 he was back in London at the original Bolt Court premises, Kenneth seems to have been too busy – as was the entire country – to fall back into the earlier patterns of family life. His training, and an attachment to the Sea Cadets, filled much of his time until the military called, towards the end of the war. By the time basic training and a certain amount of physical 'building up' had been accomplished, it was indeed April 1945. The troopship on which Kenneth embarked with the Royal

Pages 65–66 No 14747886 Williams KC, Private, was called up in 1944 and, after serving as a draughtsman in India, joined the CSE as their poster designer two years later. After some rejections ('Returned to Unit') he was eventually cast in 7 **Keys to Baldpate** as Jigs Kennedy, a police inspector. These delicate pieces of paper are all that survive of Kenneth's debut in professional performance.

Pages 67–68 The programme for **High and Low** in January 1947 said of Kenneth: 'In this production, he has quite a variety of characters to portray. Rather in contrast to his "public" demeanour, Ken's private life revolves mostly around books and "charpoys" [a light Indian bedstead]. He finds the combination of the two both comfortable and instructive.' **The poster – which he himself had designed – described it as a** 'bright new musical'.

"ALLADDIN"   *Ken Williams' Copy.*

(Princess)

(Fairy music is hear off - and Fairy Water-Melon-Seed, enters d.L. front of tabs)

          " I am Fairy Water Melon Seed fellows,
          SEALF's own godmother,
          I take a LIAP from our bloke,
          And give it to another,
          When you get into hed at night,
          You'll find I am about
          Seeing you tuck your mossy in, and take your finger out,
          But tis not of service now I speak,
          So give a kindly ear,
          But of that happy luletide thrill
          That comes but once a year
          I mean of course, the PANTOMIME,
          So sit close to your mucker,
          But let me warn you from the start
          This panto isn't pukka
          But please be kind, don't laugh too much
          At gags that may be blue
          Or with my magic wand, I'll make you all, Group 92.
          Enough of threats though, settle back, and let your minds take wing,
          Back three centuries or more, to the waterfront, at PEKING"

(tabs open on empty stage)

     ANNOUNCER :-   Moving over to the shore, we alight upon PEKING's famous
                        waterfront. What sights it has seen since China flung herself
                        open to the west,
                        With the motto of the WINDMILL, "we never closed".
                        In the daytime, it's just a peaceful waterfront ....
                        Oh! but I forget ....

                        In every show there is that bit thats simply sure to bore us,
                        Don't think that you're escaped my lads, the lusty opening
                                                                        chorus.

("Chorus of the Pantomime")

                        .... as I was saying, in the daytime its just a peaceful
                        waterfront, With the pedlars plying their wares ....

(Exit Fairy : enter Coolie with strings of ma-mee over his shoulder. He is shouting
"Ma-Mee, Ma-Mee, Ma-Mee; and finally brings the call to its logical conclusion
by singing - "I'd walk a million miles, for one of your smiles, my Ma-Mee.........
enter from opposite side another pedlar, shouting "New lamps for old" - as
they pass Pedlar One hisses "For the last time, you're not on yet," - they go off
arguing : Re-enter Fairy.)

ANNOUNCER. But when night falls ....(sinister laugh.)

(Enter Widow Twankey, d.r.)

                        (continued on Page 2.)

Page 3

TWANKEY. Then let me fest it's powers my boy ! bring out your bag of tricks
I wish to have the swimsuit of 1956.

(Black - out then full - up : GENII has appeared with tiny swimsuit, TWANKEY
screams and dashes off.)

GENII. I am the Genii Gin - sling, I'll put you all in clover,
Unlike Gordons, and the rest, with me there's no hangover.

ALLADDIN. Teek High ! Now surprise me some more !

(Trick with brassiere)

You know my secret heart Oh Slave, so take a jaldi hint,
And bring me from the Palace grounds that sweet and luscious bint.

GENII. You mean de heir presumptive - oh ! give dat dame a break,
She's just back from the Union, and besides, she's not your cake.

ALLADDIN. Don't quibble you base infidel, but speed her 'oer the land,
Remember I'm a civvy now, so jump to my command.

(Black - out and Gong - Princess appears, singing "Some day my Prince will come")

PRINCESS. Aren't these Dakota's wonderful ?

ALLADDIN. Ah! erotic Edna ! I wonder how many week-ends you've lost recently ?

PRINCESS. (Pointing to Genii) Who's the Chan-wallah ?

ALLADDIN. This is the Genii by whose lamp, all pleasures I may know,

PRINCESS. Is that a lamp ? I thought at first, that it must be a ....

(Gong sounds, Genii appears and claps a "censored" notice over Princess's mouth)

PRINCESS. I know you not, but your attire, resembles an old curtain,
Be careful lest your head should go, subcheez for a posh burton.

ALLADDIN. These rags conceal a noble heart, so Princess have no fear !
I'll now sing of my true estate - is Billy Cotton here ?

PRINCESS. Who is your lordly master then, to whom the Nations bow ?

ALLADDIN. The great and noble robber-king that they call Choo Chin Chow.

(Song :- "CHOO CHIN CHOW". At end of Song, enter Genii, u.c.)

GENII. I'm the Daemon fuel and power, I'l here and there, in a trice,
This love scene's getting far too hot, I'll turn them into ice.

(Enter Fairy.)

FAIRY. I'm the Fairy of the Wood,
I go about a'doing good -
I'll foil his plan's I'll bet,
And turn our frozen lover's here, into a Swiss Clochette.

(Alladdin and Princess perform the Clock dance, and exuent U.C.)

FAIRY. Again you find me, on the scene, doing my magic rounds,
Although you've heard I'm a fairy boys, I'm strictly "out of bounds"

(Fairy produces "out of bounds" sign.)

As you can see, my plans have worked, the princess now enchants,
Alladdin, with her sweet beguile, "Oh Gawd" - these P.T. pants.
But now a song, a special treat for all the little Mary's'n
A dirty ditty by a WAAF entitled " Whoops the Fairies".

C A T S   C R A D L E

"Highaldhow
Ken Williams
(Miss Tassle.)

Miss Lillian Mawdsley.
Miss Eva Tassle.   TWO MAIDEN LADIES.

SCENE - The adjoining gardens of two suburban semi detached houses -
being late evening.

(Lillian Mawdsley appears with saucers of milk).
Min, min min, min.   Come you Here you bad cat.
(places sauces of milk down and ha a coy look over thegarden wall.
Sniffs and retires to the other side of her garden).

(Miss Tassle enters.   Wearing an afternoon gown and garden hat.
She carries a small garden watering-can with a long spout.
She smokes a cig. with a long holder.
Watering her flowers she sings in a cracked voice
NO ROSE IN ALL THE WORLD...... Came .... came -

Miss M.   : Good evening Miss Tassle.

Miss T.   : (startled). Oh, what a fright you gave me.

Miss M.   : I'm sure I am ever so sorry.

Miss T.   : Not at all.   The fact is, I've been terrible nervy ever
             since my last operation.

    M.   : Oh Indeed.   Its a fine night.

    T.   : Lovely, too lovely.

    M.   : We shall have a full moon.

    T.   : Ha, ha, ha, do you know whenever I see a full moon I do
             believe in fairies, don't you ?

    M.   : As a matter of fact I don't.

    T.   : Neither do I really.   I love to make believe.   I live in a
             world all of my own, you know.

    M.   : Oh really.   I suppose you haven't seen my Minnie about any
             where, have you ?

    T.   : (raising her lorgnettes). Your what Miss M. ?

    M.   : My minnie, my cat.   I thought perhaps you might have noticed
             her in your world, she doesn't appear to be in mine.

    T.   : No.   I fear I haven't.

    M.   : She's mousing sure as fate. Min, min, min.   I can't bear
             her to be out too late.   You never know what might happen.

    T.   : (haughtily).   Quiet.

    M.   : 'ow are your nasturtiums.

    T.   : Lovely, too lovely !   They grow so absurdly quickly, I feel
             just like Jack. and the Beanstalk.

    M.   : Can't think what's the matter with mere look !

    T.   : My dear, how dreadful.   What's that long black thing ?

    M.   : Oh that's only a bootlace ! (Business).

2

T. : Oh dear me ! I thought it was a great Black Work.

M. : Hm.   I can't think what's the matter with ~~my forget-me-not~~
They were as right as rain yesterday, but look at them now.

T. : Hm, are those forgetmenots ?

M. : What do you think, they were, Starfish ?

T. : The lights so bad, I find it difficult to see

M. : ~~Nonsense, theres nothing about in them
the they have of play~~

T. : Hm, such a pretty cat.

M. : Nice markings and intelligent, and when I say she's human
I'm under-rating her.

T. : (sarcastically).   Fancy. ~~love~~

M. : Only the other day you would laughed.   Oh dear, oh dear.

T. : What happened ?

M. : Well, you know that young couple from over number fourteen,
well they pops over quite unexpectedly like, and you know you
can't be inhospitable, so I says, Come I says, stay to supper
I says, if you don't mind taking pot of luck, I says; I knew I
had a bit of cold mutton left over from Tuesdays dinner and half
a blanc mange and some prunes.   So we all sat down and had
the mutton, then I says, excuse me, I says, then out to the kitchen
I goes for the Afters.   I look around and there under the sink,
was a glass dish with only two prunes in it.   My dear you
could have knocked me down with a feather.   I had another look
and there was Minnie under the table awashin of herself.   Minnie,
I says, what have you done with the prunes.   My dear, would
you believe it, she never even looked up at me, but went on
awashin herself.   So then I ses, very stern I ses, Min.. nie.
What have you done with them there prun. ing.   My dear,
believe it or not, she gave me one look and swept out.   You
know you can't help laughing at her.   She makes believe there
mice you know.

T. : (with a false laugh).   Charming, quite charming.   As a matter
of fact Miss M.   I ... that is, my sister and I, have for a
long time past, been wishing to discuss a certain subject with
you.

M. : Oh indeed.   In what way ?

T. : Well .... its... rather delicate.... I hardly know where to
begin.

M. : Oh, well if you're alluding to our little upset of last Teus
fortnight, as I told you at the time Miss T. it was NOBODYs
fault.   Vera took the lid offf the dust bin and what you
found on your rockery, must have blown there.

T. : (laugh slightly).   Oh, oh not at all, not at all Miss M.
That is forgiven and forgotten.   This is something quite
different.   This is something... well... much nearer my heart.

Engineers arrived in Bombay (Mumbai) just as the European war was ending. There followed a brief period of conventional war service, followed by Kenneth's well-documented career with Combined Services Entertainment and its concert parties, made famous by Peter Nichols's play *Privates on Parade* (Nichols was a CSE colleague) and the TV series *It Ain't Half Hot Mum*. Kenneth was demobilized on 4 December 1947, and the whole family got hilariously tight at Henekey's bar.

It was 1956, very nearly a decade on, before Kenneth Williams moved into his own apartment. Until the age of 30, therefore, he continued to be based, officially, at 57 Marchmont Street, the family home. There were absences, to be sure, seasons spent in repertory companies far away, but theatrical digs didn't offer much of a respite from the traditional parental strains. Sister Pat was out of the picture for a while, having married an Australian and emigrated to Sydney: one focus of conflict fewer, as long as Pat stayed away.

❛ Very bad influence on me, my brother. I didn't swear in those days, I didn't tell dirty jokes❜

Pat Williams: 'And then when I came home in '51, I came on holiday, and he drove me mad. I thought of it the other day, I saw a photograph of Ken and I, walking down the Mall one Sunday morning. And he was really, really tormenting me. Very bad influence on me, my brother. I didn't swear in those days, I didn't tell dirty jokes, I was married, my husband would no more tell me a dirty joke … He kept running in front of me and digging me, and pushing me, and then he'd come round this side and have a go. And I said, "Ken, you'll get me annoyed." He said, "Well, let it out! Go on, let it out!" And in the end I just stood there, and for the first time in my life I said, "Why don't you fuck off!" And he went, "Oooh, ooh, you said it, oh, don't you feel good, didn't you feel it come right up, and out! Don't you feel free!" And there he is, and I've got this photograph of him, waving a walking stick down the Mall. And I just stood there and I thought, Oh well, what's the good? And when we got home for lunch he said, "Mum, Pat said fuck!" And my Mum says, "You didn't. She wouldn't say a word like that.""Yes she did. Go on, tell her." I said, "No.""Mum, come in here." So he went into the dining-room. "Pat, tell Mum the truth. Did you or did you not say [it]?" And in the end I had to say yes, I did say it.'

This naked resumption of childhood hostilities would repeat itself, on and on, through their lives, though Ken passed as little comment on Pat as he could. In his autobiography, *Just Williams*, she makes no appearances at all between 1947 (when she had already departed) and the completely different world of 1964. Yet it's Pat herself who provided a glimpse of the moment when the obscure Ken Williams began to turn into the celebrated Kenneth. Pat had undergone a divorce in Australia, and she was starting again.

Pat Williams: 'Ken was just beginning to make a name for himself in *Hancock's Half Hour*. So of course suddenly out of the blue he decided we'll decorate the lounge. So everybody had to put overalls on and decorate the bloody lounge, a

'Fabulous to see my name in lights over the theatre in Shaftsbury Avenue! It is v. thrilling for me.' **(Diary, 21 September 1959)**

massive room. And then he bought a carpet. And then he bought something else, and then he bought her a fridge, and then she had a washing machine. And the ultimate was the fur coat. And of course there she is preening herself with all these lovely prezzies, the old man's saying, "Waste o' bleedin' money," and all I could do was laugh. And contribute absolutely nothing, because I was too busy paying off me debt. And I'd only been home twelve weeks … and had a barney with the old man, and he told me to piss off, so I did, and I went and shared a flat with other girls. But by this time, of course, he'd gone to *Beyond Our Ken* and *Round the Horne*, everywhere you went there was Williams. We used to go round to the theatre at night, just to see his name up in lights.'

❛ We used to go round to the theatre at night, just to see his name up in lights ❜

On occasion, Pat would be admitted to the dressing room, too, but infantile skirmishes would break out, as ever.

Pat Williams: 'In a play called *Gentle Jack*, with Edith Evans, he played Pan, and I went round to the dressing-room on the first night, he had jagged trousers on, you know, jagged suit, little Pan outfit, and of course he'd had nothing on his feet, and make-up everywhere. And when I got in the dressing-room he was standing at the sink. And I looked, and I thought, "What's he going to do?" And there was a plastic bowl on the floor. And he said, "Oh sit down, kid, pour yourself a drink." Then up came the leg in the sink, you see, and he washed all the make-up off, and then he put the clean foot in the bowl. Then up came the other leg. And he wore Aertex shorts, you know. I said, "Hey! I can see your tom tiddly!" So he said, "So? Seen it before, haven't you? You're my

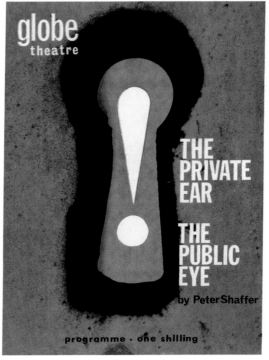

'Opening night. If I can pull it off tonight, it will be a victory indeed.'
(Diary, 10 May 1962)

Charlie Williams with Lou and friends in Jersey, towards the end of his life.

sister." So I said, "Yes, but when I saw it, it was only little. Mind you, it's not much bigger now." "Don't be rude. You've got a bloody cheek." '

By the time Pat resurfaces again in *Just Williams*, in 1964, she's living with her mother, Louie, in a flat in Broadhurst Gardens, and a couple of years have passed since the strange death of Dad, Charlie Williams. In October 1962 the Hammersmith Coroner's Court returned a verdict of 'Death by Misadventure' (due to corrosive poisoning by carbon tetrachloride) on Charlie, who had swigged the poisonous liquid from a bottle labelled 'Gee's Linctus', an over-the-counter cough remedy. How the carbon tetrachloride got into the bottle remains, as Kenneth's diary commented, 'v. mysterious'. Kenneth gave a very cool account of the entire episode, which in one way he was entitled to do, having missed the official procedures entirely, inquest included. Peter Eade, his agent, accompanied Louie to the Hammersmith Coroner's Court, and in the evenings Kenneth continued to appear as usual in *The Private Ear* and *The Public Eye*, giving one of his best stage performances. Whether this eerie calm was noted at the time is not known, but it was certainly rumoured among actors that the police had been keeping an eye on Kenneth since the death, in case he had had some part in it. There were stories of a police car parked on permanent watch outside the Williams flat. As it turned out, he merely paid off Charlie's overdraft at a bank in Notting Hill, and the case was closed.

Eventually Pat went off to live alone in Camden Town, and Louie moved into a small apartment in Marlborough House, Osnaburgh Street, across the Marylebone Road from Great Portland Street station. Kenneth arrived in the flat across the landing from Louie in 1972. It was an arrangement few friends or fellow professionals would have contemplated, yet it seemed unsurprising, since Kenny and Louie had been seen as a pair for some time, even if Louie was often chaperoned by her sister, Edith.

❛So my daughter for the first year of her life was kitted out entirely by the Williams family ❜

Barry Took: 'His Ma, dear old Louie, she was a delight. My missus was pregnant during one of the series of *Round the Horne*, and every week Louie and her sister would come up with a little box. "Summink for the baybee," they'd go, and give my wife a little box of bootees or matinée jacket or whatever it was that they'd knitted. So my daughter for the first year of her life was kitted out entirely by the Williams family.'

Much has been made of the auto-erotically charged scene in Kenneth's diaries where he vacuums his flat in his underpants. But was this a rare tableau, or part of a strict programme of household hygiene in the Williams apartments? Betty Marsden, a mother herself, had her own strong opinion on the matter.

Betty Marsden: 'I think he adored his mum, but I found I was a little shocked when I heard she was his charlady. "You know," he said, "my mum does my cleaning." I think it would have been nice had he said, "My mother insists on coming to do my cleaning. She won't let anybody else in." I would have understood that, but I hated the way he said that. I was a little open-mouthed! And his washing! Everything. Well, mums do, I know. But, "Mum comes and does my cleaning?" I didn't care for it really.'

In any society or group of people where a civilised code is held to be valuable, and one of its members violates it most profoundly — let us say in the case of premeditated murder — there are several courses open to that society. 1) He could be expelled from the country, but that raises the moral question of evasion AND whether it is right to inflict him on some other society. 2) He could be executed + have his life taken from him, in the same way that he took it from his victim. 3) He could be imprisoned + shut away from the company of those he so blatantly outraged + offended, or 4) He could be confined to a place where he would undergo some form of remedial treatment.

For various reasons, modern society tends toward the last solution — not so much because it believes in the efficacy of remedial treatment — few of us think that people like Haigh or Christie or Brady can be CURED — but because it abnegates responsibility. The argument runs from the Christian "Judge not lest ye yourself be judged" through illustrations of the non-deterrent aspect of hanging, to the accusation of society becoming vengeful and in taking life, doing the very thing they're supposed to deplore. "Give them the chance to redeem themselves" we are told — though what we are to do with unrepentant assassins who proclaim their rightness and actually refuse psychological help, — I do not think they know. In the last analysis they seem to feel "better alive than dead — better incarcerated, than have the guilt of his death on our hands ..."

Pages 74–76 'We talked about the "Moors Case". It has touches of Gilles De Rais and the Marquis de Sade and sounds quite revolting. One feels in cases like this that people should be painlessly put away. All one's carefully proposed arguments about capital punishment being wrong drain away on reading about this sort of filth.' (Diary, 23 April 1966)

Thus we are led back to responsibility — or the lack of it, in Society. For it was Responsibility (or the lack of it) that caused the crime in the first place. In the Western World (as opposed to the Communist World) we have come to value a concept of INDIVIDUAL FREEDOM and to say that there are certain areas (limited though they may be) wherein MEN must be free to make choices, make selections, and act on their free will — of their own volition — without coercion + pressure. This freedom has been fought for over many years IN EUROPE (the concept of Individual freedom to all men is something that was unknown in the ancient greek civilization) and it has been won for us by some of the noblest + most honourable names in European liberalism. This freedom carries Responsibility + but it is — one must repeat — Limited. Of course it is. It has to be — as all human Societies are limiting. But if, within the LIMITS of that Freedom an adult member of Society willingly chooses to flout one of its cardinal tenets — if he chooses to outrage public morality by murdering another individual, (who has all the same rights that he is so shamefully abusing) then Society is acting properly in destroying him. If it did NOT it would be failing to uphold the very values of responsibility

Individual freedom, and the necessary responsibility
attendant upon it, for which it has fought so zealously.

All the other arguments are spurious — the
rubbishy dictum 'This hurts me more than it hurts you'
with its inference that those punished are more harmed
than the offender, is foolish indeed. If it were
true, one should possess a very impartial Judiciary
in Britain.

The other argument — the one that says Society
becomes as evil as the Criminal in Taking
revenge, is also untrue. Vengeance is personal
and barbaric, and is concerned with an ostensible equalizing
process which is supposed in some primitive way
to RIGHT a wrong.   This is totally at variance
with what a civilized society does in its law courts.
The judgement there is carefully weighed — prosecution
+ defence present learned arguments + the jury has
the benefit of a sound legal mind to sum up for them,
and if the criminal is found guilty, + sentenced to death
it is — it is nothing to do with revenge — upon society's concern for others, and for
their protection against such wickedness, in the future.
That is why it's written over the CCC — Defend The
Children of the Poor + Punish The Wrong Doer —

But Louie was not without strategies for clawing back a bit of compensatory hospitality, according to Pat's slightly jaundiced testimony.

'That was what Hat was for me: somebody who was "as sweet as a kiss on a winter's day". She was the most heart-warming of persons.' (Kenneth, **An Audience with**, 1983)

Kenneth at a fundraising event with Hattie Jacques, Lou and Aunt Edith (far left).

Pat Williams: 'People used to come and knock at Ken's door, and she'd open her door. "Yes, what did you want?" "Oh, er, hello Mrs Williams, I've come to take Kenneth out to lunch." "Oh hang on then, I'll get me coat." So Ken would come out and say, "Where are you going?" "Oh, this gentleman's invited me to lunch." He didn't invite her at all! But he couldn't very well turn round and say, "I didn't, Ken, honestly I didn't." '

Out on his own, Kenneth would tend to treat all senior ladies as if they were his mother and possessed of the same raucous, pseudo-shockable glee.

Derek Nimmo: 'He'd come here for dinner and hold court, and one would have, say, people like Peter Rawlinson who was Attorney General, people with fine minds, and Kenny would outmanoeuvre people, really, in conversation. He always had the weapon of putting in something rather shocking. There was an old marchioness sitting here one day, and he said, "Oww, I was sitting on a plane, I dropped all gin all over me cock. Have you ever had gin on your cock? No, you haven't got a cock, have you, no," and then turned to some rather grave political problem in the next sentence.'

'Orton asked George Borwick, who took the photograph, for his handkerchief to put down his pants. I don't think Joe gave it back!' (Peter Cadley)

Joe Orton (1933–1967).

Pages 78–79 Tangiers, Morocco, May 1967.

The fact that the cock featured so largely in conversation and fantasy surely reflected its lack of active engagement elsewhere. But it was rare for Kenneth to talk to a fellow performer about the desolations of his private life.

Sir Clement Freud: 'He had a sort of slightly naughty voyeur side to him, and talked every now and again in the third person about things which were clearly done by him but attributed to others. I mean the Joe Orton friendship and Morocco and indeed what comes out in his diaries. He was not ever confiding about anything. He would confide about being High Church, about thinking that Thatcher was a great Conservative leader. His digestive tract, all sorts of physical ailments and failings, were common currency. His mother's well-being, or not, took up a bit of time. His hospital visits: he'd been to see people, we

Tangiers, June 1966, with George Borwick (bottom right).

heard about that. But nothing personal came out, nothing that would bring you closer to him.'

Barry Took reckoned he'd got about as close as it was possible for a fellow professional to go.

Barry Took: 'I think it was a traumatic thing when his agent died, Peter Eade, who had the brilliant idea of only having ten clients, ever. And had very good clients: Ronnie Barker was one, Joan Sims was another, and when he died I think Kenneth always felt deserted by dominant males, I think because his father really didn't care for him terribly, I suspect … It strikes me that in Kenneth Horne he found a father figure, in Peter Eade he found a father figure, and later in his life me, even – or at least a sibling that he could trust. I mean he would confess all sorts of things to me that he wouldn't say in public. He said to me on one occasion, "I went to the doctor," he said. "I don't know what to do, I've got these health problems, and I'm upset emotionally, I know I'm unstable emotionally, and the doctor said, 'Why don't you get yourself a petty officer, a retired petty officer of the navy, somebody to live with you, look after you, old chap, get my meaning?' I couldn't do that, I couldn't, I couldn't have that." He said, "I admire Charlie Hawtrey, envy him rather than admire him. He can go into a pub, pick up a couple of sailors, and be happy for the rest of the day. I couldn't do that!" He was too fastidious, that was the aesthetic part of him. And yet he would say all sorts of outrageous things, and be unaware that there was a barrier that he'd gone through.'

Pat Williams: 'But I asked him, was he a homosexual. And he said, "Why, does it make any difference?" So I said, "No, but I just wondered." So he said, "Well if, because I prefer men's company to women, if that makes me a homosexual, yes I am. If you're asking me, am I a practising homosexual, no I'm not." So I said, "Well, that's good enough for me." So he said, "What are you looking like that for?" So I said, "Will you tell me, what do homosexuals do then?" So he said, "How old are you?" I said "44". "And you don't know? Well, I'm not going to give you a demonstration." And then all of a sudden he'd stick his arm through mine on the settee, and said, "I'm ever so glad you're my sister." '

Sir Clement Freud: 'But Gordon Jackson, whom I knew reasonably well, with whom I spent a few days in Hong Kong, mostly talking about Kenny, was very interesting about him. You know, saying that what you can't do is change him, you accept him and you love him or you're frightened of him, or whatever.'

Derek Nimmo: 'I remember I had a heart bypass operation about eight years ago, and I suddenly received a very long letter from Kenny, about six pages, saying how fond he was of me and how much he hoped his old mate would get well soon and things, the sort of thing he would never say to you in the flesh. It was terribly touching really, coming from him, because you felt he wore his heart on his sleeve, but there was a deeper person underneath.'

❛The tears are running down our faces, we were in absolute hysterics. Now that's lovely❜

You could never tell which Kenneth you were going to get, or what the chances were that a moody Kenneth might turn abruptly into a sunny entertainer. His sister recalled a classic instance of that switch of personalities.

Pat Williams: 'I had a party at one stage – this is the sort of thing he'd do – and he rang me and said, "I understand you're having a party." So I said, "Yes, how do you know?" "Marvellous, isn't it, when your own sister's having a party, and your own brother's not invited." So I said, "Well, if I invited you would you come?" He said, "Yes," so I said, "OK, you're invited, come." Bang, I put the phone down. And of course he arrived. He sat down on the chair, we were all milling around, music going, not loudly, I don't like loud music. And he came in, sat down on the settee and he said, "You can turn that row off." "What row?" "That music, turn it off. I don't want to hear it." "Don't start. If you're going to start, and do a moody on me, there's the door." He just looked at me and glared. So I said, "Right, what would you like to drink?" "Nothing." So I said, "You've

Page 83 Kenneth doing an Orton in Tangiers.

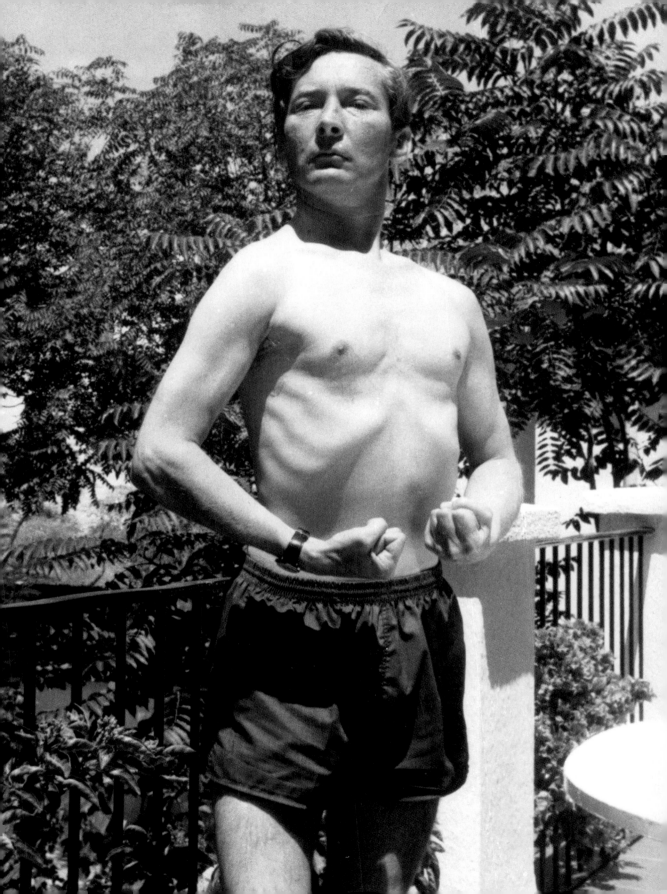

got to have something." "Give me one good reason why." So I said, "It's nearly Christmas, you could drink your sister's health." "Oh, all right, I'll have an ouzo." Now he picked an ouzo because he thought I wouldn't have it. So I said, "Certainly." Got the ouzo, got the water. I said, "Would you like it with or without water?" He went, "Oh, you've got some." And he burst out laughing. And for the next three hours we didn't have the music on, we all sat round the floor in a semi-circle while he entertained us. The tears are running down our faces, we were in absolute hysterics. Now that's lovely. Another time I would ring up, "Oh hello love, it's me." "I'm busy." Bang.'

❛He was angry with himself, sometimes the world, he was fed up. It was like being with a manic-depressive who goes through all the cycles of bipolar in one hour!❜

Gyles Brandreth: 'Towards the end of his life Kenneth became impossible. He became very difficult to know and almost impossible to work with except as a solo artist. He screamed too much, he shouted too much, he was angry with you because he wanted to smoke and you didn't want to. He was angry with himself, sometimes the world, he was fed up. It was like being with a manic-depressive who goes through all the cycles of bipolar in one hour! You have an enormous high, then an enormous low, and unfortunately it was made worse by alcohol. Not that he drank vast amounts, but a little went a long way. So it actually became quite a strain to go to a restaurant with him. It would begin so pleasantly, in the corner of a restaurant, he'd be amusing, but as the wine slipped down he would become a bit of a monster. He'd begin playing not to you, but to the waiter, then the next-door table, then the entire restaurant. By the end of the evening you wanted to disappear, you wanted him to disappear, and everybody in the restaurant wanted him to go home. He then did go home and sobered up and felt desperate. He also felt that thing that Cyril Connolly describes in *Enemies of Promise*, that "despair that comes to the wit who's given his energy out in verbal fusillades and comes back exhausted having just spoken all night, brilliantly, but achieved nothing". It's a low *after* the high.'

Kenneth at home,
Marlborough House,
April 1974.

'The same mistakes made. I just went on and on, and talked too much. O! I wanted to be dead. I drank a bottle of wine. It is my undoing.' **(Diary, 17 August 1963)**

Was Kenneth Williams sensitive to other people's views of the way he lived? There's a certain amount of evidence that he felt more challenged than he admitted when an adverse view was uttered. His ever-steadfast friend Michael Whittaker tells the extraordinary story of a journey undertaken entirely to enable Kenneth to retaliate in kind.

Michael Whittaker: 'One day he said he wanted to go to St Neots in Cambridgeshire, so I said, "Why are we going there?" He said, "Mind your own business!" We got there and he jumped out of the car in the town, got a local map and found a particular street, number 47 or whatever it was, and we sat outside whilst he made notes about this house: that the garden gate had no latch on it, that the paint was peeling off the front door, that the curtains were dirty, the garden was overgrown. All the while I didn't ask him what it was all about.

Now, I knew that he got hundreds of letters a week, 95 per cent were complimentary — lots from children about *Jackanory* — and the other 5 per cent were attacking or obscene, nearly always anonymous. But this poor man in St Neots had put his name and address, so Kenneth wrote back to him, a very severe letter, saying, "I do not indulge in whatever you accuse me of and I hope on receipt of this letter you drop dead!" Just in case he hadn't dropped dead, and because Kenneth hadn't heard anything, he wrote another letter after our trip saying, "Your house at number 47 is as filthy as your mind, your garden gate has no latch on it, the paint's peeling off your front door, the curtains are dirty, and your garden's overgrown!" And of course this man would know that Kenneth Williams had come and looked at his house, so Kenneth got a reply saying, "Please forgive me. May the Lord Jesus Christ forgive me for making these allegations!" Our expedition was all for that purpose.'

Usually their outings were more benignly cultural, and if made in the company of Kenneth's mum, hilariously so.

Michael Whittaker: 'One day Louie said she'd like to go to Lichfield, and when she saw the cathedral she said, "Oh, it's beautiful, isn't it? And they're lovely flying buttocks!" And so from then on we couldn't look at any gothic buildings without Kenneth going wild about flying buttocks. She was famous for her malapropisms.'

It's a lovely story, but it illustrates as well as any the way the spirit of Marchmont Street clung to Kenneth's life. He never did get away from it, to the end of his life, except in the deepest throes of work. And his life's work began on the stage.

Enter
stage right

'The trouble with Kenny, he would change characters in the middle of a sentence. He might start as one character and finish up as some total anarchic figure at the end of the sentence. He was very strange'

Derek Nimmo

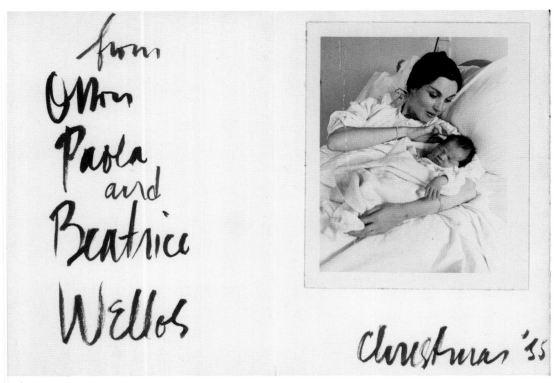

'Orson Welles once directed me in **Moby Dick**, and afterwards he said: "I want you to come to New York, I have three plays for you." I was frightened to death of going to America so I told him I wouldn't be able to because I was going to do a musical where I had to wear short trousers [**The Buccaneer**]. He said: "Why do you do such rubbish? You should aim for quality. You will tread a road to oblivion." And I thought, ooooh, how dreadful. But then, of course, he went on to do nothing but ads for beer and stuff, didn't he?' **(Kenneth, interview, 1984)**

Christmas card from Orson Welles, his third wife Paola Mori and daughter Beatrice Welles-Smith, 1955.

It's difficult to convince the many fans of Kenneth Williams who know him as a radio funny-man and the soul of the *Carry On* series that he thought of himself primarily as a theatre person. The theatre is one of the senior arts – in the old days of Fleet Street, to occupy the post of Drama Critic was to be the aristocrat of the review pages – but its triumphs belong to the moment. Even when a hit stage production is televised or filmed, nobody pretends that the essence of the piece has been truly caught. Plays are events, full of nightly accidents, small or large, and to have caught their real flavour 'you had to be there'.

With Kenneth, the liveness of the drama brought both exhilarations and dangers. He could be quite brilliant on stage, but the very ease with which he could

Page 88 'We thought it'd be a good idea if I photograph some well known people and we did a big display in an empty shop on Hampstead High Street with very big prints and statements by each one saying why they supported the Hampstead Theatre Club. It was all to raise awareness of our club. I photographed four people: Kenneth, Margaret Rutherford, Kenneth Tynan and Heather Sears. I expect the connection with my grandfather – who was an innovative stage designer, terribly important in the history of stage design, and the son of Henry Irving and Ellen Terry – was quite nice for Kenneth and I think that may have endeared him a bit to me anyway.' (Helen Craig)
Backstage at the Globe Theatre, three weeks into **The Private Ear** and **The Public Eye**, 1962.

switch from voice to voice – the thing that brought him a new career when he played the Dauphin in *Saint Joan* – could undermine both his performance and the play as a whole. If he felt the evening was foundering, or if he was getting fed up with a long theatrical run, he would begin to misbehave, importing bits of himself into the rehearsed proceedings. Suddenly his onstage character would be queasily coexisting with a music-hall comedian.

Derek Nimmo: 'The trouble with Kenny, he would change characters in the middle of a sentence. He might start as one character and finish up as some total anarchic figure at the end of the sentence. He was very strange.'

Backstage at the Lyric Hammersmith for **The Buccaneer**, 1955.

After *Saint Joan* his stage career had run healthily just the same. It can't have been easily to manage, either in practical or emotional terms. At one deeply ironic point in 1955 Kenneth was rehearsing *Moby Dick* during the day, and wrestling with the whims of Orson Welles, one of the more spectacular show-business tyrants of his age. But at night Ken would traipse home to Marchmont Street, to be under the thumb of the rather more limited Charlie Williams. It was Kenneth's versatility that recommended him to Welles, but versatility is no guarantee of stardom on the stage. On the other hand, what specialism could Kenneth offer? Where was the natural niche for such an idiosyncratic player? Derek Nimmo, a theatrical impresario as well as an actor, perceived the problem.

❛ In **The Buccaneer** when he was playing a schoolboy he was at his best, because he was sort of mischievous and naughty ❜

Derek Nimmo: 'The first time I saw him was in a musical, I think, called *The Buccaneer*, which was written by Sandy Wilson, and there was this extraordinary talent. You see, he was terribly difficult to cast, really, he was a wonderful Dauphin in *Saint Joan*, and then there weren't very many stage plays for which he was really suitable, he was a sort of hobgoblin, will-o'-the-wisp, Robin Goodfellow, he wasn't a proper person. He did that play *My Fat Friend* which was written for him really, and after about a year, I think, when it was playing to absolute capacity, he suddenly hated the character he was playing, which was a homosexual, which he didn't like, and he left the play, to everyone's horror because it then came off. And that was probably his last really big stage success. But he was terribly difficult to cast. But in *The Buccaneer* when he was playing a schoolboy he was at his best, because he was sort of mischievous and naughty and totally new, one hadn't seen this extraordinary creature before.'

Pages 93–94 'This could have been done at Kenneth's prompting to be considered for one of the revues he did, such as **Pieces of Eight**. He was always, generously, trying to get [Michael] Codron to include something of mine but they never did. It's not much good is it? At the time I must assume this was written, I was pretty low spirited, impoverished and coping with our first severely handicapped daughter.' **(Peter Nichols)**

PIECE OF HIS MIND
A double-act sketch for Kenneth Williams and Peter Nichols
by Peter Nichols.

(DESK WITH DRAWERS; ON IT A TELEPHONE, PAPERS, A PLASTER HEAD
~~LOOK~~ WITH CEREBRAL DIVISIONS. A COMFORTABLE CHAIR BEHIND THE DESK,
A COUCH DOWNSTAGE; A FEARFUL CONTEMPORARY CHAIR OTHER SIDE OF DESK.
DOCTOR BEHIND DESK, HIS FEET ON IT, A HANKIE IN HIS COLLAR,
EATING A PAPER OF FISH AND CHIPS; RADIO PLAYING JAZZ. PAUSE. PHONE
RINGS. HE ANSWERS IT, CAN'T HEAR, SLAMS DRAWER SHUT WHICH STOPS
RADIO)

DOCTOR: Didn't I tell you I was gone to lunch? Well? A gentleman to
see me? Why didn't you say so at once? Might be a patient. Has he
got an appointment? You - didn't think it mattered? What d'you mean
didn't think it mattered? Isn't this a psychiatric surgery, aren't
you employed as my receptionist, don't I pay you to know such things?
Well, ~~don't promise~~ haven't I promised to pay you as soon as we get
some patients? (ENTER THE PATIENT WITH A SMALL WORK-CASE? WHICH HE
PUTS DOWN AND WEARING A TRILBY HAT. DOCTOR DOESN'T SEE HIM.)
Expecting me to see people who haven't made appointments - any old
Tom, Dick or Harry - What? - He's gone! You mean you let him go -
well, for Heaven's sake run after him and catch him before he gets
away! What? Gone - in here!
(HE LOOKS UP AND SEES PATIENT, STANDING OVER HIM. HE SLAMS DOWN
PHONE AND JUMPS IN FRIGHT. CHIPS FALL)

PATIENT: Now look. Dropped your din-din all over the floor.

DOCTOR: You startled me, creeping in here like that. I feel quite
shaken up - (HASTILY SWALLOWS TWO PILLS WITH SOME WATER) What d'you
mean by it?

PATIENT:(PICKING UP CHIPS INTO PAPER, BLOWING ON THEM, DUSTING
THEM) -And what a thing to be eating. These won't make your hair
curl, you know. My Mum ~~~~ always says there's not a scrap of goodness
in fish and chips..all starch, she says, and grease.

DOCTOR: It was an experiment - a patient of mine, keeps a fish
shop, says the smell follows him everywhere, thinks it's a stygma
ruining his social life. ~~~~ He's coming to see me this afternoon,
so I thought I'd fill the place with the smell and make him feel
at home. I wasn't really eating them -

PATIENT: NO?

DOCTOR: Just toying with them. (STUFFS THE PAPER AWAY) You haven't
any appointment, I believe?

PATIENT: No. I've come...

DOCTOR: What's your name?

PATIENT: Desmond.

DOCTOR: Desmond what?

PATIENT: Bigger.

-2-

DOCTOR: Pardon?

PATIENT: Bigger. Plus grand. Maggiore!

DOCTOR: Oh, Bigger. Please, Mister Bigger, take a seat.

PATIENT: What? Why?

DOCTOR: BEFore we can discuss anything, you must relax.

PATIENT: I haven't got time for relaxing.

DOCTOR: First take off your hat and make yourself feel at home..
(PATIENT TAKES HIS HAT OFF, PUTS IT ON THE PLASTER HEAD.)

PATIENT: You seem to have..

DOCTOR: I want you to understand that if I undertake to treat
you, it will be as your exclusive psychiatric adviser. You must
be frank and co-operative with me, I shall be discreet and
circumspect..

PATIENT: Hold on a second..I haven't come here to listen to you.

~~KENNETH~~DOCTOR: Of course not. You shall do the talking. But all
in good time. First you must relax.

~~PETER~~PATIENT: I haven't got time for that ..things to do..

DOCTOR: They can wait, Mister Bigger, they can wait.

(~~PATIENT, SHRUGGING, PICKS UP PHONE~~) PATIENT: They can't, you
~~PATIENT~~ ~~PETER~~ Hullo, Terence, that you? know —

DOCTOR: (~~SEIZING TELEPHONE~~, PUSHING HIM BACK) Do as I say, Mister
Bigger, as I say. (Now sit down.

(KENNETH SITS IN THE FEARFUL CHAIR. DOCTOR DOESN'T SEE, ~~REPLACES~~
~~PHONE AND~~ BEGINS TO FILL OUT A FORM, TALKING BUT NOT SEEING.) There
can be no possible question of help unless you place yourself
enitrely in my hands.

PATIENT: I only wish I could.

DOCTOR: What?

PATIENT: I wish I'd placed my- self anywhere but in this ruddy
chair.

DOCTOR: Oh, d'you like ~~that~~ it? (LOOKING UP) So do I. Present
from a Chinese patient..

PATIENT: What was his trouble?

DOCTOR: Had an obsession for bending pieces of wire.

PATIENT: I think before he left, he might have straightened this
one out...(THE DOCTOR HELPS HIM OUT. IT HAS BEENSTUCK ON HIS BEHIND.)
You sure that's a chair?

DOCTOR: Why, what else d'you think it is? Well, my Mum could work wonders using that for an egg-whisk.

PATIENT: ~~Television aerial - egg-whisk. Political Prisoner..~~

DOCTOR: Perhaps you'd find the couch more comfortable. Just loosen
your tie and lie down and relax completely. Now. ~~Who~~ Who was it
that ~~told~~ told you to come to me? Your Mum? PATIENT: No. Terence

~~PATIENT: No. My foreman.~~ ~~Doctor: is Terence!~~

~~DOCTOR: Ah! You've been overworking?~~

~~PATIENT: No. Can't complain really. We got on very well really.~~

There was at that time one refuge left in the theatre for the versatile actor of mercurial disposition, and that was the (often misspelled) revue tradition. The succession of sketches, musical items and dance which goes to make up a revue seems to the modern eye a weak form, and it can indeed be painfully inconsequential; but in the 1950s it was still thought of as 'sophisticated' — partly because attempts at social and political satire were encouraged, and partly because revue tolerated material that would have been considered too 'adult' (or sexually alert) for other theatrical forms.

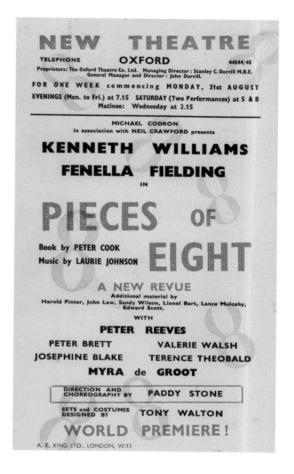

Derek Nimmo: 'He liked revue better, I think, because then he had an opportunity to change when he was in the run, and friends of his like Maggie Smith — you see, the only women he liked were people like Maggie, and Sheila Hancock could give as good as she got. She played as a man to him, really.'

Kenneth's co-stars in revue were a formidable trio: Maggie Smith (in *Share My Lettuce*), Fenella Fielding (*Pieces of Eight*) and Sheila Hancock (*One Over the Eight*). All stood up to him successfully, though it was Maggie Smith who became his special friend. Their sense of the absurd overlapped so much that for a time a sharing of style was sensed between them.

Betty Marsden: 'Their campery was similar. Not as an actress. But you know, in "Share My Fetish" — *Share My Lettuce*, that revue they were in together — I think they each picked up a little of the other. But Maggie is absolutely superb. And I think if anybody understood him, she did. And knew him.'

'I went down to Broxbourne by minicab. Mags and Bev at cottage down there, we sunbathed on the lawn. A really lovely Sunday, my first for ages. The Aga had gone out and Bev had a terrible job relighting it and consequently Mags' casserole was a bit dicey but it tasted v. good to me. I was starving. Beverley took the photograph.' **(Diary 3 June 1962)**

With Maggie Smith and Tuffet, 1962.

Kenny and Maggie were reunited later in Peter Shaffer's double bill *The Private Ear* and *The Public Eye* at the Globe in 1962. In an excellent cast, Kenneth found another fast friend.

Richard Pearson: 'Before we worked together I'd only met him once, at the Television Centre. I'd been in the first production of Pinter's *The Birthday Party* and he was one of the few people who saw it because we only lasted a week at the Lyric, Hammersmith – the one where the critics dismissed Pinter as a cheap imitation of Ionesco, you know. And he was one of the few people who thought a lot of it as a play, and so he came up and we were both doing different plays.

But I didn't work with him until 1962. That was the only time I did work with him, but it was for eighteen months, so we got to know each other very well, and we remained friends. Close in a way, because he knew my family and that sort of thing, but in fact I hadn't seen him for years when he died, and very often would go long spells without seeing him.'

Some of his contemporaries felt this was Kenneth's finest performance, in the sense that in the course of it he got furthest away from the personality nature had bestowed on him.

❛ I went to see him in **The Private Ear** and **The Public Eye**, in which he was brilliant, he was absolutely flawless ❜

Richard Pearson: 'Funny thing, he looked upon *The Private Ear* and *The Public Eye* as a real benchmark in his career. You could joke about it latterly, 'cos my wife said to him, "That was your finest hour, Kenneth." He would have hated that at the time. But he roared with laughter at that, he said, "You're absolutely right, it was." Shaffer of course was delighted with him in that.'

Betty Marsden: 'I went to see him in *The Private Ear* and *The Public Eye*, in which he was brilliant, he was absolutely flawless, it was the most brilliant perform-ance. Not just because I knew him, funny thing, I find it quite difficult to say a friend of mine, because I never really considered him a friend of mine, he was an acquaintance, he was someone I knew, and admired greatly, as an actor. And certainly I stood on my feet and cheered at the end of this, it was the most fan-tastic performance. And when I went round to see him, he was taking me out to supper to the Seven Stars or wherever it was, all he could say when I was telling him, 'cos I go over the top if I think someone's good, I just can't stop, I said, "The notices you had …", no, no, one. Kept it in the drawer. The *Spectator*. Given him a bad notice, told him he was camp. Now he wasn't, he was not. In fact, I was quite knocked out by the performance because I could quite see him falling in love with Maggie Smith, it was quite a possibility, which of course in reality it was absurd! But that was how he disguised what he really was. But that was the only notice he would talk about, which was really very sad.'

Richard Pearson: 'He was awfully pleased with the cast, and he was thrilled with the play because up till then, although he had done things like the Dauphin in *Saint Joan*, and other straight plays, this was such a good play he really thought it would change his line altogether. It nearly did, he had a great personal success in it. And Peter Wood bullied him into stopping some of his vocal things, which were one of the reasons he was such a success, you know, and he always wanted to do them, but he bullied him and kept him very much on a line. He really did hold back on this. But as the run went on he got a bit naughty. But not very naughty, not as bad as he was before. But he would like to have taken off again as a straight actor. He was very self-critical, oddly enough, and I remember him saying, "I'll never really be a good actor, because I won't expose myself". That should be rephrased, but you know what I mean. He didn't want the audience to see Kenneth Williams. He liked to hide behind those characters ... He was not the best chap to tell a story to. If you said a funny line, he said, "Oh yes?" But he did actually listen, and he got his characters from life. He'd listen on buses, and things like that. I think he had very good imagination, really. He liked doing grand characters, too, as you probably remember. When he was beginning to get ill and go to surgeons and things, he used to do wonderful Harley Street doctors and drawing little maps and saying, "Well, that's where it is, you see?"'

But, as that naughtiness indicated, Kenneth didn't have the temperament for an open-ended run.

Richard Pearson: 'In fact he left. It went on altogether for nearly two years, and I was contracted and had to stay. But he hated long runs, like all actors. We're always complaining, aren't we? Either we're out of work or we're stuck in something. He really didn't like long runs.'

But the friendship with Richard Pearson persisted, extending quite soon to the Pearson family in Beckenham. In a small way, Kenneth actually collected families. He loved the shared domesticity that his temperament denied him.

Richard Pearson: 'Gordon Jackson, and Rona Anderson his wife, he saw more of them then he did of us, particularly latterly. He first came down with Maggie Smith to Beckenham, but when he started to come on his own, he pictured being in suburbia, he thought it was so peaceful and everything. I drove him round, looking at places. But he would go home; he was a real Londoner, he would have been bored stiff. Yes he liked the idea of family life. He was a gift for children, all the funny voices and things, they absolutely loved him. My children were absolutely crazy about him, and they would be leaning out of the window, waiting for him to arrive. He used always to come in a big hire car. He gave all that up, though, and he used to come on the train after a bit. He liked that too, in a

'Today is the start of this awful filming job. Walked to Cromer St. We did shots outside the block. In the afternoon we did the stuff in Sandwich Street – dirty bloomers – and then on to Duke St Drill Hall, shots in Woburn Walk and Euston Road and St Pancras Church and then to the school in Camden St. Shots in the playground with children which I didn't know they were taking! I was just chatting away to the children!' **(Diary, 7 June 1983)**

way. He was a great letter-writer, as you've probably heard. He wrote very very good letters, he must have had time. I never seem to have time to write letters, I don't work as much as he did. When I was in Russia he wrote me tremendous long epistles, and so amusing. And he wrote them straight off, you know. He wouldn't do a draft, I'm sure.'

In spite of these successes, Kenneth hadn't really escaped the casting problem that had originally faced him. He was now a big enough name to encourage managements to skew existing plays in his direction, or have parts written especially for him, but he never felt fully comfortable. Leading ladies, in particular, had his memories of Maggie Smith to compete with, and they were unlikely to win. One modest success that pointed the way to future calamity was Charles Laurence's play *My Fat Friend*, which arrived at the Globe Theatre in December 1972 after a couple of weeks out of town. John Harding made his West End début in the cast.

❛He was a gift for children, all the funny voices and things, they absolutely loved him❜

John Harding: 'It was kind of weird, right from the beginning, because Kenny and the director did not see eye to eye. And there was this "Chekhovian" approach from Eric Thompson who did all the voices in *The Magic Roundabout* … Eric was terrified that Ken would just take the ball and run and turn it into a broader production, and really, he should have trusted Kenny better. Although Ken is one of the funniest men in the world, he had a huge respect for theatrical technique. He was able to be hilarious and outrageous for the coach parties, but pull it back — in an instant — for the play itself: the pathos and subtlety of it. All the audiences adored him. He had this fantastic technique and charm and kept it fresh every night, would pull it back and not go for the obvious gags. He knew exactly how to do away with the small gags in order to go for the big one. He knew how to take ten minutes off a matinée without anybody thinking they'd been short changed.'

Actors can enjoy such manipulations of the play, but unilateral actions on the part of the star player are unlikely to appeal to a director, who naturally hopes

'Kenneth and Pete were great friends, so Ken came down here and we all went to Brighton pier. He was very fond of the family. It was a very happy day because of his enjoyment with Tyler and Emma. I once went with Pete to go up and see him and when we went in it was so stark. He opened the door to his bedroom and there was nothing in it, more or less, but this bed and a light above it and I didn't know what to do because, normally, you walk into somebody's place and say, "Isn't this lovely?" So I've never forgotten walking straight to the window and saying, "Oh, you have a good view from here Kenneth, haven't you?"' **(Janet Brown)**

Kenneth with his co-star in 14 **Carry On** films Peter Butterworth, his wife Janet Brown, and their two children, c.1970.

for a consistent faithfulness to the interpretation he's built up. And Kenneth's diary suggests that he not only controlled the piece through his performance, but adjusted his attitudes to fellow players quite capriciously, too. It was inevitably his leading lady who suffered most.

John Harding: 'I think [Jennie Linden's] confidence was shaken a bit by this. They'd have stand-up rows in which he'd try and get her to perform better. He was a terrible misogynist, Ken. He had ladies he loved, the sort of Joan Simses of this world, that he had camp fag-hag relationships with, but a straight young woman, with a child, wanting a life, was not a great camp comedienne; he didn't

Rehearsing
My Fat Friend at
St James's Church
Hall, Piccadilly,
with Jennie Linden
and John Harding.

know how to cope with her. And I think she, in some ways, didn't know how to rise to the level of performance he wanted. When it was his birthday we all bought him a cake and a bottle of champagne and left it in his dressing room. We never really saw Ken before the show, he'd prepare himself quite privately and then we'd all meet for the first time properly in the interval. We expected him to say, "Oh, come and have a piece of cake and we'll have the champagne after the show!" But he said nothing and kept himself to himself, slamming the door to his dressing room, and we didn't see him until we went back on for the second act. The dresser came to us and said, "I'm sorry but he's cut the cake up and flushed it down the loo and poured the champagne after it." The next night, though, he threw a party for us. Everything had to be on Ken's terms.'

Privately, Ken was complaining that he had to provide all the energy for the whole show. And he was suffering (no doubt partly psychosomatic) trouble in the colon. In the end he took the medical way out, and the whole thing collapsed.

John Harding: 'It ran and ran until Ken got ill and then it closed with about a month before its run was up, in some disarray. He got paranoid basically – it was the most successful play he'd ever done, built for him, made for him, and he kind of blew it in the end.'

My Fat Friend later made a reasonable showing on Broadway, with Lynn Redgrave as the female lead, but by then Kenneth had put it out of his mind. He later admitted in so many words that he'd walked out of the play, as he had from Roger Longrigg's *The Platinum Cat* in 1965: a worse fiasco, from which Kenneth almost literally ran away, to – of all places – Beirut, where a photograph commemorates a moment of consolation (and a generous tableful of grub) in the company of Stanley Baxter. In a shorthand résumé of his life he characterized the whole episode as a 'nervous breakdown'.

Derek Nimmo: 'He was one of those people you could give a meaningless sentence to, and he would make it wonderfully funny. But he'd have had to go back to the classics, I think, to find room for him, to a style of theatre that was probably more expansive than it is today. He was not a naturalistic actor at all.

'This was taken in Beirut. I was playing in a farce in Australia and I'd planned my itinerary for going home, via Hong Kong and Beirut, and then this distressed call came through from Ken. He had just come out of a play, **The Platinum Cat**. He was very upset emotionally and he said, "I believe you're going to Beirut?" I said, "Well, that's one of the stops: I'm going to Hong Kong for several days before that." "Oh dear," he said, "oh dear!" In the end I went back to this woman who'd booked my flights and said, "Can we change all that and can I get to Beruit by Christmas morning and I'll only spend one night in Hong Kong to break the journey?" So I arrived there on Christmas morning, just to keep him company, because obviously he was very distressed about having come out of this play. The management were absolutely furious because they were playing to capacity business and, of course, as soon as he came out the whole thing flopped.' **(Stanley Baxter)**

You see, after that initial success with the Dauphin, one's sorry that he didn't go on and play Malvolio, so many characters he could have done, really. Andrew Aguecheek, he'd have been wonderful at. Being in period costume would have given him the licence that he needed.'

A limited run of Shaw's play from 1900, *Captain Brassbound's Conversion*, proved an interesting diversion with Ingrid Bergman leading the cast, and suggests that Nimmo was right: Kenneth would probably have thrived better in established

Page 104 Publicity shot for **The Platinum Cat**, 1965: what would become his third West End flop in a row, and the cause of a 'nervous breakdown' (see page 244).

pieces than in newly written vehicles. His last stage play in an acting role was *The Undertaking* by Trevor Baxter, in 1979.

Isabel Dean: 'I went to see that with Ian McGarry, who was the Assistant General Secretary [of British Actors' Equity], and I can remember we went out to supper afterwards, and I can remember that the evening was really – I think he'd had to face up to something really bad, which he wasn't prepared for. Because those personalities, even if they're in something bad, they come out of it all right. And he didn't.'

When short lists are made of the women for whom Kenneth reserved a special fondness, Isabel Dean is often left out. Yet in her way she was one of the loves of his life. In his diary he goes so far as to say (and such wording is rare): 'She is the most attractive, elegant and most intelligent woman in England. She never ceases to delight me' (6 March 1979). She was indeed a beauty, and

Page 107 'Had to go to Ingrid for an autograph (…) I should think Bergman is the BEST PERSON I've ever met who is an International Star.' **(Diary, 11 June 1971)**

Ingrid Bergman as Lady Cicely Waynflete in Bernard Shaw's **Captain Brassbound's Conversion**. Kenneth played the role of Drinkwater in what he described as a 'creaking play and rickety production.' It ran from February to July 1971 and actually, thanks to the presence of three-time Academy Award winning Bergman, broke box-office records for a short-run play.

CAMBRIDGE THEATRE

UNDER THE DIRECTION OF EMILE LITTLER

CAPTAIN BRASSBOUND'S CONVERSION

By BERNARD SHAW

PROGRAMME 10p

To Ken, with the "kind face" thanks for the laughs and support from Lady Cicely and

Ingrid Bergman

an actress who should have been much more celebrated, but a dispute with the West End's dominant manager-producer 'Binkie' Beaumont (she had turned down a touring role he'd offered) had seriously blighted her career on the London stage. Popular in the profession, she was regularly elected to the Equity Council, where she and Kenneth Williams became colleagues and very warm friends.

Isabel Dean: 'Absolutely. I never felt so close to anyone, you know, without having any sexual sort of . . . it was an extraordinary feeling. And he did give out a lot, I think. He once said that he was very close to Maggie Smith, and he said, "I know you're not as famous as Maggie Smith," he said. "You have the same quality, for me." That's what he said. He really was a remarkable person. We had a favourite poem which was George Eliot on friendship. He said it was one of his favourites, and it happened to be one of mine.'

The piece in question is often attributed to George Eliot, but it was actually written by another Victorian novelist, Mrs Craik (Dinah Maria Mulock):

> Oh, the comfort.
> The inexpressible comfort of feeling
> Safe with a person,
> Having neither to weigh thoughts,
> Nor measure words, but pouring them
> All right out just as they are.
> Chaff and grain together
> Certain that a faithful hand will
> Take and sift them
> Keep what is worth keeping.
> And with the breath of kindness
> Blow the rest away.

Kenneth's arrival among the administrators of the actors' union came as a surprise to many. It hadn't been generally known that he had strong feelings about the way actors were represented and organized.

Using a few of his favourite, most poignant quotes, including Craik's poem, in a letter to Nick Lewis: 'He always mentioned the theme of friendship in his work, in interviews and in the autobiography, so I wrote to him asking what advice could he offer to a young man, in his 20s, going through a period of self-doubt at university.'

8 MARLBOROUGH HOUSE, OSNABURGH STREET, LONDON NW1 3LY

24.2.81

Dear Nick

Impossible to advise about 'co friendships are matters for individuals — there are no rules. The friends are those who take the chaff & grain together, keep what's worth keeping & with a breath of kindness blow the rest away. Emerson saw his friends "came to me unsought, the good God that sent them to me..." And that's a lovely thought for someone with Faith. Sometimes I think there is a benign influence for our good & sometimes I don't. Sometimes I think 'this is a vast orphanage where no one knows his origin & no one comes to claim us. The old have no superior knowledge — if you'd read all the books they've read you'd only know as much as them. In the end, it comes back to Rilke's — Only ENDURE — "we all have to find our own way to Endure & to accept mortality'.

Your old chum

Kenneth

Isabel Dean: 'No, Peter Plouviez [General Secretary] knew, and so did Ian McGarry, but I think the General Council didn't really know, because he really was always making faces and sending people up, you know, and so they didn't know that underneath that there was a really strong feeling that he really wanted to help young people coming into the profession.'

Kenneth's private record of his Equity encounters was sometimes caustic, and he was clearly regarded as a potential troublemaker ('At coffee break, as I took my cup, the President [John Barron] asked Peter Plouviez, "Have you put cyanide in his?" '). But in general he was inclined to respect the Chair.

Isabel Dean: 'Usually he was, and when he took the chair he was brilliant. We always hoped that he would become President. But he was inclined, if he thought somebody was trying to be too self-important, he'd send them up rotten, you know. If he met you, if you were on the Council with him and if he met you out-side, he'd send you up … At Annual General Meetings and things, the sort of speech he gave was very different from the sort of speeches that are given now. We do miss him very much indeed. He was able to switch from being very funny to being dead serious, as opposed to the extreme Left who took themselves des-perately seriously all the time and didn't have many laughs. It was a great relief and it meant you did think about what he was saying. He didn't altogether agree with the side that voted for him, you know, in Equity.'

But then Kenneth Williams was complicated by nature. When he and Isabel spent time together, generally in restaurants during the Equity Council's long lunch breaks, she felt the two-way current of his temperament.

❛He could be heard all over the restaurant, and the waiters would be screaming with laughter. Oh, he loved the limelight ❜

Isabel Dean: 'It sounds awful, but he would say something terribly nice, and you'd feel, oh, how wonderful, and then there'd be a sting in the tail, because he couldn't bear to think that he could only be nice about somebody or some-thing. That was too simple.'

Restaurant life had always been a bit of a lottery with Kenneth, as Betty Marsden had discovered years before.

Betty Marsden: 'The waiters, how they ever served us I don't know, 'cos he had them all in hysterics, all of them. I must say, he sat with his back to the "house", as it were, but to sit facing him was quite an eye-opener! As he was saying, "Don't want any of *that* rubbiiish!" you know, he could be heard all over the restaurant, and the waiters would be screaming with laughter. Oh, he loved the limelight.'

Isabel Dean: 'If he was in a good mood it was marvellous, but if he was in a bad mood it was extremely awkward, because he would make … it would be very

'I remember he wore the same tie and suit to rehearsals every day and, in front of the studio audience, would delight in breaking wind to roars of laughter whilst proclaiming, "Well – you like your own don't you, admit it!" He took to me in a genuinely friendly way and always said I'd go far! I found him fascinating, funny, outrageous and a little bit scary. He could fly into a tantrum and five minutes later completely forget it. Example: after recording the show one evening, Kenneth asked if I was going over to the Granada bar – I agreed. He said, "We'll take our make up off and walk over together." I wandered off and couldn't find him and strolled over to the bar about 200 yards away and joined the rest of the crew. Half an hour later someone asked where Kenneth was and I said I would go and find him. I discovered him in high dudgeon, sulking in his dressing room, ignoring me and saying to the costume lady, "Well its a fine thing isn't it when you make an arrangement with somebody and they stand you up?" I apologized fulsomely and he agreed to join us all at the bar for more hilarity and farting!' (Ted Robbins)

Kenneth, Lulu and Ted Robbins, promoting **Some You Win**, at Granada Television, Manchester, May 1984.

noisy. Anything he objected to would be definitely brought out into the open and talked about. In a loud voice. And he could be quite rude to oneself, you know. It was his marvellous sense of humour that made one accept that, it never really worried me.'

There was a conscious bond of loneliness uniting these two: it was a theme of their conversation.

Isabel Dean: 'He knew that I was quite solitary, too, and he knew that I'd had a divorce, and everything, so he was very open about all that.'

Of course, the possibility lay before them that their lonelinesses might be pooled, a stratagem Kenneth had contemplated with other women before. And in fact he did mention the idea at the lunch table.

Isabel Dean: 'Yes, he did, but I think if one had made any sort of suggestion he'd have run a mile.'

As things were, there was comfort to be derived even from these intermittent meetings. For Isabel Dean, it was Kenneth's way of coping with the vicissitudes of an acting career that helped most. Not many friends of Ken's felt that he had set them an example, but she did.

Isabel Dean: 'If he'd been a failure, he could have accepted it as well as he accepted being a success. And it helped me a tremendous amount, because I've had a lot of disappointments in the theatre, and quite often I'd feel so fed up that I'd really feel I'd like to pack it in. He was very encouraging about that side of the theatre. He didn't underestimate his success, but he said that he'd gone straight out for it and got it. And he wouldn't even look down on people who hadn't, which was very nice for me because I'm not in the same category as he is.'

There is a *Brief Encounter* sense of sadness and unfulfilled longing to the whole tale. Isabel never visited Kenneth's flat, though, unusually, he seems to have wished that she had.

Isabel Dean: 'I can remember I delivered some sort of notification from 'Act for Equity', that list of all the people who were not wanting to make it a political union, and I can remember delivering it to Osnaburgh Street, and the next Equity meeting he kept going on "You actually came round to my flat!" he said. "Extraordinary. But why didn't you ring the bell and come in?" And I thought, Yes, why didn't I? But he never invited me, so I didn't. But he made a big thing about that. I wish I'd known his mother. I wasn't part of that side of him. And all the *Carry On* films and everything, I didn't know him in that way. And I wished I had, because it would be something to cling on to when he went. It's a pity the National [Theatre] didn't do something to put his career on a different note, really, because I think that's what he would have liked.'

❛If he'd been a failure, he could have accepted it as well as he accepted being a success ❜

Derek Nimmo: 'He didn't really like the theatre very much in the end, I don't think. He didn't need much in terms of money to exist, he used to have an old raincoat on. I mean if you'd passed him in the street you might have given him 50p, really, if he'd held his hand out.'

Richard Pearson: 'It was quite a shock when he died. I was in another Shaffer play, *Lettice and Lovage* with Maggie Smith at the time, in the same theatre.'

By that time, Kenneth Williams had for some years been a name nobody expected to see in West End lights. For good or ill, he had become a broadcasting person. Everybody knew as much, but nobody knew of the struggles he'd endured to establish that strain in his career, forty years before.

From CSE to the BBC

' The chap playing the Dauphin's name is Kenneth Williams, and if he hasn't got comedy, I'll eat my hat '

Peter Eade

India c.1945. Kenneth fourth row, eleven from right.

'I haven't come all the way from Great Portland Street to be treated like this!' Kenneth Williams used to utter that line, and its several variants, with such terrible relish on *Just a Minute* that listeners outside London might have believed he'd been put to some genuine inconvenience. But of course Great Portland Street and the Paris Studio in Lower Regent Street, where recordings generally took place, lay only a brisk walk apart, and none of Kenneth's apartments was ever more than a short stroll from Broadcasting House itself. The proximity was no doubt accidental. It so happened that the BBC's headquarters lay within the St Pancras / Fitzrovia / Bloomsbury borders that defined Williams's lifetime 'patch', give or take a three-year excursion to the Edgware Road. Much though he scorned the limitations of his upbringing, he was never able to put any significant distance between himself and his childhood home, the barber's shop (which is still a hairdresser's, as 'CV Hair & Beauty') in Marchmont Street, WC1.

Page 114
Kenneth as
Grole in
**Pieces of
Eight**,
1959.

Gradually, though, the BBC did become another kind of home. For all the notoriety of the *Carry On* films, and sundry stage hits, it was the Beeb that carried on Kenneth's reputation from decade to decade. Without his connection to the Corporation he would have made no Hancock series, no Jules and Sandy or

Rambling Syd, no variety shows or poetry compilations of his own, and indeed no *Just a Minute*. His talent for straight drama tended to go adrift on stage, but BBC radio recordings preserve some fragments of it. And he became a chat-show and magazine-programme fixture, not only because he was reliably entertaining and informed, but because he was usually available, just up the street, ready to be called in at very short notice if another star dropped out.

The files on Kenneth Williams held by the BBC's Written Archive tell a long and complicated story, beginning as early as 16 December 1947. Released by Combined Services Entertainment and only recently returned to England, Kenneth had no professional standing at all. He had returned to his former employment with Stanford's, the mapmakers, of Long Acre (another walkable destination). But his experience in the ramshackle forces troupe out East, plus a few bouts of microphone work under the same auspices, emboldened him to try his luck with Broadcasting House. His target was Val Gielgud, brother of John, the famous actor. Gielgud had been Head of Productions at the BBC since 1929, responsible for all radio drama, and he was well enough known to have published his autobiography (*Year of the Locust*), earlier in 1947. 'Dear Sir,' wrote the 21-year-old Kenneth, from the family home in Marchmont Street:

> I have recently been demobilised from the army, and am anxious to obtain work in the field of broadcasting.
>
> Whilst in the service, I worked entirely under Combined Services Entertainment, and through them, the opportunity presented itself to me of broadcasting over the forces network of the B[urma] B[roadcasting] S[ervice] in Rangoon, Radio Malaya in Singapore, and latterly ZBW Hong Kong, in various dramatic features and etc.
>
> The experience has served to make me eager to devote my career to it, in England, if possible, and I should be terribly grateful if you could offer me any advice or help on the subject in any shape or form (or, if this is impossible, pass on my letter to anyone who might be interested).
>
> Meanwhile I am,
>
> Sincerely Yours,
>
> Kenneth Williams

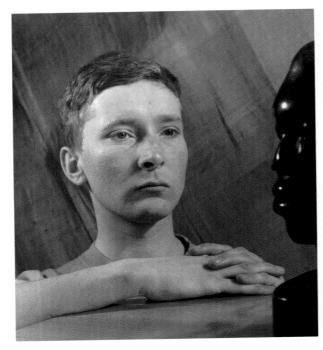

Pages 118–119 & 121 Kenneth's first set of publicity shots photographed by his army friend, aspiring photographer, later Academy Award winning director, John Schlesinger, in May 1956. Kenneth had written 'Property of Ken Williams, 817 Endsleigh Court, London WC1' (where he lived from March 1956) on the reverse of one, whilst another had typed, 'Please return to Peter Eade' (Kenneth's agent from 1951 until Eade's death in 1979).

Val Gielgud was by now a little bit grand to be dealing with this kind of supplication, and besides, he had moved over to Alexandra Palace to supervise the post-war re-emergence of BBC TV drama. So it was radio's Drama Booking Manager, David Manderson, who replied.

> *Dear Mr Williams,*
>
> *Your letter to Mr Gielgud has been passed to me for attention.*
>
> *Before considering you for an audition I should be grateful for further particulars of your professional career, pre-service experience, if any, and details of what you have done since your demobilisation.*
>
> *You will appreciate that, except to a very few experienced broadcasters, radio work offers little prospect of regular employment, and can only be regarded as an occasional source of income by the majority of artists.*

Manderson added that he was 'returning your testimonial forthwith'; presumably a record of Kenneth's satisfactory contribution to the CSE.

This was a discouraging reply in several ways. For one thing, Kenneth had very little in the way of 'further particulars' to add to the résumé he had already given. He also knew very well that Manderson was right about the amount of work on offer, even to a successful applicant. The BBC's output in the immediate post-war years was minute by modern standards. There was only one very limited television channel, confined to the evenings, and seen by few, and three national radio networks: the Home Service (very roughly equivalent to Radio 4), the Light Programme (a more obvious forerunner of Radio 2) and the Third Programme, a high-cultural service with genuine intellectual ambitions. Williams himself was a diligent listener to the Third, which for him, as for many, became an informal 'university of the air'.

And yet because the BBC enjoyed a virtual monopoly of the airwaves, disturbed for many years only by dodgy-sounding offshore popular-music stations, work at Broadcasting House was hugely desirable for young performers. There was no better professional shop-window — not even the cinema, where a small-part appearance could flash by almost unnoticed and even uncredited.

The *Radio Times*, by contrast, was at that time very diligent in printing complete cast lists, and many listeners took a pride in recognizing voices by name. A radio reputation could be made quite quickly. For newcomers, however, there was only limited space. Fresh young comedians, it's true, tended to thrive in BBC Variety, because the world was changing fast, and they could reflect its newer madnesses, which many of them had undergone in His Majesty's forces. But for straight plays the BBC was already well supplied with seasoned actors, including the most distinguished Shakespeareans and classical performers of the day. There was a sizeable radio-drama elite, which had further enhanced its reputation during the war years. Between them, the radio veterans and the theatre greats had the radio drama business largely sewn up.

In spite of all that, Kenneth Williams pressed on, though not very urgently. His excuse for taking his time (below) does not sound true, and it wasn't. What was really happening was that he was firing off letters in all directions to all possible employers, mostly theatrical, and failing to follow them up systematically.

> *Dear Sir,*
>
> *With reference to your enclosed letter, my sincere regrets for not having been able to reply sooner, but I have been away from my home for some time, on business connected with the decease of a relative. Please accept my apologies.*
>
> *My pre-service experience? None, as far as radio is concerned, for I was with the Tavistock Rep., and learned voice training with them. And as I have only been back in this country for a few months, I have done no regular work, as yet.*
>
> *Mr Anderson [sic], all I am asking for is a chance to prove to you that I have a good voice for broadcasting, and that [if] you see me, I promise I shan't waste your time. This means everything to me, so please don't cast my letter aside, but be immeasurably kind, and help me.*
>
> *Very sincerely,*
> *Kenneth C. Williams*

Sadly, this entreaty failed to move the Drama Booking Manager. Kenneth's misreading of Manderson's signature can't have helped. The archived letter is marked in pencil across the top: 'Put off'. But it must be said that in putting Kenneth off Manderson did his best to let him down gently. On 22 March 1948 he wrote:

Dear Mr Williams,

Thank you for your letter.

The audition situation is virtually at a standstill for the time being as the rate of application has been so great since the end of the war that we have accumulated a very large list of artists who have succeeded at auditions but for whom we have not yet been able to find suitable openings. Until such time as these artists have been given an opportunity under actual broadcasting conditions, therefore, I regret there is little I can do to assist you.

It is no longer considered essential for an artist to have had an audition with us before being offered parts in broadcast plays and features, and I suggest you let our producers know whenever you are appearing on the stage in the London area, in the hope that they may be able to spare the time to see your performance. You can see from the 'Radio Times' those producers associated with the type of programme in which you are interested.

That explains why there is no formal audition-card for Kenneth Williams in his early radio file. Producers were no longer assessing general abilities, but casting specific parts, and in the light of that Manderson's advice was good. Indeed, by the beginning of the following year it had worked for Kenneth. A busy producer called Alastair Scott-Johnston (later in charge of *The Navy Lark*) cast him in the second episode of a Light Programme series called *Gordon Grantley QC*, by John P. Wynn. His contract, for 5 guineas, bears a scribbled note of his Marchmont Street telephone number: TERminus 4870. And the performance must have been a success, since Scott-Johnston invited him back to play a different character in the same series, four episodes later. 'Good part in *Gordon Grantley* today,' Kenneth remarked in his diary. 'Very drama.'

A torrent of work did not follow. Scott-Johnston used him again that spring, and another producer, Hugh Stewart, gave him a role in 'Virtue', a Somerset Maugham story. It wasn't much, but at least the Scott-Johnston work gave him a new way of approaching further BBC programme-makers, like the producer David H. Godfrey, who received the latest 'Dear Sir' letter in early April. It showed Kenneth realizing that modesty had been getting him nowhere.

Mr Scott-Johnston has suggested to me that I might write to you, asking for an interview, with a view to your using me in any future production you may be planning.

As far as voice is concerned, I have a remarkable range, and can play juveniles and mature men with equal success. Am able to handle all types of english [sic] accent (my best being Welsh), a good French accent, and a working knowledge of German. Also sing very well. (Baritone). I am twenty-three years old.

At the moment, I am playing at the New Theatre, Bromley, but am free during the day. My telephone number is TERminus 4870. If there is any chance of your seeing me and you will name a time, I shall be there.

Many young actors were involved in letter-writing campaigns of this kind (Kenneth's future *Carry On* colleague Charles Hawtrey was sending in near-identical pleas). It says a lot about the sheer slog of it all that Kenneth C. Williams found himself virtually repeating his letter to David Godfrey, well over a year

Pages 123–125 Unknown repertory theatre productions.

later. And on it went, from season to season, producer to producer, with nothing changing except Kenneth's ability to drop the odd name of a colleague from his latest repertory-theatre experience: 'Mr Richard West says that he has spoken of me to you and how desperately anxious I am to obtain an engagement … (Don't suppose you will remember, but we did meet once – rather fleetingly – on the train to Beaconsfield in 1949).'

The name of Richard West wasn't a bad one to drop, since he was the son of Gladys Young, one of the topmost senior radio actresses. But the best thing West did for Kenneth was introduce him to an agent, Peter Eade, on 1 February 1951. Agent and client would stay together till Eade's death (and beyond, since Kenneth remained with Peter's deputy, Laurena Dewar). Eade began impressively by

arranging an instant audition with Laurence Olivier, and although Kenneth privately scorned it ('I never got anything out of an audition in my life') he did appear in an Olivier film the following year. But for now, life in 1951 was rough. 'My 25th birthday and still *unemployed*,' Kenneth recorded on 22 February.

It was not until early the following year that an unlikely upturn seemed to have occurred. What few parts Kenneth was getting in radio by now came from a producer called Norman Wright, and it was to him that Peter Eade communicated the news:

Dear Norman Wright,
In case you don't know, KENNETH WILLIAMS is playing the part of
the Angel in a television production of H.G.Wells' 'The Wonderful Visit',
transmitting on the 3rd and 7th of February. This is his first television
appearance and from all reports it sounds as if he is going to be very good.
So sorry to have missed you at Michael Harald's party recently.

It's possible that the TV career could have begun sooner. There are no audition notes for Kenneth in the archive, but there is an official 'Record of Interview' form, and it is disconcertingly marked 'Did not attend 26/4/51'. Kenneth seems to have been rehearsing at Guildford Rep on that day. Nevertheless, some details were collected:

Agent: Peter Eade.
Colouring: Fair. Voice: Deep
Classification: Juvenile char.
Height: 5' 8

Chief details of experience: Stage
Swansea: 6 months
Worthing: Mr Inspector Jones
Guildford
Broadcasting: The Immortal Lady
Accents, dialects: Welsh (native)

The Immortal Lady had been Kenneth's best radio opportunity so far – a Norman Wright production of a Clifford Bax play. 'Special fee,' his contract read, 'ten guineas for leading part'.

By the turn of the year the Ally Pally staff had rounded Kenneth up, and in January 1952 he took his first step into the television world.

Dear Mr Williams,

Mr Douglas Allen has asked me to say how pleased he is you are playing the part of the Angel in 'The Wonderful Visit'. I enclose herewith a script, and we look forward to seeing you at the King George V Suite, Alexandra Palace, on Thursday 17th January at 10.30am, when there will be a Wardrobe and Make-up Conference prior to the read-through. A special bus will leave Broadcasting House at 10am each morning, calling at 27 Marylebone Road (round the corner of Luxborough Street, opposite Madame Tussaud's), en route to Alexandra Palace.

> *Yours sincerely,*
> *Rosalind Pool*
> *Secretary to Douglas Allen*

Wardrobe and make-up should have been a doddle, but they were the worst of it: producer Allen required the full cherubic look for the Angel, so Kenneth was fitted with a curly wig which bestowed on him a dangerous resemblance to Harpo Marx. But he bore up bravely, and *The Wonderful Visit* went ahead as cast and as a piece of live, not recorded, television. The two transmissions mentioned by Peter Eade, on 3 and 7 February, were two separate live performances, as in the theatre. The inconvenience to actors was offset by the opportunity to make genuine improvements to the second edition. And word of mouth after the first transmission could be powerful: if a promising actor had appeared, the profession was alerted in time to catch him or her the second time around. In Kenneth's case, this could have been really useful. But there was no second version, as Norman Wright signalled in his reply to Peter Eade: 'I had intended seeing him in "The Wonderful Visit" last evening, but, of course, owing to the present tragic situation, this was cancelled, but I will continue to keep Kenneth Williams in mind when doing any future casting.'

The tragic situation was the death of King George VI, from a coronary thrombosis, on 6 February. Normal programming throughout the BBC was abandoned, *The Wonderful Visit* never recurred, and Kenneth lost his chance to impress the producers and casting directors who, like Norman Wright, had been advised to watch him. Presumably he was paid his full 32 guineas for the two intended performances. Oddly enough, the Welles piece had already cost him another television appearance, in a production of *King John*, where he'd been double-cast as a Messenger and the English Herald. But the two rehearsal periods had collided and the contract was annulled. The one consolation for Kenneth took a long time coming. The producer Douglas Allen went on to cast him as Bentley Summerhays in Shaw's *Misalliance*, but that didn't happen until July 1954, more than two years later.

In spite of Peter Eade's help, Kenneth was still writing his 'begging letters' (as he called them) to producers, and their tone had become more desperate in the meantime. 'It's tortuous writing an unprovoked letter anyway,' he groaned. 'For me it is.' Now 26 years old, he may have felt ashamed not to be further advanced in the profession, hence perhaps the otherwise meaningless falsification: 'my voice age is somewhat mature, about 30 to 40ish, though I am myself 24 and at the moment I am desperately in need of some work'. This particular letter closes with a wretched bout of emotional blackmail:

> *While I know I've no right to burden you with worries of a purely personal nature, you must believe that I am a young man of unusual talent & belong in the theatre. I won't tell you about stage experience because it wouldn't help at this juncture. But really I assure you I shall not be wasting your time if you see me and you'll hurt me terribly if you don't.*

Kenneth was of course right, and the broadcasting world would eventually recognize him as a person of 'unusual talent'. But by 1954 he must have been close to abandoning the struggle to convince them. There was a horrible moment when Peter Eade even had to ask Norman Wright if he would release Kenneth from playing Beau Brummell in Conan Doyle's Rodney Stone, because some work in provincial rep had come up:

> *He has had a most unfortunate year so far with no work whatsoever since the beginning of January and he has now had an offer to go to a Repertory Company in the West Country for eight weeks starting on 3rd May. I know you will understand how galling it is for any ambitious young actor to be out of work for any length of time and I feel it would be a wonderful opportunity for him to have some steady employment. Consequently, as*

your offer to him is only one day's duration, would you consider releasing
him from this commitment under the circumstances?

Wright replied that he would be 'delighted' to release the young man, which was perhaps not the ideal way of putting it. So Kenneth went off to Bridgwater Rep, and on his return had no choice but to resume the letter-writing in the same tones as before. His plea to Peter Eton, of the Variety Department, caused the stunned recipient to scribble in pencil on the letter: 'This bloke appears to want a job!' Alas, Eton wasn't able to do anything about it. But in midsummer at least, Kenneth had the TV production of *Misalliance* to think about. He didn't enjoy the prospect much ('it reads very drearily, and I suspect it won't act much better') but the day after transmission he admitted to his diary that there had been 'generally good reports about last night's play'. The same day, he also recorded that John Fernald had offered him the part of the Dauphin in Shaw's *Saint Joan*, with Siobhan McKenna, and that he had accepted. He didn't know it, but this was the beginning of the rest of his life.

'Dress reh. and opening of **Painted Sparrows**. The dialogue is such filth that I feel like vomiting continually. The whole thing is deplorable. There were only a few people out front – 30 or so – and the evening was very much a flop.' **(Diary, 24 May 1954)**

Kenneth as Syd Fish in Painted Sparrows.

Saint Joan opened at the Arts Theatre Club on 29 September 1954. The initial notices were middling, but the top critics, Kenneth Tynan in the *Observer* and Harold Hobson in the *Sunday Times*, came through with praise for Kenneth. The play transferred to the St Martin's, and ran till the end of the following May. This was success, but even as it happened it was being engulfed by the beginnings of Kenneth's real career in broadcasting and in broad comedy.

The man who changed everything was a BBC producer called Dennis Main Wilson. A slight man with a deep, urgent voice seemingly borrowed from a body twice the size, he had already had a remarkable career, including a spell writing anti-Nazi propaganda while still in his teens. After training at Sandhurst, he was among the first to land on Juno Beach on D-Day, and somewhat later, in Hamburg, he took over the former broadcasting citadel of the Nazi propagandist Lord Haw-Haw. Back in Britain, he rejoined the BBC and did much to bring together and propagate *The Goon Show*, among other enterprises.

But Wilson had also served a spell as the BBC's Head of Auditioning, and it must have been the instinct accumulated in that demanding post that drew his attention to Kenneth Williams in the cast of *Saint Joan*.

Dennis Main Wilson: 'I'd been doing *The Goon Show*, and while I was doing that I'd met up with Tony Hancock, who was direly in need of scriptwriters, good ones. And I'd found these two youngsters, 19 years old, [Ray] Galton and [Alan] Simpson, and I knew that there was something great there … He needed his own show, and we wanted to get away from catchphrases, and you do a sketch and there's a band number and another sketch and there's a singer and there's another sketch. This was the old, old formula in radio comedy … And in May 1954 I confirmed that we'd got Hancock his own show, to start in October. And I was well cast, I had Tony, Sid James, Bill Kerr, Moira Lister, and we were well set. But I still needed the odd voice-man, you know "'Allo 'allo, what's goin' on 'ere, then? How *dare* you, sah!" and things like this. So I wrote to all the major artists' agents in London saying "I've got a great show coming up, there's a chance for an unknown youngster" … Not a dicky bird from one of them! Nothing. But there was a phone call from an agent called Peter Eade, whom I didn't know, who said, "He isn't one of mine, but you should go down to the Arts Theatre and see Shaw's *Saint Joan* with Siobhan McKenna, and the

'Since I got a lot of laughs during the run, it all started going to my head and I began to develop a comic persona which wasn't always appropriate for the production.' (Kenneth, **Just Williams**)

By Candlelight, Salisbury Repertory Company, 1952. Kenneth considered the role of Bastien a favourite of his.

chap playing the Dauphin's name is Kenneth Williams, and if he hasn't got comedy I'll eat my hat."'

If Peter Eade really did sell Kenneth as 'not one of his', it was a disingenuous ruse, because he had been acting for him since early 1951, even if there was no signed contract to show for it.

Dennis Main Wilson: 'There's nothing really comedic in *Saint Joan*, is there? And then I realized why he'd phoned me. For the last scene of the last act the Dauphin has to age about twenty-five-odd years, which is accomplished in different ways, depending upon who directs it in the theatre. Kenneth Williams had done it his own way. There was no pause, no break, no turning back on the audience, he just changed gear, wah! Aged twenty-five years, *instanter*. The voice had changed, the face, the body language changed, and there was this malevolent old

Suspect, Bridgwater Repertory Company, early 1950s. Kenneth as Doctor Rendle, an obvious forerunner to his acclaimed performance of the aged Dauphin in **Saint Joan**.

man with an evil underlying humour. It was quite frightening, beautifully done. I was very impressed. So as usual I took him round for a drink afterwards, congratulated him, and explained that I was doing this new series starring Tony Hancock, and offered him a part. And he went into a sort of not quite "God-for-Harry, God-for-England", but jolly nearly. And he was "*awfully* busy", and "didn't really *fancy* the wireless, you know", and anyway, a bit of comedy was not really his scene, "it's not great theatre is it? And anyway, the BBC couldn't afford me, so there." And I thought, The rotten bastard, you know, I'm offering him what I think is the chance of a lifetime, and he's turned me down. And I suppose my face must have looked pretty woebegone and disappointed. He wet his knickers laughing! He hooted, and he'd got this tremendous laugh. He'd been sending me up all the time. This is Williams the Outrageous. I said, "How the hell did you manage that tremendous vocal and physical gear-change for the last scene?" "Oh," he said, "simple, duckie, the man was a syphilitic." Williams the Intellectual … But the voice, it was incredible, this great sonorous, Felix Aylmer-type voice, if you know, it could go up to a high-pitched squeak, camp little Boy Scout. And the laugh, this huge roar, when he was really amused his laugh was incredible. He and Hancock had two of the greatest laughs in show business.'

‘ The show is now almost K. Williams' Half Hour ’

Wilson was too experienced, and too honest, to be entirely satisfied with what BBC contracts at first called 'The Tony Hancock Half Hour'. For many years the first episode of all was presumed lost, but it was rediscovered in the 1990s. By common consent, the most memorable line in a lumpy and hesitant episode comes from Kenneth, playing Lord Bayswater, whose stately penthouse has been invaded by partying squatters. 'My God, there's jelly all over the Rembrandt,' wails the aristocrat.

Dennis Main Wilson: 'Listening to it now, forty years later, it's not very good, it's terribly old-fashioned. But then, when you think we were all … I'd just turned 30, and I'd never done a show like this before, Galton and Simpson had

Kenneth with Tony Hancock, during rehearsals for the television series of **Hancock** in 1957.

never written a show like this before, and like most new things certainly that I've done over the years, it takes a good two series. It usually begins to mature round about the third series. *The Goon Show* didn't really settle down until four or five series in ... But Kenneth? I have an occasional guilt thing, whether in fact by going down to the Dauphin and switching his career virtually from legit to comedy, in retrospect whether I did him a disservice or not. I think with his very slight physical stature, because he was physically quite puny, his body belied his voice, or vice versa. Whether he would have made a great dramatic actor with that slight frame is interesting to ponder on.'

From the start, Hancock, Wilson, Galton and Simpson were set against 'formula comedy' of all kinds, but the catchphrases did build up over time. Hancock himself was not innocent of them. 'Stone me, what a life' did recur, as did 'You must be stark raving mad!' But it was Kenneth's 'No, stop messin' about!' that became regular enough to be expected. For the first time the public had something to remember him by, and it's a tribute to the pungency of his comic voices that he was also able to turn a phrase as banal as 'Good evening!' into a memorable radio slogan. But the 'Snide' character, whose call-sign that was, eventually became the focus of Hancock's desire to rid his show of what he regarded as its ready-made elements.

It took a while for Hancock to build up the clout to express such preferences, and he didn't strengthen his bargaining position when he disappeared from Series Two of his own programme, in April 1955.

Dennis Main Wilson: 'We'd done the first series of *Hancock's Half Hour* which the BBC liked, and they rebooked us to start again within ten weeks, which is quite a compliment, for kids. And I took the first script of the new series down to the Adelphi Theatre stage door, the first of the new ones, 'cos I was rather pleased with it, it read very well. And I went down to the stage door, and there was old Fred there on the door, I think Tony had described him, he had "a full snooker set" for teeth in terms of colour. And he said, "If you're looking for the boy, sir, he's gawn." "Pardon?" "He's gawn." "He can't have gone, the first house is still running. You haven't done the finale to the first house yet." "No sir, he went off during his solo act. He couldn't stand it no more." I said, "You're joking!" He said, "No, we got Dick Henderson Jr coming in second house." So I shot down to Jimmy Edwards's dressing room. Jim said, "He's gone." I rang his wife; nothing; his agent, Jack Adams; nothing. Went round the local pubs, hadn't seen him. After the second house was finished, Jimmy Edwards and I scoured every sort of night club and pub where he might have gone, rang everybody we could think of; nothing. I got home in the small hours of the morning, and heard from an old friend of mine, Chief Inspector, Special Branch . . . I'd invited him and his wife to the [radio] show the following day, the Sunday. And the phone rang about half-past three, four o'clock in the morning, and he said, "Ginger here. What's the bloke we're supposed to be seeing tomorrow night doing catching the last plane to Rome?" '

Hancock had indeed decamped, and for a time proved untraceable. His place was taken on the air, at less than a day's notice, by Harry Secombe, which gave rise to the bizarre announcement: 'This is the BBC Light Programme. We present *Hancock's Half Hour*, starring Harry Secombe.' Harry started his stint as a pure Neddy Seagoon, all lunatic energy, but by the third show he had really got the hang of playing it, according to Dennis Main Wilson, and it went very well. It's one of the great sadnesses of BBC Archive history that these bizarre, anomalous but no doubt fascinating shows were at some early stage junked, never to reappear.

But one of the effects of them must have been to strengthen Kenneth Williams's position on the show, since he was one of the faithful regulars keeping the pot boiling in Hancock's absence, seemingly the most prominent of them, to judge by an informal note from Wilson in the BBC Archive. 'What about series No. 3 in October,' he enquired of the Variety heads. 'The show is now almost K. Williams' Half Hour.' This view was echoed a short time later by a note to Wilson from Patrick Newman, the Variety Booking Manager: 'In view of the fact that the new show looks like being entitled "The Tony Hancock and Kenneth Williams Hour Each", I'm sure Drama Booking will now be only too agreeable to review the question of Kenneth Williams's fee.'

It was the end of the begging-letter era. Henceforth the producers would be coming to him, and remembering the thinner times with a ho-ho-ho and a pat on the back.

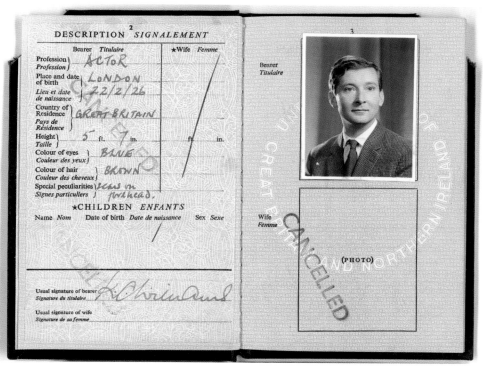

'This passport photo looks startled and plump to me. V. nasty.' (Diary, 29 September 1960)
Kenneth's passport from 1955 until 1965.

Radio star

'If you did a sketch that built up to some surprise
ending, a monster coming upon us or something, he
just said "Ooh hello, don't be like that…" '

Eric Merriman

The brilliant cast that could 'make a telephone directory sound funny'. Kenneth and the cast of **Beyond Our Ken**: Hugh Paddick, Betty Marsden, Bill Pertwee and Kenneth Horne.

In a remarkably short time Kenneth had gone from scratching around for the odd small part on air to overbalancing the budget of one of the best-known comedies in broadcasting. By mid-1956 he was being paid 20 guineas per programme, and in October could afford to give notice that he had moved to a flat of his own, in Endsleigh Court, Upper Woburn Place, WC1. The following March a contract was issued to him for a TV version of *Hancock's Half Hour*, at a rate of 40 guineas for the performance, with 12 guineas on top for rehearsal time. What's more, he was working in the theatre almost throughout this period, and every time he was heard on radio his current stage activity was marked by an obligatory credit, both on air ('Kenneth Williams is appearing . . .') and in the *Radio Times*.

To round out this considerable bounty, a new strand in his broadcasting life appeared in early October 1957, with an offer from the producer Jacques Brown of a part in a production called *Beyond Our Ken*, at 15 guineas, 'special 75 per cent fee for trial recording. Should the records be passed for broadcasting, a further fee of 5gns will be paid under this contract.' That same month Kenneth gave what seems to have been his first television interview, at Studio M, the former Viking film studio in St Mary Abbott's Place, Kensington, for the famous early-evening magazine programme *Tonight*, produced by Donald Baverstock. Kenneth was emerging as 'a personality', though chiefly, so far, on account of his theatrical life. In fact, the reason for this TV appearance was not at all to his credit. The previous day he'd completely forgotten the 5.30 p.m. performance of his current revue (*Share My Lettuce*, recently transferred to the Comedy Theatre) and gone to sleep. By the time he got to the theatre at 6.00 the matinée had been cancelled. The news had made the front page of two national papers, and page two of the rest, launching Kenneth, and it was bound to happen one way or another, as one of the 'characters' of his profession.

Beyond Our Ken, of course, was gratefully received by BBC Light Entertainment. The later success of *Round the Horne* has served to mask the reputation of the pioneering *BOK*, which shared several cast members. But the formula – a kind of verbal maypole dance around the central totem of the perpetually suave and tolerant Kenneth Horne – was developed and thoroughly established by the earlier show. There was no visible social bond between the Kenneths, and yet Kenneth Horne had been born in St Pancras, right in Williams's home 'village'. The pilot programme Williams took part in was not quite the beginning of the story, as the late Betty Marsden (ever-present in both *Beyond Our Ken* and *Round the Horne*) revealed in 1994.

Betty Marsden: 'I had heard of Kenneth Williams. He was doing a play, I think, with Alec Guinness, at the Winter Garden. I think that's when I first heard of him, saw him, that sort of thing. Hugh Paddick I didn't know, but I knew he was also a revue actor at that time. Hugh and I became very close friends, we still are now. Ron Moody, you see, was originally in the cast, and Ron Moody was almost bigger than Kenneth at the time. He was doing impersonations and doing cabaret, that sort thing. It was a very interesting cast altogether, and Kenneth Horne of course was wonderful. It was old Jacques Brown who got us together, because the original pilot I did with Jacques was not to do with Kenneth Horne at all, it was supposed to be for Max Wall. And Barry Took and myself and Eric Merriman, we sat waiting with a lot of other people for ever and ever, and Max didn't turn up at all. But there was a lot of Merriman's material in this particular show, and in the end Jacques Brown said, "Oh, come on, let's put some of it on tape," and that was the first chance I'd ever had of doing various women and various voices. And then when the pilot came up for *Beyond Our Ken*, Jacques remembered me.'

The writers of *Beyond Our Ken*, in its early stages, were Eric Merriman and Barry Took. Took had not long been released from a wobbly career as a stand-up comedian (with trumpet-playing finale) on the variety stage.

> ❛ He came in and he shrieked with laughter at everything I did, whether it was funny or not. And he didn't laugh at anybody else ❜

Barry Took: 'I first met Kenneth in a television studio in 1956. We were both in revue, I was in a thing called *For Amusement Only* with Ron Moody and Hugh Paddick and people like that, and he was in *Share My Lettuce* or whatever that was [This would make it 1957.] and it was Gilbert Harding who used to present these things on Sunday, people in the West End theatre, can't remember what it was called, *Hello, West End!* or something, and Kenneth and I got on very well in the Green Room. We gossiped away. We liked each other, obviously, performers are drawn to each other anyway. And then on a matinée – by then I was in a thing called *For Adults Only* which was the follow-up – he came in and he shrieked with laughter at everything I did, whether it was funny or not. And he didn't laugh at anybody else, with that terrible laugh of Williams's. And then Miriam Karlin would go out, absolute stony silence; got very angry by the end of the performance. He was like that, he was vicious in a way of putting people down, quite unique. And then of course *Beyond Our Ken*, he'd just been ditched by Tony Hancock, and came to us. BBC said, "Would you like Kenneth Williams?" and we went, "Oh my God, yes," Eric Merriman and I.'

In their different ways, Merriman and Took were both quite difficult men, prone to bear a grudge, and their partnership was not destined to last. The friction between them increased when they took on the additional task of perpetuating the vintage series *Take It from Here*, whose long-established writers, Frank Muir and Denis Norden, had departed for television. Under this additional strain the Merriman/Took partnership dissolved, and the long history of *Beyond Our Ken* was carried on by Merriman alone. From the start he'd been looking for a way to use Kenneth Williams.

Eric Merriman: 'He was one of the names that I selected when casting for it. I said I wanted him desperately. In fact, I seem to recall that the powers that be then at the Beeb weren't so mad about him. It's funny. At the initial meeting after a pilot they queried, and I said, "Oh no, he must do it," you know. I suppose he'd done Hancock, he was well known as the voice; the Man of Many Voices.'

Some of the voices, of course, were already in the Kenneth Williams repertoire, ready-made. In the troop shows he had done impressions, and the remnants of his act stayed with him. Sir Felix Aylmer, one of the senior stage actors of the day, much in demand for playing hanging judges, resurfaced regularly as a voice.

Barry Took: 'Marty and I wrote a series, Felix Aylmer was one of the stars … He was high up in Equity, the actors' union, and he used to do the obituaries every year at the Annual General Meeting: "Those who are no longer among us, Fothergill, J.R." and all that. Williams caught all those, and he had a sort of hybrid creature that he called Sir John Gingold … He used to get quite indignant with the stars that he'd worked with, like Alec Guinness. "How dare he think I would come on with my flies deliberately undone!" But anybody who knew Williams would think, Well, it's quite likely that he would have gone on in *Hotel Paradiso* with his flies open to get an extra laugh. When Guinness was rather disappointed by that, Williams thought he was being strange. Odd chap.'

His 'snide' character was his best known, and he was only too pleased to use it again, since in the Hancock environment it had been causing trouble. In Hancock's own opinion it was a generator of automatic, catchphrase laughs, the kind he was aiming to purge from his comedic outlook. But for a scriptwriter in search of a guaranteed weekly round of applause it was a gift not to be spurned.

Eric Merriman: 'Obviously one utilized that character, and that was a great boon and blessing to me because it was such a wonderful voice. And if you did a sketch that built up to some surprise ending, a monster coming upon us or something, and he just said, "Ooh hello, don't be like that …", which was very funny. But then we added things to it. I had this character I wrote, the old man who's "bin in the biznis for thirty-five yeeears" and that wonderful face of his just used to crinkle up and age, visibly age. It was wonderful.'

❛ That wonderful face of his just used to crinkle up and age, visibly age. It was wonderful ❜

Both writers laid claim to the invention of that character. The bad feeling later generated between them by the series coloured much of what they said about it in later times. Took tended to disparage the quality of the scripts as a whole, though he loved writing for Kenneth from the start.

Barry Took: 'Most of us, I could say, were revue artists, I mean we were all theatre people, all our friends were theatre people, and it was very much a theatrey type of show. And he of course revelled in that, 'cos he liked all that. And we were able to find things for him to do. I invented a couple of catchphrases like "thirty-five years" and my favourite which was "The answer lies in the soil." And that worked very well. People loved catchphrases, and Williams loved catchphrases. You didn't have to write anything after a while, just hopped from catchphrase to catchphrase. Not a thing I enjoy personally, but actors like it.'

Betty Marsden felt she recognized the source of the 'thirty-five years' character in some of Kenneth's rehearsal-hall grumblings about his father, whose decrepitude and lack of ambition emerged in his domestic habits, as described by Kenneth, at any rate. Betty Marsden reproduced his dramatization of a typical scene.

Betty Marsden: 'He said, "Point me to the television." "Silly old fool, there's nothing on the television. There's nothing on the telly, Dad." "Never mind, I like the [test] card. Let me look at the card, then I'll be all right." And this is where he got the old man from, you know, the "thirty-five yeeears", that was his father.'

It's perfectly true that Merriman and Took were listening out for real-life character clues in what they heard Kenneth say in conversation.

❝ From a scriptwriter's point of view, you knew that whatever you wrote, he would find something to fit it ❞

Barry Took: 'From a scriptwriter's point of view, you knew that whatever you wrote, he would find something to fit it. And if you listened in the coffee breaks of the recordings and so forth, you'd hear him doing these extraordinary anecdotes, and you'd make a mental note and then you'd write something that had that voice in mind. If I had one word to sum him up, it would be "versatile". You could give him anything to do, he could handle it. And handle it in one take.'

Like every other series known to radio, *Beyond Our Ken* took some time to settle down. Indeed, it took a little time to start at all, since Kenneth Horne suffered a slight stroke in the early weeks of 1958, and the show was briefly shelved. Ron Moody was a cast member in the first series, replaced by Bill Pertwee when they reconvened for Series Two. Kenneth Williams didn't join in the general welcome.

Bill Pertwee: 'Kenny Williams was a little bit sort of offhand with me, "What's he coming in for", you know. He actually said one day, "What do we want him in for? What's he in for, Ken?" he said to Kenneth Horne. So Ken said, "He's our utility man, going to do two or three voices when we need them.' "Mmm, well, I could have done them, couldn't I?" I think it was a bit put on, I think it was to test me out. And I wasn't bothered about that at all, I was just enjoying being with that marvellous company. I used to love knowing that Ken was going to make us laugh immediately you got in, about some terrible thing. "Well I went to the doctor, you see … Ooh, he put this thing, shocking, stuck this needle, ooh it was awful, and of course I'd had the diarrhoea, you know." It went into *all* that, you see, which used to make me roar with laughter.'

The show ran from mid-1958 to early 1964, though Eric Merriman and Barry Took quarrelled and parted during the third series, with Merriman, after the sundering, in sole charge of the scripts. It was then that Took's opinion of what had been going on took a sharp dive.

❛ Of course, Kenneth was brilliant, and was always over the top and disgraceful ❜

Barry Took: 'I thought that *Round the Horne* was infinitely better because the characters were firmer and better founded. It was better written, let's be honest. I was a pretty new scriptwriter at the time, Merriman who was the other writer was more experienced than I but not fantastically so, and we wrote fairly simple material. And I found it a bit of a strain after a while, because Merriman had a drawer full of joke books, and if we were stuck he would open the drawer and we'd have to plough through these books, finding a suitable joke. And I used to say, "It's much quicker if we invent one." '

Eric Merriman: 'Socially, he was an extraordinary person. For instance, I asked him up here once, to come for a drink or a meal. "No, I won't do that. I'll come for Sunday afternoon tea." So I said, "Fine, come. I'll give you a ring." "No , don't do that. Write to me." Because he had a pathological hatred of the telephone. So I had to write, "Dear Kenneth, Will you come …" you know. To which he replied, "I'd be delighted …" And he came up here for tea, and then, "Yes, very nice, very charming. Bloody suburban, of course," and all that sort of thing, you know.

But that's one occasion when one managed to sort of lure him out. And the other one, which was really quite funny, was the time the whole cast of *Beyond Our Ken* went to see Hugh Paddick, another member of cast, who was on stage in a revue. And throughout the whole of the first half Williams was laughing that laugh of his, that rasping machine "hehhehhehhehhehheh" – which to all intents and purposes seemed false, but it wasn't, you know. Anyway, it unnerved the people on the stage completely; a lone laugher affects an audience. And in the interval the management asked Mr Williams either to restrain himself or leave the theatre. He did restrain himself, and stay. It wasn't done for attention-getting, I think it was just a natural exuberance. He was just enjoying it so much.'

Hugh Paddick, Kenneth, Kenneth Horne and Betty Marsden recording **Round the Horne**, 1968. 'Half an hour of crap with not a memorable line anywhere: well – perhaps the odd one. Well of course one goes on and flogs it gutless and gets the rubbish by.' (Diary, 5 February 1968)

What Kenneth and Hugh Paddick later perpetrated, in the roles of Jules and Sandy, tended to blot out their earlier achievements, but they were already well known in *Beyond Our Ken* as Rodney and Charles, a more sedate pair of aesthetes. Paddick's contemporary contribution was the figure of Ricky Livid, an unenlightened pop star. It was assumed, then and later, that Paddick and Williams must be close friends, but Paddick in particular was wary of his fellow broadcaster.

Betty Marsden: 'Hugh was a very quiet man. He was no exhibitionist. I think they were members of a certain club, I don't know where it was, but Hugh always used to go to the doorman and say, "Is Mr Williams here?" Albert, or whatever his name was, would say, "No, no, Mr Paddick, he isn't." He'd say, "Thank God," and he would go in. One day he asked and the man said, "No, sir, he's not," and of course he was. And Hugh walked in and suddenly saw him at the bar, surrounded by a load of little fellas and things, holding court. And he shouted out to Hugh, "Oh, Hughsie Paddick. Come along, Hughsie Paddick. There you are, come and join me, Hughsie Paddick, here I am." Hugh said, "Yes, I can see you're there, surrounded by your rrring of confidence . . ." I don't think either of them would have really chosen to work one with the other, any more than Kenneth would work with Stanley Baxter. He was a great friend of Baxter's, but what? Not likely! They were too similar, they'd both want to play the best parts, have the best lines, and expect them.'

In a way unmatched by any other 'host' figure on the air in those days, certainly in the comedy field, Kenneth Horne was the show's centre of gravity. You could hear an organizing discipline in his voice, and yet he did nothing to suppress the tiniest fraction of the available hilarity. Horne always sounded delighted by the efforts of the cast. He'd been a successful businessman, and still maintained, offstage, a spectacular managerial flair.

Betty Marsden: 'In that first lunch that darling Kenneth Horne gave the whole company, and the orchestra, everybody, which I think we had at the Hyde Park Hotel, in the restaurant. Well, that was Kenneth Williams at his best! But next time we had a private room. Kenneth Horne was so wonderful, he didn't remark on it, he said, "I think it'd be better to have a private room, then we can all behave as we wish." He was so marvellous, and understanding. And really, I think Kenneth Williams adored him. I think he was one of the people he really had a deep, deep affection for. It was almost like a father-figure, I think. We hadn't all got that patience, I'm afraid.'

Such patience as they did have quite often came under strain, although the memory of those occasions turned out funnier than the day-to-day reality had been. Kenneth was not one of those performers who would leave his troubles at the threshold of the rehearsal room. He would tend to bring his moods in with him, obliging Kenneth Horne to do his best to anticipate the worst of the Williams sulks.

Betty Marsden: 'Oh yes, he sulked. He was a very sulky gentleman. I think we were doing a recording on a Boxing Day, or something, I can't remember whether it was *Beyond Our Ken* or *Round the Horne*, and Kenneth Horne said, "Whatever we do, do not let us ask Kenneth what sort of a Christmas he had, because I'm sure he's going to say it's dreadful." 'Cos he wasn't looking forward to it at all. So of course he came in and "Mnaah, morning everybody … Where's the script? Is this it? Filthy paper, look at it. Morning, morning, *morning*." And of course somebody said, "Did you enjoy your –?" "Don't talk to me about Christmas! My old man, let me tell you, he's a *bastard*. I can't stand the old …" and every word in the book came out. Apparently, what had happened, he said, "I had bought him the most beee-au-tiful coat, it was all a sheepskin lining, it was beautiful, leather down to here, showed it to him at Christmas, took it out, here you are, Dad. 'I don't want that! Is that for me, I don't want that! That's a poof's coat, that is. That's a poof's coat. Give it to a poof.' So I did!" he said. I can't tell you, we had that terrifying presence all day long.'

Barry Took: 'He responded to warmth with warmth, he responded to affection with affection. He was very likeable. He could be acerbic, he could brush people off if he didn't know them, if he felt it that way, because the tensions of performing are quite considerable. And if you're getting all your emotional life out through your performances, as Kenneth Williams did, then obviously you're highly charged at the end of a performance. I remember my daughter, who was about 12, came up to him after something, I think it was *Just a Minute*, and she

"ARKWRIGHT   V   MRS. EMERSON (deceased)".

When pond'ring over B.O.K.,
(the Series that's just past)
I often think how bright we were
Assembling such a Cast.
Ken W: perfectionist,
Who thinks it is a crime
To do a Show unless we've read
The Script time after time;
Provided he remains with us
We know the Show will thrive
For many years - I'd even take
A bet on thirty-five.
Then Betty Marsden - many voiced -
Each role a tour-de-force
Exaggerating nothing
Except everything, of course.
Now Betty is my passion
And I can't think how I missed
The boat and lost the battle
To a plain Anaesthetist.
Hugh Paddick: He's the man
who Cecil Snaith thinks is a hit
While Stanley Birkinshaw says "No,
I think he's just a spit".
Yes, B.O.K. could never run
Without Hugh, all agree
And if the B.B.C., can't find
The Cash, we'll use H.P.
Bill Pertwee - uncomplaining type
We couldn't be without.
He never beefs when both his lines
Are altered, then cut out.
He keeps Ken W. in check
And that's one reason we
Will answer the old question with:
'Pertwee!' not 'Not Pertwee!'
And now let's turn to Janet
(That's a nice thought by the way)
How lucky "Minnehaha -
Laughing Waters" came our way.
From letters we've received we know
That all admire her voice
And now she runs an early morning
Show: "Househusbands' Choice".
To have the surname Merriman
Is suited to a scribe
And Eric lives up to it, so
He'll never diatribe.
We hope to hear more brilliant wit
Suffusing from his pen
Who knows? Perhaps the B.B.C.,
Will one day tell us when?

- 1 -

Kenneth Horne's personal tribute to the cast and crew of **Beyond Our Ken** and
performed, perhaps, at one of his celebratory parties at the Hyde Park Hotel.

We Actors are quite busy folk
Who have our plans to make
Don't leave it to the last - then rope in
Hutch and Charlie Drake.
Or just imagine Douglas Smith
(That stalwart of our Team)
Announcing that 'our Singing Group
Was led by Julian Bream'.
Or saying, "Here's 'Beyond our Ken' -
Starring old shiny dome -
Anonymous as always, yes!!
It's Kenneth Wolstenholme!"
But I digress - I always do
When something gets me down
Let's talk of something happier -
To whit to whoo, Jacques Brown.
The corner stone on which the Programme's
Built. At every stage
Imploring us to do our nuts
And lift it off the page.
With Winnie egging Williams on
And fetching tea and buns
And noting down the stories
(All the risky doubtful ones!).
The Hornets, Eddie Braden,
The V.O., with John and Paul
Without these kindly folk
There'd be no B.O.K. at all:
Ron Belchier's essential - plus
Steve Allen or Jo Young
Now who have I missed out?
Or have I all the praises sung?
Oh yes, there is one other bloke -
Not worth a lot of fuss
For after all, as always, he
Remains anonymuss!

------ooOoo------

Hugh Paddick, Kenneth, Kenneth Horne, Betty Marsden and **Round the Horne** announcer
Douglas Smith, 1968. 'Did Round the Horne at the Paris. It went very well. The writing is
really good I must say. I only hope they keep up the standard.' **(Diary, 12 February 1968)**

went up to him and said hello, and he said, "Go away little girl. Go away. I don't
want to talk to anybody after the show. I've just been performing, you know."
She was quite abashed. She came over and stood with her mother and me, we
were talking to somebody else. And he went, "Who's that girl? Is that your daughter?" I said yes. "God," he said, "how embarrassing." And he wrote her a wonderful letter the next day, saying, "how bad mannered I was, how appallingly
behaved, and will you accept this signed photograph as a little tribute?" which
she treasures, of course.'

In any top-class performance there are touchy egos present, and Eric Merriman
even found himself offended on one occasion by the sainted Kenneth Horne. For
once, it was a situation not caused by Kenneth Williams, but defused by him.

Eric Merriman: 'During the run of *Beyond Our Ken*, at its height, when it was
a really successful show, Kenneth Horne was interviewed by the press, and was
asked to what did he attribute the success of the show. And he very kindly said
to them, "Oh, well, it's the brilliant cast, you see. They could make a telephone

directory sound funny." Now I did take a bit of umbrage at this, because there I was, turning out a pretty good script every week, so I thought, Right, I'll get my own back, and the next week, when we convened in the little room at the back of the Paris Cinema for the scripts to be handed out, I said to the producer, "Let's hold them back a minute, and I'll produce telephone directories." And I said, "Right, there we are. There's A to K for you, S to Z, L to R," and I felt I'd made my point. There was a bit of a stunned silence and then Williams picked up one of the books and went, "The Pneumatic Drill and Tyre Company ..." and made it hysterically funny.'

He certainly had the technique to do so, but it wasn't the sort of technique some of his fellow performers expected from a conventionally rep-trained player.

Bill Pertwee: 'That's what rather amazed me, the fact that he was an actor. He's a very well-read man obviously, he's no idiot. Yet he's communicating with that audience like a seaside comedian does. I was very surprised at that. And where he learned that art of communication, I wouldn't know.'

But Kenneth's relish for communication had strict boundaries. As Eric Merriman suggested, he was difficult to coax into a simple social visit, and anything resembling an official function, with polite conversational duties attached, was usually shunned. One of the few who could cajole him into participating was Kenneth Horne, and even he was given an embarrassing public tutorial on the limits of Williams's tolerance at a suits-meet-talent reception organized by the BBC.

Bill Pertwee: 'On one occasion Ken Horne said, "Now come on, we have to go up. We don't have to, but it's very nice for us to go up and have a nice lunch and meet the people who are employing us. Ken, you forget that, don't you?" And we get up there, and there's this very nice chap who I'd met two or three times, he was a Controller, quite big up there, and his wife, and I remember they lived in Tunbridge Wells, and after five minutes you see Ken getting very anxious to go. And he went up to this lady, and he said, "Ooh, this morning," he said, "I've come down walking past Selfridges, and this bloke, shocking, he opened his coat, he had nothing on, showed the lot he did, ooh, all hanging out!" And this poor lady, she didn't know what to do. Ken Horne said, "You'd better go, I think," and Williams looked at me and winked. He'd done what he meant to do, and off he went.'

And this unscrupulous manipulator was the same Williams who, only a few years before, had been humbly petitioning the BBC's producers for a stray part here and there. Incidentally, any collection of Kenneth Williams anecdotes would have to devote a well-stocked section to the theme of self-exposure. In his lexicon of bourgeois-baiting, there was no quicker way to startle the innocent punter than to flourish the genitalia, if only notionally.

Eric Merriman: 'I was at a party of Betty Marsden's, loads of people there, and I was pushing through this crowd with a couple of plates of something, and he caught my eye. He was holding forth to a group of people, who were not show business, you see, and he just caught my eye, and I just called across, "You behaving yourself?" and he turned round straight away and said, "Is my cock out?" I said no. "Well, I am behaving myself" and he went back to them and their faces were a picture. Because they weren't expecting that kind of thing, you see.'

❛ Come along and see it and grab 'old of it, with your 'and. It's all right, it won't bite cha ❜

The most rhetorical of his self-exposure fantasies unspooled backstage at a pantomime. Kenneth was already leading a compartmentalized life, and it was not often that a friend or colleague overlapped with him in more than one personal or professional environment. His radio chums were not, on the whole, his fellow stage-actors. But Betty Marsden counted, briefly, as an exception. She shared the stage with Kenneth in the Christmas season of 1958/9, and exacted a curious revenge for all his goosings.

Betty Marsden: 'I beat him to it, though, when we were together in *Cinderella* at the Coliseum, with Tommy Steele: the Rodgers/Hammerstein *Cinderella*, beautiful book. I was playing the Godmother, he was one of the Ugly Sisters.

He dressed in the dressing room next to me. And every day, every day, he'd get out there and he'd say, "Well I've *got it aht*! I've got it aht. Anybody want to see it? Come along and see it and grab 'old of it, with your 'and. It's all right, it won't bite cha." It went on like this night after night, till one day I said, "All right, Kenneth, I'm coming out." And I went out, and I chased him all up the corridor, and grabbed him! I literally grabbed him. He'd never been so frightened in his life. He didn't come out of his dressing room for days after that. It was really very funny, so I got my own back.'

It was during the long run of *Beyond Our Ken* that stories began to circulate within the profession about the way Kenneth Williams lived, in his spartan flat. At that stage it was not unknown for numbers of people to enter his little domain and see it for themselves – indeed, occasional visits were built into the *BOK* timetable.

Bill Pertwee: 'We used to go round to one another's places – not mine, actually, 'cos I was living in Brighton – we used to go round to either Ken Horne's flat, or Kenneth Williams's place, or Hugh Paddick's, to have a get-together before we started a series, just to say, well, there's a new character in here, that'll be nice, and how's everybody, have you had a nice break, whatever it was. And when we went up to Kenneth Williams's flat, above Baker Street station, we'd arranged to get there at eleven, and knocked on the door and it was about five to eleven. And Ken Horne said, "Morning, Ken!" and Williams said, "Go away. It's only five to eleven. You're too early. Go away. I'm listening to the radio." And wouldn't let us in till eleven o'clock! He only had cushions on the floor, you know, things like that, to sit on, and he wouldn't let anybody use his toilet, any stranger or anything like that, you had to go down to the Baker Street Station to use the gents. Oh yes. I think it was his way of saying "I'm the guv'nor."'

It was certainly a gesture of assertiveness in a strangely passive world. 'These radio shows,' Kenneth told his diary, 'leave me feeling quite dead. I feel as if I'm moving in a soporific dream. There is a curious feeling of apathy about all radio entertainment. A negative feeling.' But he kept at it, and his radio fame still had room to grow.

Cordwangles and JAM

‘Oh will you love me Mary Oh,
when my futtocks be bended low? ’

Rambling Syd Rumpo

MONO | ffrr LK 4393 | ONE OVER THE EIGHT | ORIGINAL CAST | DECCA

MICHAEL CODRON PRESENTS

KENNETH WILLIAMS IN

one over the 8

A NEW REVUE

AN ORIGINAL CAST RECORDING

SETS AND COSTUMES BY
TONY WALTON

DIRECTED AND CHOREOGRAPHED BY
PADDY STONE

The 1961 cast recording of **One Over the Eight**, inscribed to George Borwick (1922–1994).

Kenneth Williams's contribution to *Beyond Our Ken* had become one of radio's unmissable turns. Yet it had completely failed to register in the upper levels of the BBC hierarchy, to judge by an internal memo from yet another Kenneth, Kenneth Adam, Controller of Programmes (Television), in the spring of 1960. Adam still associated Williams with earlier achievements.

> *To Head of Light Entertainment, Television:*
> *I was reminded again this weekend by friends of how funny Kenneth Williams*
> *is — an old member of the Hancock radio team, remember? I wonder if we*
> *could not interest him in a situation comedy series?*

Eric Merriman: 'I have a theory that I don't think he quite made it on television. It's strange, but I don't think they ever did the right thing with him. I mean, he was basically an actor, he had this wonderful array of characters and voices,

Page 156 'Read a lot of poems aloud from the Larkin Oxford collection. The Flecker one about the [Oxford] Canal is fine. I sat, revolving many memories and weeping.' **(Diary, 9 March 1974)**

'He always was a believer for most of his life and he was an expert on something called the Ontological Creed. But towards the end of his life the poet Philip Larkin talked him out of his religious faith – because they were in correspondence – by saying he'd read the Bible and it didn't impress him at all and in his opinion it was all a load of rubbish. Somehow that affected Kenneth very badly, at the wrong time really because it coincided with him becoming more and more depressed and suffering from his various ulcers, headaches and pains. It was through Larkin that his faith collapsed.' **(Michael Whittaker)**

and what did they do, they put him in a white tuxedo, to compere I think it was called *International Cabaret*. And although of course he did make it quite amusing, 'cos he had some monologues which he did, I don't think that was the real Kenneth Williams.'

The 1959 cast recording of **Pieces of Eight**.

But that extraordinary, misshapen effort, one of the BBC's most shambolic entertainment concoctions, awaited Kenneth's attention a few years later, in 1966. Back in 1960 he was still feeling his way in television. The nearest he'd come to a TV sitcom was Tony Hancock's show, from which he'd been initially excluded anyway, and then subtracted after the second series, in the course of Hancock's doomed search for truer, purer comedy. His notoriety had now been much enhanced by the success of the last of his West End revues, *One Over the Eight*, in which he starred with Sheila Hancock. Written in the main by Peter Cook, it contained the famous sketch about a verbally bungled bank robbery, 'Hand Up Your Sticks', which became a much-requested record on BBC radio. (The original running-order also featured Cook's famous 'one-legged Tarzan' sketch, which later adorned *Beyond the Fringe*, but it was cut from *One Over the*

'I continually wonder about how London will take this revue. I pretend that I am prepared for a flop – but secretly I'm frightened of one – and at the same time equally frightened of a mediocre success!' (Diary, 20 September 1959)

Pages 160 and 161, publicity shots for **Pieces of Eight**, the revue show that became a West End hit, spawning a sequel in 1961.

Eight before the London run on grounds of taste.) In his diary after the first night Kenneth laced into the show mercilessly and at length ('a revue of pathetic trivia'), but it charmed the public, contributing to one of the most exhausting work schedules Williams ever undertook. His status as a 'personality' in public life was now confirmed by the emergence of a press release about him, put together (in a more cautious tone than these things usually generate) by a firm called Baron Moss Public Relations. It was part of a general effort to publicize *One Over the Eight*, but even with that topical peg to help them in their task the boosters evidently found Kenneth quite tricky to sell. 'Off stage,' their text confided, 'he is a much more serious person. Fame placed restrictions on him and he claims that if he had an ambition it would be to be a hermit ... One matter disappoints him. He has no opportunity to sing in the revue. "Nobody seems

to realise that I have a marvellous singing voice," he says. "Once I get through the first few bars there is nobody, in truth, like me." The truth will not be revealed to the audience of *One Over the Eight*.'

Peter Eade's letters were envisaging ever more grandiose undertakings for Kenneth. In the midst of all this activity he communicated some vague and fanciful warnings to Jacques Brown of the BBC.

> *I am returning the complimentary card for BOK for tomorrow in case someone can use it.*
>
> *Incidentally, can you tell me whether the BBC are planning to bring back BOK for another series? I mention this as it seems Kenneth is in much demand in America and I have already had to turn down a season for him at Las Vegas because of his revue commitments. Nevertheless, as soon as this revue ends in London I have agreed that Kenneth should appear in it in New York if the offer is made, but, alternatively, he is wanted for film and TV commitments over there so it looks very likely that he will be making the trip anyhow.*
>
> *Just let me know if you hear of any future plans.*

❛I have a theory that I don't think he quite made it on television. It's strange, but I don't think they ever did the right thing with him❜

A scribbled note by Brown at the bottom of the page remarks 'And K. Williams is not the only one in demand.' However, so far from taking his marvellous singing voice to Las Vegas, Kenneth never made a trip of any kind to America. In the event, *Beyond Our Ken* not only reappeared in the autumn, but returned for two more series after that, the last of them with John Simmonds producing in place of Jacques Brown. Eric Merriman continued to write the scripts, seemingly undisturbed by a controversy behind the scenes in mid-1960, when Barry Took had proposed a radio show called *The Proudfoot Family*. This was a Kenneth Williams series we never heard, for reasons set out by Kenneth in a letter to the Assistant Head of Light Entertainment (Sound), J.H. Davidson.

*I decided for various reasons that it would not be a good idea for me to
proceed with this project The Proudfoot Family and in conversation with
Eric Merriman he said he would rather I didn't take part in it, as it would
be practically impossible not to give vocal qualities to the new show which
were obligatory to Beyond Our Ken. I wrote to this effect in a personal letter
to Barry Took, and he has replied saying that he has conveyed this letter to
you. I cannot understand such an unethical procedure as this, for a personal
letter to be used in this fashion is unthinkable: but if indeed he has sent
you my letter, I would ask you to remember that it was a personal &
confidential letter.*

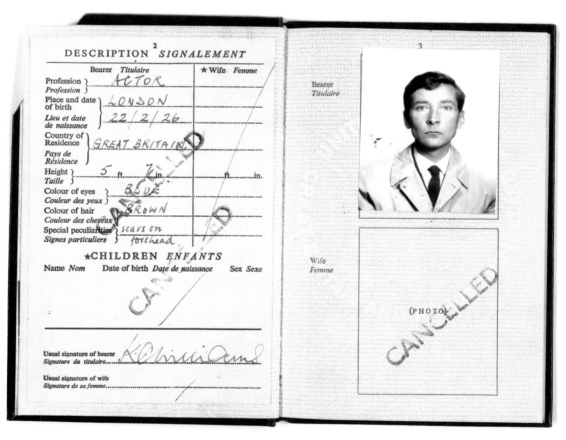

'Had passport photograph taken at the same place as I originally went to in 1950! And it came out as I
wanted it. The camera operator said "You must smile!" But I ignored the stupid fool, I must look as I
usually look, and that is NOT smiling.' **(Diary, 4 May 1965)**

Davidson's reply registered both shock and disgruntlement:

> *I am truly sorry you have found it expedient to withdraw from this project. Whilst I understand your dilemma and sympathise, I find it difficult to agree with your reasons for withdrawal. Upon reflection it can be seen that all we had proposed was a trial script from Barry Took, based upon an idea of which you were aware and if the subsequent script had been acceptable, we proposed to make a trial programme. I cannot for the life of me see why this in any way concerned Eric Merriman as it is quite unlikely we would have taken any action parallel with Beyond Our Ken, thereby causing a 'double banking' of your efforts. However we must perforce let things lie for the time being. When and if an appropriate opportunity arises I shall again contact you.*

Clearly, Kenneth's vocal resources were not infinite, and he did fear an over-exposure of certain effects. At the same time, it's not hard to imagine that Barry Took perceived Merriman's role in the affair as that of saboteur. He had provided Kenneth with a persuasive reason not to go ahead with *Proudfoot*. This was the sort of thing that poisoned relations between Took and Merriman. When *Beyond Our Ken* ceased, in the early months of 1964, Merriman went off to television, having obscurely incurred, according to Hugh Paddick, 'the wrath of the BBC'. Barry Took moved into the vacated place, alongside his new writing partner, Marty Feldman.

Their creation, *Round the Horne*, featured a completely refreshed assembly of grotesque characters, but nothing very new in the way of format, and Merriman (who was unwilling to talk much about these matters in his later years) was incensed. Even the title had been contemplated years before, at that stage in the form 'Around the Horne'. Williams's diary records an irate phone call from Merriman, accusing Kenneth of disloyalty simply for taking part in a series reconstituted, as the writer saw it, by two usurpers. At that moment Merriman seemed to be contemplating legal action, presumably for plagiarism, though nothing came of the threat. A pilot programme went ahead – contractually under the feeble title *It's Ken Again*, with Kenneth Williams receiving a comfortable 55 guineas for his trouble – and, as the world knows, the show was approved.

7.

<u>MARY-OH</u>!

1.   KENNETH &   OH WILL YOU LOVE ME MARY OH
       GUITAR: WHEN MY FUTTOCKS BE BENDED LOW

WHEN MY ORBS GROW DIM

AND MY SPLOD BE WHITE

AND MY CORDWANGLE MAKES AN UGLY SIGHT

AND MY FUTTOCKS BE BENDED LOW-OW-OW

MY FUTTOCKS HAVE BENDED LOW

AND SHE ANSWERS:

YOU ASK ME IF I LOVE YOU OH

WHEN YOUR FUTTOCKS BE BENDED LOW

WHEN YOUR ORBS GROW DIM

AND YOUR SPLOD BE WHITE

AND YOUR CORDWANGLE MAKES AN UGLY SIGHT

IF I FEEL THE WAY I DO TONIGHT

MY ANSWER WILL STILL BE - NO!

<u>KENNETH OVER</u>/

Pages 165–167 'On the 3rd of July I did the Rambling Syd recording at EMI studios in Abbey Road before an audience of about two hundred people. It went like a bomb. The laughter was so intrusive that it broke up the rhythm of some of the songs.'
(Kenneth, **Just Williams**, 1985)

THE TERRIBLE TALE OF THE SOMERSET NOG

(Trad.,Took,Fledman=EMI=B.Rhodes)

1. KENNETH: (SPOKEN INTRO.)

well Hallo me dearios! my song Tonight

~~My next ditty~~ is about a fabled horse, the Somerset
Nog, so called 'cos it's a cross between a nag and
a dog. It's half Suffolk Punch and half Dachshund,
well it gets very foggy on the moors. Anyway,
this nog is a strange looking creature, three hands
high and eighteen foot long. They're not pretty
to look at, but the rhubarb in that part of the
world....it really is magnificent. My song tells
of a man who wants to go to the great fair at
Gander Poke Bog. So he asks this farmer for a
loan of the nog so he can take all his friends
with him, and it proceeds in this fashion:

2. GUITAR: IN: 'WIDDICOMBE FAIR'

3. KENNETH: REG PUBES, REG PUBES, LEND ME YOUR GREAT NOG
ROLLOCK MY FUSSET AND GRIDDLE MY NODES
FOR I WANT FOR TO GO TO GANDER POKE BOG
WITH LEN POSSETT, TIM SCREEVEY, THE REV. PHIPPS,
PEG LEG LUKE, SOLLY LEVI, GINGER EPSTEIN,
ABLE SEAMAN TRUEFIT, SCOTCH LIL, MESSRS KATAMO
MOUSEHABIT AND DEEPTHIGH AND TRUSSPOT:
SOLICITORS AND COMMISSIONERS FOR OATHS,
FATHER THUNDERGAST, FAT ALICE, DAVID HATCH,
YETI ROSENCRANTZ, BARBARA WOODEHOUSE
AND UNCLE DICK FRANCIS AND ALL
OLD UNCLE DICK FRANCIS AND ALL.   (Cont'd Over/)

1.   KENNETH: (SPOKEN)

So they all got on, except for Alice, who don't
get on with no one and off they go.   But ⸍sad to
relate, the horse snaps in two and expires.
But they do say as how its ghost walks abroad in
two halves, and if you be passing Gander Poke Bog
at midnight, they do say you can hear the two
ghostly halves of the nog singing in duet:

2.   GUITAR: IN:

3.   KENNETH: REG PUBES, REG PUBES, YOU LENT YOUR GREAT NOG

ROLLOCK MY FUSSET AND GRIDDLE MY NODES

AND NOW MY REMAINS ARE IN GANDER POKE BOG

WITH LEN POSSETT, TIM SCREEVEY, THE REV. PHIPPS,

PEG LEG LUKE, SOLLY LEVI, GINGER EPSTEIN,

ABLE SEAMAN TRUEFIT, SCOTCH LIL, MESSRS KATAMO

MOUSEHABIT DEEPTHIGH AND TRUSSPOT:

SOLICITORS AND COMMISSIONERS FOR OATHS,

FATHER THUNDERGAST, FAT ALICE, DAVID HATCH,

YETI ROSENCRANTZ, BARBARA WOODEHOUSE,

AND UNCLE DICK FRANCIS AND ALL

OLD UNCLE DICK FRANCIS AND ALL.

Kenneth Over/.......

Barry Took: 'Kenneth Horne was the stabilizing factor, he was very, very much the boss, and very fatherly, and Kenneth just loved him to pieces, thought the world of him, and therefore relaxed and was at ease. He enjoyed the scripts – after initial suspicion – he enjoyed what Marty and I wrote for him, and we loved writing for him, so there was quite a rapport among the whole crew.'

Kenneth's 'initial suspicion' towards *Round the Horne* was indeed characteristic of Kenneth. When the mood was on him he was prepared to be limitlessly reckless in the cause of his own conversational rudery, but when confronted with a startling new script he could display something oddly like prudishness.

Barry Took: 'He had to work himself up into a mode where he could perform by telling a series of jokes, and they all followed exactly the same sequence: they started at one joke and went through about another four or five, and they were exactly the same and exactly the same order every week. I can't quote them, they were filthy, and they grew in filth, you see. There's jokes about breaking wind, jokes about erections and jokes about mishaps of a sexual nature, and they mounted in fury to the climactic joke about a man losing his penis. And that was it. But he was primed to perform, he was like a surgeon getting into his rubber gloves and the green outfit and the mask. He had to go through this routine in order to perform. It was so mechanical and repetitive, and then he'd go out and be thoroughly original.'

'We created very theatrical people. Knowing the theatre background we were able to do Julian and Sandy, which was all camp slang. And Charles and Fiona, very theatrical, Noel Cowardy type of stuff. And Rambling Syd Rumpo was an absolute fraud of a folk singer. And all those things were excellent.'

In most successful comedy shows there's an element that seems to take on a life and an impetus of its own, and in the case of *Round the Horne* it was always the Julian and Sandy section (the names a tribute to the musical-comedy writers Julian Slade and Sandy Wilson, writers of *Salad Days* and *The Boy Friend* respectively). To most of the huge radio audience, the strange language issuing from this florid pair was new and hilarious, but mysterious in terms of its origins. Had the scriptwriters made it all up, or were there real people who spoke like this? Or was it, as most people probably thought, a mixture of actuality and invention? In point of fact no invention was required.

❛Kenneth Horne was the stabilizing factor, he was very, very much the boss❜

Barry Took: 'Both [Kenneth] and Hugh, being theatrical people, knew all the slang terms, as indeed did Marty and I from our theatrical experiences. And what we didn't know, they added. They just thought it was a great treat, to have something that they could really extend themselves doing. We didn't make any up. We used whatever was available. "Lallies" was legs – circus slang, and fairground slang, with ballet and dancers' slang, and the whole thing arrived in the West End as a terrible mixture of all these origins, a mish-mash. "Riah" is just hair backwards, it's back-slang. We used to have a list of all these words when we were writing, we'd have a list on the thing, and go, "Oh, we haven't used lallies yet, we'd better put that in." They were all genuine words. With Rambling Syd Rumpo they were all made up, none of them meant any-thing. And we just used sounds, we wanted sounds, knowing that strange voice of his, we wanted to capture that. We did an LP for EMI, this was in Abbey Road [in June 1967], and very wisely they gave them wine and cheese. I don't know how much cheese was consumed, but a lot of wine went down, I know, and it was absolute euphoria. And it was just him and a guitar player, terrific rapport between the two of them, 'cos they'd done twenty or thirty *Round the Horne* shows. And an evening of absolute delight. It still sounds good on the LP.'

Rambling Syd's ''Ullo me dearios' still stands as one of radio's truly instant character-establishing phrases. Naturally the show's general display of rudery was not accepted with equanimity by all listeners, but the BBC in those days was both confident and combative on behalf of its output, very ready to face its would-be censors.

KEN:

Of course I've been in trouble round behind.
No, stop messing about, missus. I'm serious.
Well, you see, I had this phone call from a
man who was watching the programme and he said
"I'm very annoyed at you running down
advertising. Let me tell you, he said, it's
done me a lot of good. That's how I got
married."
I said you're joking - he said "Straight up.
I put this ad in the paper saying 'Handsome
bachelor desires wife'
I said really - what happened ?
He said "Sixteen husbands sent me theirs".
I put the phone down..leaving *m him to
his seraglio..because I had to get back here
to introduce 4 young ladies fr. Germany to sing for you
The Yarcob sisters.

Thank you .... from ....
As a matter of fact, talking about France, I
was particularly interested in that news item
in Paris-Soir - I always go to this French
fish and chip shop..it keeps me au fait...
anyway, that's where I read it - a news item
about Picasso being knocked down by a hit and run
driver in France. Apparently, the police asked
Picasso to draw a sketch of the driver, and do
you know, they have already arrested three suspects.
A nun, the Eiffel Tower and a television set.
But I digress. It's time for me to introduce
our next guest from Italy - Ladies + Gentlemen
GINO DONATI.

KEN:

I said but we did
about "I like Kenne
and the first prize
Bermuda. The only e
reading "I like Kenneth
want a dream holiday in
humiliating. She said "O
different with Hilary. Af
got the S.A., when he's sob
for the Laureateship."
didn't you say
can all

DEC 3

..BARET.............12

Good evening and welcome to another edition
of International Cabaret, the show that's
a pot pourri of the polyglot - where the sari
meets the sweater, the burnoose meets the
bowler, and the kimono meets the kilt and says
"Brother, you could have fooled me." Of
course, you get the odd reactionary saying
"Why present a programme full of foreigners ?"
Obviously, they don't realise the British
themselves are a load of foreigners.
Originally, there was only a small group of
natives on the island. They wore their hair
in bangs, and were known as the lunatic fringe.
Most of the time they were hiding behind
bushes, terribly embarrassed at their own
nakedneds ; but they all turned over a new
leaf when this queen came along to rule them.
She was called Ethel and she cried out to them
"I am your new ruler, Queen Ethel." And they
all said "Ethel be the day" and she said "No.
Stop messing about. I am your actual royalty."
And one of them said "Oh, get the madam" and
she bashed him and said "Lissen - I've got a
divine right." And he picked himself up
and said "You've also got a very good left."
She said "you will show me obeisance" They
said "We have no basins - we wash in the river."
She said "I was coming to that. Look at you -
I've never seen such a load of scruffs. All
the women get their hair washed. That's my
first decree. Except you four." She said to
this group of drears standing near... "Stop
scratching yourselves - you shall be my hand-
maidens. You can give me the wash and set and
a henna dye. I fancy myself with a henna."

grab
mustn't be bitter. Though
why not. The producer's on
much as I am - and his wife
of Montreal. That's her mai
of course. I could tell you
make your hair curl...but I
the law of libel. And anywa
time to introduce our star
Ladies and gentlemen, Inter
Dabaret is proud to welcome
the Atlantic - PAUL ANKA.

Thank you .... Well, tonight is
rather a special occasion. It's my birthday..
and I sent the usual telegram to my parents -
congratulations on having a genius. Well, they
~ the flattery...and I spent the day quietly
'~v fashioned stocking feet, going throug]
~wering the odd telephone call
~e lady called me person to
odd name but she never
~ said "I can't believe ~~
~y in show bus~~

KEN: No, of course, nothing underneath -
that would be cheating. All during
the summer months I do quite a bit
of practising over here on Hampstead

Oct 8   ll, I say I do, but I mean
ads of the British Skulki~
But we never get the
le Skulker Nabbed" like
Switzerland. We don'
all on Hampstead Heath
ere unrestrainedly.
"Hulle and what are y
out "Skulking, that'~
g - skulking unrestra
"And what, pray, is
y "It's knowing wha
alf an hour ago."
them up. Interfer
u'll be glad to he
too... and introd
ladies and gent.
te-Valente.

INTERNATIONAL CABARET............5

KEN:

Good evening ladies and gentlemen and welcome
to another edition of International Cabaret,
the show that makes everybody happy - except
perhaps the postman. The weight of my fan
mail - he veritably staggers. And no wonder.
You should see the contents...heavy with passion.
One of them actually said "Would that I could
kiss the hem of your garment." Well, she
knows I affect the nightshirt. And another
was even more obeisant. It said "I would
deem it an honour to scrub your doorstep,
polish your paintwork and shiver your timbers."
I thought it was very nice of her, but I
haven't got any timbers to shiver. I'm more
your laminated plastic and uncut moquette.
But it's a pity her offer hadn't come a few
days earlier, cos I'd put the advert in for -
Girl Friday-cum-daily wanted to run bachelor
establishment for west end celeb. Out
Thursdays. Automatic boiler - no stoking.
The only answer I got was from a lady who
signed herself Florrie Plume, late of Roebuck's
Family Hotel and Gaming Parlour. I thought
hullo, that's a funny place to have games.
Still, in for a penny, in for a pound so I
asked her to come to an interview at her
convenience. She turned up at eight o'clock
in the morning. I don't call that convenient,
either for her or me. I was desharbille -
still in the nightshirt - and she walked in,
took one look round the hall and said "Oh, it's
green." I said no...lime crush. She said
"It looks green to me." Unless it's your
nightshirt reflecting." I said madam, let's
go through to the drawing room where we can
talk. So we did and she said "Oh, it's quite
big, isn't it. Room enough to swing several
cats, or a cheetah or a jaguar or a cougar."
She went right off - we were halfway round the
zoo.

14:3

Thank you ....
telling you abou
ask for a signe~
for a lock of ~
touch me are t
cos you're on
every night,
and a boiled
instance, I
plead the '
farthinga]
in it...~
this dir
your ol
think c   But
Gabor.
manif~
next

16:

k you ~
about g
pulle
poked
ff ou
~m..~
ell,
' A
aid
~u'
ve
in
b

sartorial e
is just as

Barry Took: 'We had Hugh Greene as Director General. There were a lot of complaints about *Round the Horne*. Mary Whitehouse sharpened her teeth on us, and would write and complain. And there was a man called Sir Cyril Black MP, a one-man crusade against filth. And they used to write to Hugh Greene, and he'd say, "Send me a script," and we'd send him a script and he'd read it and write, "I see nothing to object to in this. Pass it back down the line," and we'd do it. And years later I was talking to him, and I said, "Why did you protect us and stand up for us in that way?" He said, "I like dirty shows." He didn't really, but he liked adventurous shows, he liked dangerous broadcasting. So do I. If it's all safe and secure it becomes pretty dull after a time.'

By the same token, relentless 'smut' (as Mrs Whitehouse was fond of calling it) could also be dull, causing even Barry Took some censorious moments. They were observed with interest by Kenneth Williams.

Barry Took: 'He quotes in the diaries, in 1968, "Barry Took in a very funny mood, and snappy about filth. He kept shouting 'We might as well write a series called *Get Your Cock Out*.' I think he's a bit demented." I probably was. It was one of those things. Marty had gone off performing to become a star, and I was writing with Johnnie Mortimer and Brian Cooke, and it did get a bit dirty. It's very easy to go too far. There's no fun left if it's dirty all the time. And I was probably getting very cross about something.'

Such moments were uncommon. Four largely untroubled series were completed, and remained so vivid in the public mind that in the new millennium, a full quarter-century after the last show was aired, *Round the Horne* was able to take successfully to the London stage as *Round the Horne . . . Revisited*, with a cast of skilled impersonators replicating show-time as it had been in the BBC's Paris Cinema studio. (If the Corporation had not sadly vacated the Paris in 1995, the performances could even have been put on in the authentic setting.) Robin Sebastian played Williams, and Jonathan Rigby took the difficult role of Horne. Barry Took did not live to see the recreation and bemoan its inclusion of newly written material.

Barry Took: 'God help me for the cliché, it was a happy show, the happiest I've ever known, full of laughter among those of us involved in it, and with Kenneth Horne benignly leading the way. And Kenneth Horne would cry with laughter, tears would run down his face with laughter, at the antics of Williams and Paddick ... And then Kenneth would go and sit down and shriek with laughter at other people. He loved other people's performances. The thing I remember possibly most about him is his generosity of spirit. He loved other people's performances. When he thought they were good, they were wonderful.'

Like everything else, it seemed, the climate of British comedy was changing in the late 1960s. Old heroes were disappearing, among them Tony Hancock, whose suicide was followed by a BBC Sound Tribute, broadcast in the summer of 1968 (10 guineas to Kenneth 'to cover your part in these excerpts'). And it was Kenneth Horne's sudden death from a heart attack, on St Valentine's Day 1969, that put an end to the fairly short history of *Round the Horne*. After some deliberation the cast felt inclined to try extending the tradition under a new title, which turned out to be a Kenneth Williams catchphrase from earlier times. The exception was Betty Marsden, who left the group at this point, to be replaced by Joan Sims, with whom Kenneth had by now appeared in almost a dozen *Carry On* films.

Barry Took: 'They did *Stop Messing About*, which I was not involved with, I hasten to add. It was written by a sort of miscellaneous gang of writers who didn't really understand what they were doing. It didn't work. He wasn't a leading man, it has to be said. I mean, he was a wonderful support. He was Montgomery to Kenneth Horne's Alexander.'

After two series (between which *Monty Python's Flying Circus* arrived on television, ushered in by the new BBC comedy advisor, Barry Took) it was decided in the summer of 1970 that *Stop Messing About* had no future. In the absence of other outlets, that would have been a serious setback for Kenneth, but he was fortunate in already being involved with another radio success – one whose run from decade to decade has not yet ended, even in 2008. It's often forgotten that the early history of *Just a Minute* overlapped considerably with the run of

Kenneth Williams talking about "Just A Minute"

David Hatch produces the radio series 'Just A Minute' and when
he approached me last year, with an invitation to take part in it
I was apprehensive and told him so. "Not to worry" he said breezily
"your nerves will vanish after the first programme". As it turned out
he was right, but I had to learn for myself what made it so. One
goes into any job with pre-conceived ideas; the notion of speaking
for sixty seconds on any given subject is one thing, but to do it
without hesitation, deviation, or repitition, is very difficult
indeed as far as I'm concerned. It was only after being in one
episode that I realized no one else was very good at it either;
they simply plunge in at the deep end and try to succeed, but
inevitably the challenge occurs, and another player gets the subject.
In a way, the game is about vulnerability, and in this sense, actors
are better prepared for it than anyone else. Ofcourse there are
gimmicks; Clement Freud has developed a knack of speaking so slowly
that he's immune to the challenge of hesitation, but that carries an
inbuilt penalty as well, because this measured delivery sounds very
monotonous indeed. If I've told him once, I've told him twice about
this, but its water off a ducks back; he lives in a world of his own.
Derek Nimmo's dulcet tones soar into romantic flights of fancy and
when he's challenged, always appears to be mildly surprised at the
sheer impertinence of it all. I just start talking without ever
bothering to think about the rules - if I thought about Pedestrian
Laws I'd never cross a road - and inevitably a lot of sense gets
mixed up with nonsense and this makes some people very cross. I have
received some castigating missives from irate listeners, telling me
to keep my mouth shut; a difficult injunction for any actor to obey!
But we all get comfort and our just deserts, from the debonair
chairman - Nicholas Parsons, who rebukes, praises, prods and pushes
us, so that the show bubbles along, and I'm always a little surprised
to hear the Minute Waltz starting again and the announcer saying
we're at the end of another 'Just A Minute'. I keep moaning to the
producer "No matter HOW you play it, that Clement Freud ALWAYS wins!"
but he smilingly refutes it "No Kenneth - it just seems like that to
you, and it doesnt matter who wins or loses anyway...its only a game!"
And I ruefully agree that it is.

Review most probably for the Radio Times, 1969.

Round the Horne. The first *Just a Minute*, devised by Ian Messiter after the pattern of his much earlier invention *One Minute Please*, was broadcast in Christmas week 1967, between Series Three and Four of *Round the Horne*.

The inaugural series of *Just a Minute* was a wobbly one, trying out many panellists, some of them veterans of too many previous radio parlour games. Kenneth Williams made his début at the start of Series Two, recording in mid-September 1968 with a panel of only three instead of four, Clement Freud and Geraldine Jones being the others. It didn't seem an important gig. 'Unfortunately it means working with that Parsons fellow, but I said yes 'cos it will be a nice fill-in,' wrote Kenneth in his diary. Though Nicholas Parsons would soon be confirmed as chairman – a job for life – that role was experimentally circulated among the cast, with Kenneth taking his turn in October. The show still lacked the absurd confidence it later acquired, but there's little doubt that Kenneth's presence helped to bring it into focus.

Derek Nimmo: 'Often one found, funnily enough, just before one went on, standing in the wings to do a *Just a Minute*, he'd then come out with something really quite profound, quite deep, something quite caring; almost as though he wouldn't give you time to reply to it. He'd suddenly flip something at you, just before he went on. As soon as he got on stage, of course, he became completely manic, because the sight of an audience made him twist his body and pull faces and all these noises came out and he's sticking his bum out. The sadness really is, recently we've been doing the programme on television, and it would have been much more televisual with Kenny there, because he always used to sit next to Clement Freud and used to flaunt his ankles in Freud's face when Freud was talking, or nuzzle up against his beard and kiss him on the nose and things, which were extraordinarily entertaining. Of course the radio audience never knew really what was going on.'

Sir Clement Freud: 'I think Kenny must be the only person who used radio as if people could watch, and a huge amount of his comedy was played out before the microphones were switched on. When Nicholas Parsons warmed up the audience, Kenny would stand behind the curtain shouting, "Get on with it! Get on with it!" and then he would make an entrance, and always an entrance pretending that he had appallingly bad piles. And managed this walk in which his bum stuck out and he shuffled on, to make people laugh.'

The pre-performance escalating sequence of rude jokes had by now been abandoned in favour of something chattier and more autobiographical.

Sir Clement Freud: 'He would then do a two- or three-minute routine, again the microphones were not switched on, and he would talk hugely entertainingly about how he'd come and what had happened to him. He didn't want Parsons to warm up the audience, but he was very good at it himself. It would have been absolutely all right, had it been broadcast, but it was totally irrelevant to anything except the warm-up of an audience. At the end of each programme he would then use his funny walk to disappear upstage, and shout "Bravo!", "Encore!" "Williams was brilliant," or whatever. And at the end of a show he would either disappear or announce that he would be giving autographs, and would people please come from the right, and he'd only have five minutes. So, very much running the show.'

❝ Bits had to be cut out because his mother would laugh the loudest ❞

Kenneth's reputation for erudition, on historical topics in particular, arose in large part from the dark-brown-voiced mini-lectures that adorned his *Just a Minute* appearances. The subjects offered to the panel did not come completely out of the blue: contestants who wished to do so had time to prepare, and an element of last-minute swotting entered the game.

Sir Clement Freud: 'Unlike politicians like me who get a brief, master it in ten minutes and have forgotten it half an hour later, I think Kenny's erudition probably lasted two or three hours. I mean, he never referred to a subject he'd asked for two weeks ago again. He had, and this is probably where the programme has changed most for us who are contestants, he had a genuine clique. He had thirty or forty people who queued up outside whatever studio he was going to appear in. And they were the same people. I met one, and she was a keeper in the elephant house at the Zoo, but they were all people whose lives revolved around Kenny ... They were people who never applauded wholeheartedly but their hands just met, and they did it like butterflies, all the time. And they came into their own when Nicholas Parsons said, "If you think Kenny Williams was right will you cheer for him, and if you think [otherwise] boo for him," and then it was no contest: if ever Nick asked the audience to adjudicate between somebody's claim and Kenny Williams's, it was always Kenny who won.'

The honorary president of the clique was of course Kenny's mum, Louie, whose presence, some thought, was actually integral to the show in progress.

❛It was part of his persona to be anti-women❜

Derek Nimmo: 'The funny thing was that his mother used to come to every single recording and she used to sit in exactly the same seat, and he used to direct every line to his mother. Didn't used to look at the audience much. And particularly when he got rather rude sometimes, bits had to be cut out because of that, his mother would laugh the loudest, and he would always try and put in more bits to shock her a little bit more. And then they would leave separately. She would go off through one door and he would go off through another, and they went their separate ways.'

Sir Clement Freud: 'I think Kenny's mother was very much orchestrated by him, because if one had had a less than really happy *Just a Minute* the week before, Kenny's mother would barely speak to you. I think she was less forgiving than Kenny, who was not particularly forgiving. I don't think he played to her, but he certainly looked at her after every contribution that he made. He was in charge of his mother, rather than the other way round.'

Although the collective cast of *Just a Minute* is very large, there was an important time when a fixed and classic panel of four males established the programme in the public affections. Kenneth Williams, Derek Nimmo, Clement Freud and

Peter Jones (the classic underplayer and counterpuncher) were seen as the A-team, though it was also recognized that the absence of female voices might offend a good half of the available audience. Williams sensed the slight tension in the air over this matter, and played to it.

Sir Clement Freud: 'He certainly started coining the expression, every time Aimi Macdonald or Sheila Hancock or anyone contributed anything he didn't like, "I don't know why we have women on the show anyway." It was part of his persona to be anti-women.'

He became notorious for his on-air rages, which, though synthetic, could be alarming enough to threaten the equilibrium of the programme.

Derek Nimmo: 'Well, he'd have a rage at Nicholas, but a lot of people did.'

Sir Clement Freud: 'I think the huge strength of Nicholas Parsons is that he has total faith in himself, and therefore doesn't believe anything that anybody says about him.'

When genuinely peeved, Kenneth would sometimes fall silent and sulk, even in cases where it would have been worth his while to fight back.

Derek Nimmo: 'He was totally self-educated really. He left school when he was quite young, and he was quite conscious of this really. He used the language terribly well, but I remember in a round of *Just a Minute* he said "rhododendrons" and I corrected him and said "rhododendra", and he then sulked for the whole of the programme, hardly said another word, because I'd exposed not an Achilles' heel exactly, but something that he felt badly about.'

Michael Whittaker: 'He had intellectual aspirations. He was very interested in the English language, obsessively so. He read a lot and liked to be in the company of educated, intelligent people but didn't particularly like to argue with them. Maybe that's some sort of insecurity. I know that he was absolutely obsessed with words and the pronunciation of words, etc. At a quarter to two

Assassin group urged by MP

An original idea for reducing the Armed Forces to improve Britain's balance of payments came last night in the Commons from Mr. John Lee, Labour M.P. for Reading, who suggested that British soldiers should be trained for political assassination, our Parliamentary correspondent writes.

Mr. Lee, who said he was a nuclear disarmer but not a pacifist, argued that the various tyrants scattered about the world would be more likely to take notice of a small force of political assassins than of a country possessing nuclear weapons which they knew could never be used.

all on rec 14/11/69

Chair: 60 seconds on 'The Advantages of Living'

Ken: In order to discuss this properly we'd obviously need to know the advantages of dying. And since no one's ever returns to tell us —

Nimmo — Deviation. That is untrue. K.W. is forgetting what happened to Orpheus.

Chapman — Well the world consists of Muslims + Buddhists too and many other beliefs don't subscribe to the theory that Christ arose from the dead — so it's not proven for many —

Clement Freud — Why not put it to the audience — ask them if they think Christ rose from the dead — fact or fiction

Laughter

Ken W — I think the question should be put again so that this can all be cut from the programme. I think its offensive and irrelevant

Kenneth's claim that 'it's only a game' is at odds with the handwritten transcript he made about an episode broadcast on 17 November 1969. Maybe it has something to do with the levity with which Clement Freud treated the resurrection of Christ? (Diary, 15 June 1974: 'Saw Ronnie Corbett on television. The blatant denigration of religious practice made one sick. I turned it off.' And 19 January 1987: 'Wogan being blasphemous with Cliff Richard.')

The recording was indeed halted and replaced with another topic. 'The Advantages of Living' cropped up again on 9 March 1970 with Clement Freud being given 'Just a Minute'. In the event Kenneth buzzed in within six seconds, reclaimed the subject and rode into victory. As for the significance of the newspaper clipping, paper-clipped to the page, who knows?

in the morning I was in bed and the telephone went and it was Kenneth and he said, "Disaster, disaster, something terrible!" and I was half asleep, thinking Louie had fallen down the stairs or something. I said, "What's the matter?" and apparently he'd been to dinner that night and had sat next to a grand lady who'd been a bit rude about other people so Kenneth said, "You shouldn't be so pejorative about people!" And she tapped him on the knee and replied, "I think you'll find it's peej-rative!" and turned away. That upset Kenneth enormously and he couldn't wait to get home to look up all the authorities, Fowler and the rest, and then to ring me and say, "Yes it is! It's pe-jorative. There's no R in it!" '

❛ He had intellectual aspirations. He was very interested in the English language, obsessively so ❜

Evidently he had assumed that 'perjorative' was the spelling, as in 'perjury'. But for most acquaintances it wasn't his obsessiveness so much as his volcanic unpredictability that made him a difficult companion.

Sir Clement Freud: 'I think I would willingly have spent more time with him if there wasn't a steady feeling of unease in his company, because you really didn't know what he was going to say next, and you didn't know how he would react to anything that you said to him. Whereas he was totally polite – the courtesy was there – his desire to shock, and his desire to shoot down anything that had come up without being manipulated by him, I think were steadily in the forefront. It is quite exhausting. It also gives you the feeling that "Let us quit while we're winning," so if one had had an hour and a quarter with him, in the Green Room before the show, sitting next to him, getting the odd hug, playing to the audience he would use me, when I was speaking he would suddenly put his tongue in my ear, and the audience laughed and his clique was delighted, and then he would buzz me for hesitation! It was fine. It was a great part of *Just a Minute*. But I think he was so unpredictable that in a way, you didn't hang around afterwards to see whether you could cement this bonding which you'd established. You knew it was Kenneth Williams, and you said, "I'll see you next week."'

Radio Times, April 1974: promoting 'The Crystal Spirit', his radio anthology of poetry, which has since been wiped from the BBC's Archives. © BBC

And the weeks went on and on and turned eventually into decades. In the last years of his life, when the *Carry On* films were no more, it was his only regular series commitment. Some friends wondered how his finances were holding up.

Sir Clement Freud: 'He didn't talk a lot about money. He certainly didn't seem to have any money, but then as far as any of us knew he never spent any money. We bought him the occasional cup of tea, but he wasn't the sort of person who would put his hand in his pocket. He smoked a bit. It was ironic that *Just a Minute* was voted the Non-Smoking Programme of the Year, because he was always putting out cigarettes.'

Kenneth recorded 344 appearances on *Just a Minute*. His last series, the twenty-fourth, came on air on 5 May 1988, some three weeks after his death. He'd made six out of the eight episodes broadcast, being replaced for two shows on account of illness by Lance Percival. It's an astonishing fact that in 2007 the total

Page 182 Ken Williams (now missing) by John Bratby (1928–1992). As this was the only portrait painted of Kenneth in his lifetime, and because of their 'no posthumous portraits' rule, London's National Portrait Gallery have confirmed that this is the only picture they could display if, of course, it is ever found. **(Photograph courtesy of the Bratby Archive)**

programme count reached 694 — so at that point, more *JAMs* had been broadcast without Kenneth's presence than with it. Sir David Hatch (the show's producer) died in mid-June 2007. The longevity of the show owes much to the care he took in the early days to regulate the behaviour of the cast, above and beyond the obligations imposed on them by the publicly stated rules of the game. The following exchanges show how sensitive was the weekly adjustment that took place.

6th January 1969

Dear Ken, Would just like to drop you a line to congratulate you in winning the second show last Friday. I thought they were both good programmes, although I think a certain amount of acrimony began to creep in at one point. I don't know what one can do about this since every week now I define the basic rules of playing the game, no interrupting for fifteen seconds etc. and I am sure it is when those rules are broken that that ill-feeling creeps in. However, on the whole I think and hope it is a happy programme, and look forward to next Friday and making two more good shows.

 Yours truly,

 David Hatch

Dear David,

Thank you for your letter. Yes, I know exactly what you mean. The note of acrimony and undue asperity DOES creep in & I honestly don't think there's anything one can do about it that WON'T result in INHIBITION and that's death to comedy. I think the real truth is what I've always suspected (for years) that the principal offender has a meanness of spirit which basically resents the laughter caused by others and expresses this resentment by making the sort of niggling remarks which are generally of a personal nature & ill mannered. But if one replies on this level, the whole thing just gets NASTY. One must grin and bear it.

 Sincerely,

 Kenneth

21st January 1969

My dear Ken, I must just write and say how absolutely brilliant I thought you were on Friday. They were two excellent programmes, and this was very largely due to you. It seemed to me that you suddenly realised how best to play the challenging rule, this is really why you won the first game, but you did it without seeming acquisitive for points, and at the same time being funny all the way. It was absolutely masterly, and I haven't been so pleased since I persuaded you that time to be Chairman.

This coming Friday sees the end of the run, and I am hoping that after the show I can organise a little hospitality from the Corporation for which I hope you will stay, and any friends you have, of course, are invited. In case you should feel unable to come, and because I am rather shy at praising people to their faces, let me just say an enormous 'thank you' for all your work on this series, how very pleased and privileged I feel to have you in the company, and hope that should we be asked to do more, as I am sure we will, you will be with us again. I am sorry this has turned into a fan letter, but I am afraid it is unavoidable.

Yours, David Hatch

22nd January 1969

My dear David, you can't imagine how welcome your letter was! I've been in a lousy state for some time, due to some old trouble and everything culminated in a dreadful BLACK MONDAY which was all pain & worry. Landed up on Tuesday with the surgeon who originally operated and he handled everything superbly so this morning I was feeling tentative etc. and then your letter came through the box. I honestly think praise is like medicine for an actor and needless to say, your words acted like a tonic for me. My unspeakable thanks for all you say about my work in the series and for your kindness and understanding about the odd psychological difficulties we have encountered. Old Guthrie always used to say, the first criteria [sic] for a director was 'one who could create an atmosphere in which the cast is uninhibited' and think this is why I've enjoyed so much working with you. You seem implicitly to understand this. Look forward to seeing you on Friday,

Gratefully, Kenneth

'Kenneth and I had worked together the previous Christmas when I'd been cast as Aladdin in the BBC1 panto which was directed by Jeremy Swan. Yours truly played Aladdin, Johnny Morris played Widow Twankey, Jan Francis was the Princess, Christopher Biggins was one of the Emperor's sidekicks and Kenneth played the Emperor. Hardly a camp production! I'm convinced this all came before Ken's **Blue Peter** appearance. This meant we already knew each other and I felt very at ease with him and could have fun - especially during the "make". (The "make" section of **Blue Peter** was one of my favourites, largely because it was unscripted.) I was demonstrating how you could make your own Willo the Wisp, the animated character for which Kenneth provided all the voices. On programme days we always sat down to eat with our Editor, Biddy Baxter and the Head of Children's Programmes, Edward Barnes. These two were great raconteurs and enjoyed holding forth over lunch. But on the day that Kenneth joined us – they were stunned into silence by his monologue. I wish I could remember every detail of what he said – but I was so busy enjoying the sight of my bosses sitting there dumbstruck, that I really only remember his lesson in pronunciation. Or as Kenneth put it: "PrrrrroNUNciayshun!" The word "portrait" HAD to pronounced "portRRRIT" and the word "princess" HAD to have the stress on the first syllable: "PRRRINCEss". It's weird the stuff you remember...' (Sarah Greene)

On **Blue Peter**, talking to Sarah Greene about Willo the Wisp, with his characters Mavis Cruet, Arthur the Caterpillar and Evil Edna, 25 October 1982. © BBC

185

'Taxi to TV Centre where I recorded Episode IV of Galloping Galaxies for Jeremy: had to do the voice of my son in it! He is a small computer!' (Diary, 11 September 1985) © BBC

The BBC's files of correspondence closed to outside inspection, arbitrarily, at the year 1970. It is doubtful whether this rule deprives us of much in the way of juicy controversy, though it would have been pleasing to trace the further refinements Hatch and Williams between them made to their *Just a Minute* tactics. And even more pleasing, in the television files, to witness the reaction of young viewers to Kenneth's performances in children's programming. By the accepted count he made sixty-nine appearances in the story-telling programme *Jackanory*, and twenty-six episodes of *Willo the Wisp*, a surprisingly engaging animation series that grew out of an educational short made by British Gas. Almost poignantly, as it now seems, the Willo character was not only voiced by Kenneth, but based on him physically; a blue, floating spectral creature with a pointed nose. Both *Jackanory* and *Willo* have been revived latterly, but without the success associated with the Kenneth Williams versions.

Out of *Jackanory* came a friendship with the original director who hired him, the quicksilver Irishman Jeremy Swan, who has maintained an impressive output of children's television drama.

> **‘ And he was one of the presenters that the entire Jackanory team most liked working with, because they knew he'd come in and he would do it, and do it absolutely splendidly ’**

Jeremy Swan: 'We had this book, *The Land of Green Ginger* by Noel Langley, and it was a very good book, packed with the most innocent innuendo and double-entendre, that one knew Williams would make the most of. So Anna Home, who was the Executive Producer of the *Jackanory* programme at the time, and I asked Kenneth Williams to come and do it. And he was wonderful. He came in with a certain amount of reluctance because Hattie Jacques told him that if he appeared on the programme he had to wear a certain type of hat. So we had to persuade him that was not the case. And he proved an instant success with the audience, and he was the most frequently used presenter of the *Jackanory* programme, apart from Bernard Cribbins, who was

Number One, and Kenneth was Number Two … And if course it's every actor's great delight to be on the screen on your own for fifteen minutes. He had to wear a kaftan in *The Land of Green Ginger*, and he didn't like that very much. I think he said he looked like Beatrice Lillie. But I said the audience he was catering for had never heard of Beatrice Lillie, so it didn't matter too much. He used to watch them with Louie and they would enjoy them again at home, and she would enjoy them. And he was one of the presenters that the entire *Jackanory* team most liked working with, because they knew he'd come in and he would do it, and do it absolutely splendidly. And tell an awful lot of jokes, and give everybody a hilarious lunch-hour, and we'd all go home early, roaring with laughter.'

❛ Then when he was ill, it was the Boy Who Cried Wolf, because you used to get him saying, "I've been in excruciating pain all day" ❜

There was even a certain amount of diversification within the Children's Television output.

Jeremy Swan: 'I had a part of a robot in a series called *Galloping Galaxies*, which was a send-up of the HAL character in *2001* [*A Space Odyssey*]. And Kenneth played it. It was written by Bob Block, and it was very much a "hands off my floppy disks" type of robot. Kenneth rather liked that, 'cos he could come in the day before we did it in the studio and just say all the lines and the operator just played his speeches into the studio and the actors duly responded, so they never saw him, and he very seldom saw them, so it was quite a nice job.'

The two men carried on meeting for the rest of Kenneth's life, though at a certain point Kenneth started to ask for lunch engagements rather than dinner – a sign of his deteriorating gastric condition.

Jeremy Swan: 'Then when he was ill, it was the Boy Who Cried Wolf, because you used to get him saying, "I've been in excruciating pain all day. I haven't been able to touch anything proper to eat and I haven't been able to drink or anything," and suddenly there'd be half a bottle of Soave gone and a big plate of chips, and you'd say, "Well, a miracle has occurred."'

Sadly, it hadn't, and the energy Kenneth had used to divert himself from his own woes gradually ran out.

Jeremy Swan: 'The last thing we did together was *James and the Giant Peach*, by Roald Dahl. He did that on the *Jackanory* programme. Yes, it was a shock when he died.'

The man who taught him comedy

❛ I think what he liked about his relationship with my brother is they could talk about so many other things apart from the theatre. The theatre can be a very narrow world; actors and actresses can be very narrow-minded people ❜

Isabel Chidell

'Kenneth said to me, "Your brother taught me all I know about comedy, I shall be eternally grateful to him."' (Isabel Chidell)

Kenneth's mentor in comedy, John Vere (1915–1961).

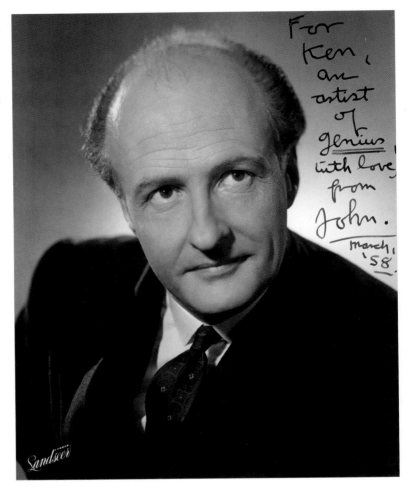

When the terms of Kenneth Williams's will became known, much curiosity was voiced about the identity of his godson, Robert Chidell. Where had he entered the story? The answer reached quite a long way back into Kenneth's career, to the character actor John Vere. The story of their friendship is brief, but it shows how much emotional investment was packed into these little-known corners of Kenneth's life. He learned from many friends whose names are not widely remembered: the writer/director Michael Harald, for example, and the poet/actor Denis Goacher, a supporter of Ezra Pound, whose rich voice Kenneth admired (Goacher once played a disembodied voice in an episode of *Doctor Who*). But with John Vere, simple friendship turned into a family involvement.

Isabel Chidell: 'My brother was a marvellous person. He was 47 when he died. He was wonderful to be with because he had so many interests, both in the theatre and elsewhere. He was one of the most generous and kind people I have ever known.'

Several of Kenneth's old friends within the profession committed suicide. Rachel Roberts was perhaps the most celebrated among them, and Michael

```
                      A Boiled Egg
                      _____

      I most enjoy, she said,
      I most enjoy my afternoon tea.
      Days when I feel more lonely
      Than at other times
      I treat myself to an egg.
      It must be boiled four minutes.
      But I take it when I fancy,
      Half past Four or Five,
      In an egg cup blue or green.
      Blue when it's a white one,
      Green when it's brown.
      Cut off its head with a sharp whack
      And the satisfaction
      Is every bit as good
      As reading in the morning paper
      That another nationalised industry
      Has gone back to its rightful owners.

      They say there's trouble in Argentina over beef.....
      Or would it be Brazil?
      The price of coffee anyway is much too high.
      There was a murder at Kentish Town, according to the papers.
      Liver is almost unobtainable.
      Rents don't seem to come down.
      Why is it that the price of everything increases,
      Except for hooks and eyes in which I've Shares
      That Uncle Harman left me, but alas
      The dividends are small.
      I'll have a boiled egg for my tea.
      I know myself a lady gently born.

                             NAN SMOOTHLEY-BROWNE
```

Michael Hitchman (d.1960) under a different guise. Just one example of the mounds of his work that Kenneth had cherished: 'Tom and Clive came at 6 o'c. I read them a lot of Hitchmania – how that good man lives ON in my life.' (Diary, 13 July 1968)

Hitchman was one whose death caused him particular pain. On his LP *Kenneth Williams on Pleasure Bent* he included Hitchman's 'A Boiled Egg': 'I felt particular delight in this, because it's my small way of [paying] a tribute to him, and a way of perpetuating his poem.' John Vere, whom he thanked in his diary 'for so much in the realm of comedy and painting', was another suicide victim.

Isabel Chidell: 'He was an intellectual and knew an enormous amount about history, and he was a very clever man who could have done many other things. But above all he was a very warm and lovely person and I was deeply fond of him and terribly distressed when it happened.'

According to Isabel Chidell, John and Kenneth met in the television cast of Tony Hancock's programme, but Kenneth's diary records meetings even before the Hancock radio series began, and the original meeting may have been earlier still.

> ❛Kenneth was a very strong personality and I sometimes thought he was too much for my brother, because he was a rather gentle person❜

Angela Chidell: 'I believe the first time he met Kenneth was when they both were called up to the army and were involved in the entertainment side.'

> *Thursday, 8 January 1953*
> *Met John Vere in lunch hour who invited me into a pub for a drink. I suddenly felt he was ashamed of me. He kept looking round the pub the whole time. I got quite confused and conversed wildly and stammered, and tore myself off to the matinée. How conscious queers are of persecution, and so gregarious.*

This unpromising meeting suggests that Kenneth was somewhat in awe of Vere, which in view of his family and personal history is perhaps understandable.

Isabel Chidell: 'He was the son of Dr H.P. Biggar, Chief Archivist for Canada and Europe, and Winifred Howland, also Canadian … He was the second son.

There were four of us: Peter, John, Isabel and Goldwin. He was born in 1915, educated at Font Hill Prep School, and Clifton College. He couldn't decide whether to be a priest or an actor. We were subjected to sermons from the arm-chair shaped like a pulpit. He then went to RADA.

'After leaving RADA in 1936 he joined the Open Air Theatre in Regent's Park in the production of *Henry VIII* with Phyllis Neilson-Terry as Queen Catherine, Vivien Leigh as Anne Boleyn, Lyn Harding as Henry VIII and John Vere playing the Marquis of Dorset – just a small part – and the Bishop. John wore the costume as though he belonged to the period. His career was cut short by the Second World War but he was invalided out of the army after pneumonia that nearly cost him his life. He then worked for the admiralty in Bath and later as secretary to Richard Hughes, the author of *A High Wind in Jamaica*.

'His godfather was Edward Knoblock, the playwright, who wrote the play *Kismet* which became a musical, first in New York and then in London at Drury Lane. My brother became involved as executor in Knoblock's estate. After the war John returned to live in London and resumed his career with film parts, theatre and radio, then television came along. He was a character actor who played small parts, studying every detail, giving the audience a clear picture of the person he portrayed.'

❛ I think Kenneth found him very helpful in teaching him a lot about comedy ❜

In terms of its connections, it was the kind of background Kenneth Williams from the Caledonian Road could only boggle at. But when they came to work together it was Kenneth who seemed, to a concerned onlooker, much the more forceful of the two. There was one traumatic reason for the difference in their temperaments.

Isabel Chidell: 'He [John] didn't have depression as a young man. He survived an English prep school and was very happy there, he didn't have any problems. It came after he was in Bath and there was an air raid and he was thrown out of the window and buried in debris. He was in hospital and he did get better but eventually it came back … Kenneth was a very strong personality and I some-times thought he was too much for my brother, because he was a rather gentle person. Kenneth was very aggressive, he would be prepared to take people on and have scenes in public. They had a lot in common about comedy, timing and that kind of thing, and I think Kenneth found him very helpful in teaching him a lot about comedy, and I'm sure that actually Kenneth taught my brother a lot.'

'Of course he was gay but he couldn't accept it. Not because being gay was abhorrent to him, but because he couldn't bear to be touched'

An explicit instance of that influence is recorded in Kenneth's autobiography, *Just Williams*, where he describes a Hancock sketch in which John Vere, playing a bishop, 'looked loftily academic and affected such grand disdain that when he was deflated the result was wonderfully funny. His look of dismay, followed by a rueful "Charming", punctuated a scene perfectly.' It wasn't long before this piece of business came in handy for Kenneth himself, during the filming of *Carry On Sergeant*, the first in the series. One scene was to be ended by Kenneth hav-ing an oversize beret plonked on his head as a prelude to his being hustled out of shot. 'In fact, when we shot the scene,' he recalled, 'I couldn't resist a touch of John Vere; as I was crowned by the hat I dropped the chin sardonically

Page 197 'Amazed as I was to find myself co-starring with him in the revue **Pieces of Eight**, I was even more amazed at an early stage of rehearsal when he rushed me into another room and declared, with great intensity, that our material was total rubbish, absolutely dreadful, that we must be prepared to ad lib it and to improvise around it, that I must trust him in this and give him my total co-operation because, in the end, it was going to be us out there on the stage and it was our reputations that were at stake. This made me quake a bit: I didn't know if I could. I'd never ad libbed so much as a "good evening". In any case, the material was marvellous in my opinion, most of it written by Peter Cook and Harold Pinter. My fear was that our "improvements" could spoil it. In the event, I went along with him. **Pieces of Eight** was a smash-hit and so were those much-abused sketches. People would come to see the show specially to hear the different things we came up with from night to night. It became a bit of a cult. Kenneth didn't like a long run, he had a very low boredom threshold and could be very competitive. But the nights when he didn't feel that it had to be war, those nights when we could just go out on a limb and egg each other on and on and on, were so blissful that in that medium I wouldn't have wished to work with anybody else.' **(Fenella Fielding)**

Kenneth with Fenella Fielding at the **Pieces of Eight** after party, 18 December 1959. Composer Lionel Bart (1930–1999) is to the far left.

and said "Charming", and then walked away. Gerald [Thomas] reproved me. "You weren't supposed to say anything there, you were practically on the edge of the frame." But he allowed it to stay in the picture and it got a nice laugh.'

Isabel Chidell: 'He was probably closer to my brother than many people because my brother understood him very well and never made any demands of him. Never asked for money or anything like that – he was a very independent man. They both had a similar sense of humour and they would have a lot of laughter when they talked together … [Kenneth] hated to be touched. Of course he was gay but he couldn't accept it. Not because being gay was abhorrent to him, but because he couldn't bear to be touched. They didn't have a sexual relationship, Kenneth and my brother, there was no question of that. They were just friends.'

Arriving for the baptism, Kenneth with Robyn Holmes (left) and Isabel Chidell (right, facing).

Sadly, the Williams diary contradicts Ms Chidell's impression of the money question. In June 1959 he records the arrival of a 'Letter from John Vere, asking for £100. I sent it off by return post.' There are signs of growing distress on Vere's part, and of some impatience on Kenneth's. About a month before the request for money there had been a very testy entry in the diary, railing against Vere for the symptoms of neurosis he displayed. 'The so-called mentally sick,' Kenneth concludes unpleasantly, 'get away with murder.' But he sends the money without delay.

Isabel Chidell: 'Kenneth was very good to him when my brother was ill and he had a breakdown, and he was very good to him after the breakdown and offered him his little cottage in the country and said go and stay there and get

'I held Robert Anthony Russell Chidell in my arms and there's no question but that he is a beautiful baby ... magnificent.' **(Diary, 25 April 1976)**

well. He was a very kind person … John's death was tragic and I think an awful lot of it was bad medical attention. In all, five members of my family committed suicide: my mother, three brothers and my youngest son. What are they up to, these useless psychiatrists? These were clever people, they weren't mad. They needed proper treatment for depression, which the English cannot cope with … Kenneth thought it a relief, as I did, because John had been unhappy for so long. He'd already had two breakdowns and I'd always gone to him, but I had a young family and husband, and we had just moved back from Zimbabwe. Twice I'd gone and helped him, he came to stay with us, and then the third time when he called for me I was going through my divorce and I just couldn't go to him. I was in such a flat spin myself. Next thing was, before I could get there, he'd taken his life. He'd decided that suicide was the best way out. He died on January 11th 1961, as a result of a drug overdose.'

But the death of John Vere was only the beginning of the attachment between Kenneth and John's sister's family, the Chidells.

Isabel Chidell: 'The one thing I didn't want to be was someone who took advantage of knowing someone famous because he happened to know my brother. But I hadn't realized when [Kenneth] was ill, how ill he was or I would have gone to him. I didn't like to intervene unless he'd called me to do so. After my brother died we kept in touch, we spoke on the phone, he offered me tickets for his shows and that sort of thing, and then he became godfather to Robert. When Robert was born, he was the fifth child of Anthony, my son, and Angela, and they had run out of godparents because they'd already had four children! They rang me up and said did I think Kenneth would like to be godfather. I said, "I don't know. All we can do is to ask him and he can say no if he wishes to." So I rang him up and said, "Think about it, Kenneth. Don't rush yourself." "No," he said, "I'd love to be a godfather!" He was a very kind godfather, I mean he never forgot Robert's birthday and always sent him a present. He couldn't have been kinder.'

Robert's christening took place on Sunday 25 April 1976. 'I held Robert Anthony Russell Chidell in my arms,' Kenneth recorded, 'and there's no question but that he is a beautiful baby … magnificent. I held him throughout the

The **Sun**, 30 September, 1988.

Stars say farewell to the king of the capers

BOY WHO GETS FORTUNE FROM CARRY-ON KEN

'Service was fun'

By NEIL SYSON

THIS is Robert Chidell, the 12-year-old schoolboy who was left a fortune in Carry On star Kenneth Williams' £538,000 will.

Robert — Kenneth's godson — joined a host of showbiz stars at an amazing laugh-a-minute memorial service yesterday to the comic who died from an accidental pills overdose.

The spiky-haired youngster said as he came out of the church: "That was good fun! I enjoyed it."

And Kenneth's frail mum Louisa, 87, declared: "It was the way he would have wanted it."

A sombre tribute was turned into a half-hour comedy sketch by Kenneth's wise-cracking showbiz pals in front of a 200-strong congregation.

Songs

Four of Kenneth's Carry On colleagues — Liz Fraser, Barbara Windsor, Kenneth Connor and Lance Percival — turned up for the no-tears service at the St Paul's Church in London's Covent Garden.

Other big-name guests included broadcaster Ned Sherrin, actress Sheila Hancock, Upstairs Downstairs actor Gordon Jackson, quizmaster Nicholas Parsons, Barry Took, Christopher Biggins, Stanley Baxter, and Derek Nimmo.

Babs belted-out one of Kenneth's favourite music hall songs, The Boy I Love is up in the Gallery.

Ned Sherrin had the church ringing with applause with a series of showbiz anecdotes.

And Kenneth Connor recited a bawdy Kenneth Williams version of Auld Lang Syne — in pidgin French!

Wise-cracking Lance Percival, using the Carry On star's catchphrase, said: "Kenneth has stopped messin' about, but the characters and voices he created will linger for many years to come."

Naughty

Derek Nimmo, in his personal tribute, said: "He was an extrovert beyond belief. He could be a sensitive scholar — and a very naughty schoolboy."

After the ceremony Nimmo hit out at suggestions that Kenneth, 62, purposely took a pills overdose when suffering a painful stomach ulcer.

He said: "The suggestion that he committed suicide is absurd.

"He was deeply concerned about his mother. He loved her above other people.

Kenneth Connor and wife . . . a bawdy recitation

Kenneth . . . drug overdose

Louisa . . . the star's mum

Robert yesterday   Picture by PETER SIMPSON

Babs Windsor and Liz Fraser . . . Carry On pals

IT'S SO SAD!

By MANDY ALLOTT and ANGELA DAVIES

CARRY On stars yesterday denied abandoning ailing Charles Hawtrey.

The comedy film veterans said Hawtrey, 73, had become a recluse at his home in Deal, Kent.

And they insisted they did NOT know he was facing death from an artery condition after refusing to have both his legs amputated.

BARBARA WINDSOR said: "I am terribly sad over what's happened but he is a very elusive, quiet man."

LIZ FRASER said: "No

one has been interested in him lately. It is not always easy to get in touch, and it takes two to tango."

And KENNETH CONNOR said: "I have seen the story about Charles's illness, but I don't want to read it.

Hawtrey . . . elusive man

"I am sickened by the news. We have just been to bury one and we have another one on the way. We have not neglected him. It has been a great year for the Grim Reaper."

Cockney star SID JAMES, who died in 1976, sent this message through medium Charles Loundon: "You'll love it up 'ere mate — it's a right old carry on.

"And far from thinking your talent was wasted you will see how genuinely loved you were and how revered you will still be as one of our comic giants."

ceremony at the font but, just at the last moment, he roared his disapproval & I handed him to Angie …'

Angela Chidell: 'Like all other occasions when you were with Kenneth it was larger than life because he just encapsulated everybody in his personality. When he spoke in church suddenly you felt there were microphones everywhere, it was his wonderful strong actor's voice coming across. At the moment of baptism I handed Robert to him, because he was a godfather and that's the usual thing to do, but it was pretty clear that Kenneth wanted to hold Robert, of whom he was very fond.'

He had a great talent for dealing with children, who responded instinctively to the ill-disguised child in the man they saw. And it was not merely a question of a professional knack, but of a person-to-person warmth, and even concern.

Isabel Chidell: 'I always remember when Kenneth came down to Weybridge when my children were quite young and all the local children had heard that Kenneth Williams was coming. So they all came rushing round after school to see him. And there he was, sitting there. They all came up to him and asked him questions and he was quite open with them all, as he always was with people in conversation. And he picked out the ones who had parents that were probably very mean, and said, "I don't suppose your parents bother very much about you, do they?" He was absolutely right, because these were very rich people in Weybridge.'

But as years went by the focus of concern moved gradually over to Kenneth and his difficulties.

Isabel Chidell: 'I don't think any of us realized how lonely he *really* was. He was a person who found it very difficult to have relationships with people. I think what he liked about his relationship with my brother is they could talk about so many other things apart from the theatre. The theatre can be a very narrow world; actors and actresses can be very narrow-minded people. But they had far greater interests and could discuss so many other things … But of course he had his own problems, because his mother, whom he'd been very fond of, became very possessive and very demanding. His mother and his sister, I think, got a lot of money out of him to buy them accommodation. He once said to me, "I wish my mother and my sister would leave me alone. They keep on going at me." He was very generous but I think he found them a bit heavy going, towards later in life.'

Angela Chidell: 'Whatever we asked of him, such as something for a school event or something, he would immediately respond with a yes. In fact the last time I saw Kenneth before he died was after one such occasion. I'd driven him back home and my last memory is of him walking away from the car across to his flat. That lonely figure that everyone sees in Kenneth anyway, was so apparent then.'

Kenneth's relationship with the Chidells had continued in the background to the end of his life – a life so compartmentalized that some friends were surprised to learn that a godson existed at all. At Kenneth's memorial service the press naturally focused on the boy's good fortune.

Isabel Chidell: 'When we came out of the church we were besieged by reporters saying how much money had he left to Robert. Well, actually it was a very small amount, but they thought it was a fortune. We just got this little boy away from all these crowds ...'

Robert Chidell: 'When I walked out of the remembrance service all the cameras turned on me and they were shouting, "Robert! Robert! Over here! Robert! Robert!" and flashed me. I was thinking, "What the hell?" and just stood there looking at them all, a thousand shots a second, like I was David Beckham or something. The next day at school all the kids were running up to me with cut-outs saying, "Is this you? Is this you?" What really pissed me off, actually, was when I left the remembrance service and this guy came up to me to do a little interview and he said, "Hi Robert, I'm so and so from the *Sun*. What did you think of the service?" And I said, "Yeah, I thought it was very pleasant and very nice. It was a very respectful service for a good man." And he put in the paper, "Spiky-haired school boy says service was FUN!" That made me more angry than anything.'

And all this grew out of a sadly short and intermittent friendship, Vere with Williams, and a shared fascination with the minutiae of the craft of acting.

Isabel Chidell: 'You'd see John showing shock, because somebody had said something to him that was very shocking. His face would give the explanation. It's very difficult to describe it, but you can see Kenneth do it in the *Carry On* films. Kenneth said to me, "Your brother taught me all I know about comedy. I shall be eternally grateful to him."'

The day John Vere died Kenneth wrote in his diary: 'He was a lovely lovely character.'

Carry on Ken

‘ Oooh Matron! ’

Dr Soaper (Carry On Camping, 1969)

Carry On Follow That Camel, Camber Sands, May 1967. (Photograph by Ian Jeayes)

BC7, the retro-minded radio network, has been generous with its replays of Kenneth Williams's work, particularly his series with Kenneth Horne. Yet one still feels as if the most accessible parts of his performing output, to the broad British public, are the *Carry On* series of films, made at Pinewood Studios between 1958 and 1978, with a dubious bonus (*Carry On Columbus*) after Kenneth's time, in 1992. The team in charge was Gerald Thomas (1920–93, director) and Peter Rogers (born 1914, producer), and the series maintained what was virtually its own repertory company. Once the format had settled down in the early 1960s, the cast remained remarkably stable. Only special circumstances would allow an outsider access to the charmed circle.

Page 204 Kenneth's second **Carry On** role: as patient Oliver Reckitt, in **Carry On Nurse**, 1958. (The film, written by Norman Hudis, was so successful that the Crest Cinema in Los Angeles screened it for over a year.)

Russell Davies: 'It almost happened to me, around the turn of the seventies, when I was a very young actor, not long out of the Cambridge Footlights. My agent was Richard Stone, known to some as "The Colonel". He was a rather formidable old-school type with one eye, and he really did specialize in comedy. He had an awful lot of actors and stand-ups on his list. I remember talking about him years later with Dave Allen, who was one of his. Anyway, I happened

'This Roman tunic I'm wearing in the film is really quite attractive. In white and gold. I continually lift it up and expose my cock and everything at the Unit. They're all rather disgusted and laugh it off, but quite a number of them have remarked "O! Kenny! Not again! – put it away ..."' **(Diary, 4 August 1964)**

Kenneth with **Charles Hawtrey, Aunt Edith and Lou** on the set of **Carry On Cleo**.

Above, and page 210 Kenneth as Captain Fearless in **Carry On Jack**, 1963, a parody of Charles Laughton's Captain Bligh in **Mutiny on the Bounty** (1935).

to be in Richard's office one morning, reviewing the prospects after a not very brilliant TV series I'd been doing, and suddenly the phone went. Richard excused himself and answered it – I didn't have to leave the room – and what followed was a stream of stuff from the other end of the line, punctuated by groans and grunts from Richard. He finally said he'd see what he could do, and put the phone down with a great sigh. And then he told me, to my surprise, because I thought this sort of thing was confidential, that Charlie Hawtrey had just been thrown off the latest *Carry On* at Pinewood for being drunk, or repeatedly drunk. And Richard must have been the likeliest agent to provide a quick replacement.'

Peter Rogers: 'Well, his love of drink was his love of drink. If you like it, you like it. And, if you like it too much you don't know when to stop. And sometimes he didn't know when to stop. But, oddly enough, at the end of picture parties, when you expect someone to go a bit over the top, he would have a pot of tea! His mother used to come down with him at times, and she was a little bit funny too, because the whole of the corridor in front of the stage was covered in toilet paper that she'd thrown around. So he had to keep her shut in his dressing room. So what with his mother, and his boyfriends and his bottle, he had quite a busy time. He was a dear man, a lovely man, very professional. I mean he would turn up and do his best. But sometimes when he couldn't stand up, he couldn't stand up!'

Russell Davies: 'Then I realized suddenly that Richard Stone was scrutinizing me rather closely with the one eye that worked, and then after a long silence he said, "No, no, you're too young. It's a pity, but you are." And that was how close I came to being sent to Pinewood to join the hallowed cast, and see Kenneth Williams on set at first hand. Possibly share a scene with him. I think about it often. Funnily enough, I can't find a *Carry On* of that period – there were several – that doesn't have Charles Hawtrey in it, so perhaps he sobered up and was reinstated. I left full-time acting for journalism not long after, so the chance never came again.'

Peter Rogers: 'The biggest problem we had with [Hawtrey] was when, you remember, a journal called the *Daily Cinema*, a fellow called "Willy" Williamson used to write for it, and he said in his column that they're going to make another *Carry On*, and of course it wouldn't be any good without Charlie Hawtrey, so Charlie Hawtrey becomes the star, the price goes up, he wants, believe it or not, a star on his dressing-room door, silver star on his dressing-room door, this was on *Cruising*. So we had to say, "Sorry, Charlie, won't do at all," and we took Lance Percival in his place.'

Actually, the record shows that while *Carry On Cruising* (1962) did indeed include Lance Percival, apparently at the expense of Charles Hawtrey, *Carry On Screaming* (1966) was the picture over which Williamson issued his troublesome endorsement of Hawtrey. It's easy to get confused, because the *Carry On*s, certainly for a time, carried the *Guinness Book of Records* title of 'Longest Series in World Film History'. Throughout its long history it remained a low-budget series, even a defiantly cheapo series, with no elaborate hierarchies, so Peter Rogers, the

producer, was not at all distanced from events on the sound-stage. Over the course of thirty films he got to know his cast as well as anyone; and of course Kenneth Williams was there from the start.

Peter Rogers: 'We first came across him in one of his revues. He was in the very first one, *Carry On Sergeant*, of course, which was written by Norman Hudis, who wrote what you might call the college-type character, which he played beautifully.'

Norman Hudis: 'The last time I saw him, he was bounding up the stairs to Peter Eade's office as I was descending them. Without pausing in movement, he shot at me: "There's never enough time, is there, Norman? So I'll say it now in case there isn't time in future. When you left the *Carry On*s the heart went out of the series."'

Talbot Rothwell took over from Hudis in 1963, so there was plenty of time for that to happen. Rogers and Thomas didn't set out with any intention of creating a British tradition, though they soon realized there was a lot of life in the idea they'd conceived.

Peter Rogers: 'I think if you go out to make a series, you're taking an audience for granted. And they'll very soon say, "No thank you, we don't want that." I don't think it was until about the third one that I said to Gerald, "I think we can do some more." 'Cos the second one was *Nurse*, which of course as you know was top everywhere; well, they all were, believe it or not, always in the top two or three, and in later life of course in the top ten. I can remember one of the trade journals coming to me and saying, "Your *Carry On* is number eleven this year, but if we say the top twelve, would you take an advertisement?"'

Kenneth grumbles often to his diary about the prospect of making yet another film in the series, and vows half-heartedly that he will do no more.

Pages 212–213 'Kenny was in great demand to make personal appearances and, being assiduous about responding to such a request, he had had printed a card that read, "Mr Kenneth Williams thanks you for your letter, but regrets that because of other engagements he is unable to accept your invitation".' **(Joan Sims)**

Entertaining the Metropolitan Police on a rare occasion, with Joan Sims.

Good Evening ladies + Gentlemen, and thank you for asking this good Lady - Miss Sims - and myself, to be your guests this evening - it is entirely due to Sgt. Van Dyck that we are here, he told me they needed someone with guts and go and virility and I said I've got the guts and the go and I'm sure we can come to some arrangement - but I should like to dispel any illusions that might be lingering in your mind about the Acting profession - we used to be known as a band of rogues + vagabonds, a sort of cross between Henry Hall and Kathy Come Home — people thought of actresses as loose women: I'd like to state categorically that no one could call this good lady 'ere - LOOSE. There is nothing LOOSE about her. The more appropriate adjective would be TIGHT — cos she is tight. She's even got a burglar alarm on her dust bin And ~~this a teacher~~ she cleans her own window's - she was up the ladder doing the front ones, dressed in some depressing decolletay housecoat and black bloomers when some passers by cried out "Ere aint you on the Telly? Well as she said herself she didn't like to be recognised in that situation - hardly your romantic film actress hardly your glamorous Maudie Fittleworth, Fun with a frankfurter But they kept on at her - some of 'em even started to rook her ladder + eventually she came down and signed their autograph books Imagine her mortification when one of them looked unbelievingly at the signatures + said 'oh! I thought you was Dora Bryan...
I myself have been asked - are - are you Kenneth Conor? + Kenneth Horne, even once an Sloane Sq. Kenneth Haig
and it has happened to me, I used to be a tenor before me voice dropped + I was evacuated when I was a flaxen haired stripling and shoved in the glass foundry at Wolverhampton - it was my job to blow the little bulbs on the end of the glass ~~baton~~ thermometer you know the bit that holds the mercury + I took this extra wind + instead of huffing delicately — I blew meself a prosefим bowl - well move your Wedgwood bowl + the foundry was in uproar - they all shouted 'Oh! you've blown a beauty... —

And the fireman said — you must have abdominal
breathing — which is true — I have — he said he could use
me in the glee club and I went down there and gave
them a few notes how they were delighted — they asked
me to sing to them — actually I wanted to do the
Fishermen of England but they said they'd never get them
all on stage — but I went from Iolanthe to Hiawatha
hardly pausing to draw breath + there was many a tear
When the time came f. me to return to London — They saw
me off to the strains of 'Will ye No . . . . but of course I
don't know + obviously neither did they 'cos the train was
on the other platform. I ended up in Ballahulish
Where they were expecting Webster Booth + Anne Ziegler
Well obviously I don't look like either of them and their
chagrin was awful to see. In fact I said to one of 'em —
eye I can see your chagrin + he said no its me fur
sporran moulting + anyway you shouldn't be looking
But I digress here — I began by telling you something about
this good lady here — Miss Joan Sims + her unfortunate experience
on the step ladder — actually she accepted Comforts invitation — she
thought Sgt. VanDyck was Dick VanDyck — I told her after
it was the C.I.D. — She's v. naive — she said whats that? I said
they're the one's that you send for when your house is burgled +
they pinch all your stuff she said there's nothing in my house
to pinch — I said what about you — you're a valuable
commodity aren't you? She said nobody would ever pinch
me, so I gave her a playful nip + enlightened her — she really
is naive you know — on this quiz game they asked her
the difference between a fly and a wasp and she said — oh I don't
know, I never undone a wasp . . . .

Peter Rogers: 'They all said that, but I don't think they meant it. You see, what they used to do, they used to get the script and ring each other up, and say, "You going to do it?" "You going to do it?" "Yes, I'm going to do it." "All right, I'll do it." Joan Sims said it was like going back to school. On the set the first day, if they weren't called, even not called for shooting, they turned up. Just to be with the crowd. And in the restaurant downstairs, the waiting staff will tell you it was the happiest table in the restaurant.'

❛ He was lying on this bed, and she was slapping some salve on his penis, and he was thoroughly enjoying himself ❜

It was observed, as the series developed, that any Kenneth Williams screen performance was subject to certain limitations. He often said, though few accepted his valuation, that his was 'just a vocal talent', but it's certainly true that the voice came first, and to some extent at the expense of other parts of his performance.

Peter Rogers: 'He couldn't do two things at once. He couldn't answer the phone and talk to you. Something about coordination that he just couldn't do. We found that out eventually. For instance, he couldn't pick up a glass and then hold it and talk to you. On one occasion, I think it was on *Carry On Regardless*, for some unknown reason he fell down the back of the flat of the set, and squeezed himself in an unmentionable part of his body, so we took him along to Medical, and in Medical at that time there was a nurse/sister who you could have cast in a Hammer film. And he was gone for so long, and Gerald and I went down to Medical, thinking where the hell is he, and he was lying on this bed, and she was slapping some salve on his penis, and he was thoroughly enjoying himself, he could have stayed there all afternoon.

'He seemed funnier to me on the radio because, like Sellers, he had this wonderful range of voices. But he wasn't the mimic that Sellers was. [Williams's] voices were original. Now you know Stanley Unwin's gobbledygook, Kenneth can invent his own, just talk to you for hours on end and you don't know what the hell he's saying. And he would invent Shakespeare; he'd come up to you and

'This was at a charity Art exhibition, that Hattie Jacques was hosting and it was at the
Chelsea Town hall. I am sure you know that the lady with the glasses is Anna Karen:
Olive from **On the Buses**, and now my sister, Aunt Sal, in **EastEnders**.' (**Barbara Windsor**)

he'd make very rude, outrageous passages which he said came from Shakespeare and of course they didn't at all, he was making it up as he went along. He was a very clever chap.'

His cleverness was naturally reflected in the casting process, which frequently required Kenneth to play senior professional men with a certain academic background. In spite of his own lack of formal education, the voice of authority came naturally to him. Peter Rogers liked him best in his several medical roles.

Peter Rogers: 'When he's a doctor going round the wards, I think. He does a wonderful throwaway on one occasion, passing the bed, I think he says something like, "And syringe his ears out while you're at it!" He just throws it away. I don't think anybody really gets it, but it's there. He threw it in himself.'

Kenneth and Lou, tagging along with Barbara Windsor and Ronnie Knight on their honeymoon in Funchal, Madeira, 1964.

This he would occasionally do, although it was not a practice encouraged by the producer or director.

Peter Rogers: 'We didn't like ad libbing in the pictures at all. You can't make comedies with ad libbing. The ad lib he did in one film or other, I don't know which one it was – which I got blamed for by the press for being so vulgar – he goes to the loo, and then he comes out and someone's waiting to go in, and he says, "I'd give it a minute if I were you." I mean, that was his own idea. We kept it in. It wasn't written.'

❛ He went on my honeymoon with me. It's a long story. I won't go into all that ❜

Though Kenneth was no romantic lead, it was not out of the question – as it would have been with Hawtrey, for example – for him to be cast in a possible male–female relationship.

Peter Rogers: 'Well, although he was, you might say, a bit of a neuter, you could always team him with a romance. And he was always being chased by Hattie, of course, round the desk.'

Barbara Windsor joined the cast when it was already well established, and so felt doubly vulnerable during her first day on set.

Barbara Windsor: 'And I knew Bernie Cribbins well, and I said, "What have I got to look out for?" and he said, "Kenny Williams. He'll get you." And I knew that he had a terrible dislike of Fenella [Fielding] at that time. And my first line was, "Oh, hello, sir!" and he had this terrible black beard around him as he was playing a spy. And I goofed, I got it wrong. And he went, "Oww, duckie, do get it right!" And I said, "Don't you have a go at me with Fenella Fielding's minge-hair round your chops!" And he went, "Oww, ain't she lovely! I *like* her!" And that was it. He went on my honeymoon with me. It's a long story. I won't go into all that.'

'I had to be photographed with the group and chat with a girl from the Evening Standard. All useless. You want publicity when the film's released, not NOW.' **(Diary, 17 April 1978)**

On the set of the penultimate – some say, final – **Carry On** film, **Carry On Emmanuelle** with Joan Sims, Kenneth Connor, Suzanne Danielle, Jack Douglas and Peter Butterworth.

Kenneth's critiques of his own screen presence often dwelt on his overactive facial musculature. A certain amount of frantic mugging came to be expected of him, but even so it was sometimes excessive. He was saved, in Peter Rogers's view, by the cinematographic house style of the *Carry Ons*.

Peter Rogers: 'He did make funny faces. Of course, we didn't go in for a lot of close-ups in *Carry Ons*. There's nothing funny in a close-up – nothing funny in a tree. That's why we didn't have much location!'

In between takes, the cast generally behaved as if they were in a doctor's waiting room. They had few long speeches to negotiate, so there was no nervous anxiety about learning lines.

Carry On Cruising with Sid James, January 1962. According to Robert Ross, author
of the **Carry On Companion**: 'Kenneth, unhappy with his lowly wages for the series,
told [Peter] Rogers that he would only make the film if he had a pay rise. Peter assured
him this would be considered (it later came into effect with **Carry On Jack**) but
promised Kenneth that the filming would get out of the studio and on to a real ship for
a Mediterranean cruise. Williams agreed to star. Eventually the cruise around the Med
became simply a cruise around Britain, which, to Williams, was better than nothing.
Finally, of course, the money wouldn't even stretch to even that and the entire interior
and deck of the ship was built at Pinewood Studios.'

'Went up to the Fort they've erected on Camber Sands. I've got the monocle which I fancy is going to give me trouble.'
(Diary, 2 May 1967)

Kenneth with Lou and Sid James at the launch party for one of his twenty-six **Carry On** films, **Carry On Up the Khyber**, November 1968.

Peter Rogers: 'They were very good studies. He'd probably do the crossword or something, *Times* crossword. Hattie was very good at that too, they helped each other. Sat in a row, Kenneth Connor would make 'em laugh about something or other. Very good artist, that one, very good. He's another one, you see, with the funny voices and everything.'

All the more amazing was how well the two Kenneths got along. They had come into radio in much the same way, and must in many producers' minds have been considered rivals, each with his own vivid set of character voices. But Williams's affection and admiration for Connor never fluctuated. Nor did his fondness for Joan Sims, or for Bernard Bresslaw, with whom he would discuss the finer points of religious dogma. Yet Peter Rogers felt that Kenneth's real intimates at Pinewood weren't in the cast at all.

Peter Rogers: 'I don't think it was another artist. His closest chums were me and Gerald. Although he fitted beautifully into the team, and other people we had tried in the past didn't, he really wasn't with them, he was different. I mean he was always talking about Maggie Smith and the things he'd done with Maggie Smith. Well, that of course didn't interest Sid James, for instance, in conversation. All Sid wanted to do was get the cards out.'

At one point in the series Sid had a serious heart attack, so his place was taken in *Follow That Camel* by the American stage and television veteran Phil Silvers, best known all over the world for his Sergeant Bilko TV character. It was probably a mistake to mix comic traditions in this way, if only because the cast seemed disconcerted by the change. Kenneth was not the only one to show hostility.

Peter Rogers: 'They all were, including the crew. They didn't like the idea of the American. In fact he was rather like a new boy at school. I'm afraid – the only time I've ever done it – I had to get everybody together and say, "Now look, he's a guest and please don't keep sending him up so much." He couldn't remember his lines. It was the distributors' idea to try an American in the series, which I didn't think would work anyway. It worked *all right*, but it stuck out like a sore thumb, didn't hurt the picture. But they were very naughty. They were rather like schoolboys – I mean, not only the cast but the camera crew, and everybody, making fun of him.

'They weren't comics, they were actors playing comedy, and comics, you see, like Phil, stick out like a sore thumb amongst those people. That's one of the secrets of casting that sort of film, not to have comics. We did have Bob Monkhouse on the first one. It didn't work.'

Phil Silvers, in fact, brought perfectly good acting credentials from a career that had featured not just appearances on Broadway but one big hit there, *Top Banana* (Silvers won a Tony award). But certainly he was in decline by 1967, which made it all the more anomalous that his agreed fee was known to be, by *Carry On* standards, colossal — at £30,000, six times the standard fee for a leading cast member. Pinewood was not Hollywood. From time to time Kenneth Williams would wonder if, for the next *Carry On*, a car would be provided to deliver him bright and early to the studios. He could have saved his energy.

Peter Rogers: 'No artist ever had transport in a contract. They had to provide their own.'

Filming a *Carry On* was an event in itself, and the kind of spectacle that could be offered as a treat to Pinewood's visitors. Kenneth's mother did not drop by in the way that was habitual with her in the radio and TV worlds, but when ladies of a certain age did appear on the studio floor it would be Kenneth, as likely as not, who would assist in their reception.

Peter Rogers: 'If he thought it was wanted of him, he would, and he'd do it in a most outrageous, uncensorable way, but nobody worried. I remember on the floor one day the Lady Mayoress of Wolverhampton came down on a visit to the studio for some unknown reason, and he told her in front of me the most outrageous story, and she didn't even blush. When he finished they just laughed. Just took it. That was him.'

> ❛ I think a lot of the things that have been said about Kenneth are his own fault, because he does love to pull your leg ❜

Away from the workplace, at the occasional dinner, Rogers and Williams would find other things to talk about, especially music. The shared a fondness for Fauré. 'But I always found him a rather vulnerable character, I wanted always to put my arm round his shoulders,' Rogers said. 'But then Kenneth was worth taking care of, because while he cost very little — £5,000 a film — he made a very great deal of money for the franchise.'

With Peter Rogers, the producer of all 31 **Carry On** films.

Peter Rogers: 'I think a lot of the things that have been said about Kenneth are his own fault, because he does love to pull your leg. I know, I haven't read it, but I've been told that in some book or article or something he said that I turned up on location with green wellies and Rolls-Royce and a chauffeur! I've never worn green wellies in my life! But it was a lovely story for him. He loved sending you up. Sometimes I'd come on the stage and he'd come straight up to me and say, "I've got a complaint." I used to say, "Well, I'm not surprised." Then he'd say he didn't like his dressing room, didn't like this, that and the other, and you listened for a little while and then you'd stare him out, and he'd burst out laughing. He's just trying it on. I liked him very much, I was very fond of him. You couldn't not be. He was a very soft, nice person.'

Beyond
our Kenneth

‘ He used to say, "When I'm gone, I shall be a cult!"
And he is. The answer is that he was multifaceted.
Different ages and different sections of society
remember him in their own way ’

Michael Whittaker

Above, and page 226 How poignant that Kenneth should wear a black tie: this was one of his final photo sessions, shortly before his death.

It's difficult to imagine how long Kenneth Williams's fame will last. Will a public who never knew him continue to puzzle over his contradictions? Each generation of comedy devours and digests the last, so that a comic personage as rare as Chaplin may ultimately come to be almost despised because his vast inventions have been recycled. His sentimentalities, which we cannot use, seem to stick out the more offensively. Buster Keaton survives better by going out of his way to 'say' less, signify less, on the screen. By that measure, the future of a gabby exaggerator like Kenneth Williams looks discouraging. But his image and reputation will no doubt survive, when the comedy itself has finally died of old age. It happens to the greatest.

One thinks, for example, of a great comedic figure of a century and more ago: the music-hall hero Dan Leno, born George Galvin, who died aged 43 in 1904, probably of a brain tumour. There are remarkable parallels here. Leno was born in St Pancras ('under Platform One', he used to say), the heart of Williams territory. His mother, like Kenneth's, was called Louisa, and when comedianship took over Leno's career from clog-dancing, one of the best characters he portrayed was a hairdresser, like Ken's dad. Small and slight, Leno became known in time as 'The Funniest Man on Earth'; but while good descriptions of his stage presence exist, and he did make a burst of recordings in the earliest years of the twentieth century, much imagination is required to recreate his manic, capering presence on the stage.

What we read of Leno, however, is strikingly consistent with what we know of Williams. Max Beerbohm, Leno's most faithful supporter among the intelligentsia, wrote of the 'air of wild determination that possessed him, squirming in every limb with some deep grievance that must be outpoured'. Only Kenneth's face truly squirmed, but his grievances were multitudinous. Beerbohm insisted that Leno was not, properly speaking, a comedian, but a magnificent actor with amazing vocal resources, from which he extracted two seemingly incompatible effects: his truth to life, and his batty surrealism. 'He knew thoroughly, inside and outside, the types that he impersonated,' Beerbohm

'At 7.30 to Boot pub where we filmed the "Signora" and "Hawkin' me greens." The pub was full of undesirables ... and a gaggle of queens who made several esoteric remarks while the cameras were rolling!' (Diary, 8 June 1983)

Comic Roots, a half-hour BBC documentary that reconstructed Kenneth's most vivid childhood memories in their actual locations.

wrote. 'He was always "in the character", whatever it might be. And yet if you repeat to anyone even the best things that he said, how disappointing is the result! How much they depended on the sayer and the way of saying!'

If there is one modern performer whose 'way of saying' is the entry point to his world-view, it is Kenneth Williams. His world does not become comically mad until you *hear* him describing it. Beerbohm's ruminations look all the more pertinent when you examine the scripts of the *International Cabaret* TV show, where, for a time, Kenneth Williams had to adopt the techniques (and flirt with the desperation) of the stand-up comedian. The scripts are frequently weak, and in the same optimistically punning way that Leno's seem often to have been; but in both cases you can see exactly how the artiste felt he could get away with them. Both men were virtuosi of the vocal swerve. Sometimes there is nothing really funny on the page, except an abrupt change of tone – the very trick that Beerbohm drew attention to in Dan Leno's standard presentation.

Finally, what Beerbohm saw in Leno was a powerful concentration of Englishness, such that nobody seeking to understand what the English were about should fail to see in him. In fact, Beerbohm used to take foreign visitors along to witness Leno at work, especially in pantomime, where the theatrical tradition was itself as ripe with local flavours as the star of the show. England at the time was already bristling with confident symbols of itself, from Queen Victoria (or her son) on down. But what interested Beerbohm was something much more organic: the compendious temperament and social mobility Leno displayed, as he flitted from character to character, always alighting on his home territory ('the sordidness of the lower middle class, seen from within'), but never actually secure anywhere.

Compare the social situation today. The English, never exactly sure of who they are, find themselves doubly baffled as they wrestle with a new role as hosts to the world, with over 250 languages now spoken within a five-mile radius of Kenneth Williams's birthplace. Though he died only twenty years ago he actually belongs to an era of settled Englishness more like Dan Leno's than ours. In those fascinating utterances where he sweeps from aristocratic disdain to raucous guttersnipery in the pace of a single sentence, Williams is drawing a quick map of the territory where the old class battles used to be fought; territory where different cultural struggles are now taking place. It's hard to say which is the more marvellous assemblage of almost bygone types – the ones he acted (doddering aristo, ancient jobsworth, snide informer, ingratiating queen, etc.) or the ones he embodied in real life (scolding autodidact, rhapsodic poetry-lover, tipsy hobgoblin, terrified sexual fantasist). You can make up as many types as you like, and somewhere, Kenneth will have been each one; sometimes as a comic character, sometimes as himself.

Having talked about him for fifteen years with interested parties of varying involvement and intensity, I get the feeling that people are in some half-realized way proud of Kenneth Williams, for having at least courage enough to act out his confusions. There is a paradox in the way he set about dismantling the whole idea of 'English reserve' – affronting marchionesses and polluting restaurants with egotistical noise – while replacing it privately with something even more stultifying. But it's not beyond understanding. John Lahr, one the wisest observers of showbiz figures, once remarked that it was in order to beat down his own panic that Williams created panic around himself, and that feels right. He was a mass of checks and balances, compensations and diversions – a whole machinery of psychological adjustment, which he drove, as if it were some fantastical old steam contraption, struggling onward under the load of its own obsolescence.

Kenneth's friend Sheila Hancock believes that we all benefited from the struggle. 'There was a fountain of venom and bile and anger, and being English that's difficult to deal with,' she once said. 'In England we have to be so proper. And Ken was a kind of expression of the demon inside all of us.' But he didn't vent those feelings altruistically, on our behalf. On the contrary, according to John Lahr, who once toured with Kenneth, advertising Lahr's edition of Joe Orton's diaries. They went to Cambridge, and entered from the back of the hall where their audience was already seated. 'And I've never seen this before in any other performer,' Lahr recalled, 'but he started talking before he hit the aisle, and he talked up the aisle, he talked on to the podium, he took his coat off. And what I found fascinating about that was that the whole performance, his language, he really used this language as a kind of shield ... He felt dead inside. People speak themselves, pronounce themselves to the world, as proof that they exist.'

Occasionally a visitor from overseas, observing the general interest in this barely exportable creature, will chucklingly say something like: 'Why do you torture yourselves about this guy, who only tortured himself?' The answer, I think, lies in an understanding that the British are somehow brought up to have: not just that that comedy and despair live side by side, but that comedy informed by despair becomes meaningful rather than merely amusing. There wasn't much personal comfort in that for Kenneth Williams, though he recognized the mechanism in others. Of Maggie Smith, he once wrote: 'She is the only actress in the world who can give you the whole coin: pathos & comedy together, sometimes teetering on the brink of lunacy; it is brilliant.' And so was he.

'Every time I see this girl act I am filled with admiration. I was so proud and privileged today to be sitting next to such an actress. Such incomparable style, such careful delineation, such vulnerable fragility.'
(Diary, 18 January 1973)
Dame Maggie Smith, DBE.

KENNETH WILLIAMS

Plan for an Autobiography, March 1969

appearance – chorus girl suggested (Gordon Jackson recent space & diary) 5 March '69.
if music looking at you – were finished then. Naked, Scene

1) 1) Labels – Errors – actor & the lines posterior
   2) Titles – Doctor –
   3) Romantic – Idealist – Realist – The realistic novel – will be written

2) School – beginning of playing –
   Poetry – master who taught it –
   Teacher opens a door to the SPIRIT
   of a subject – show QUALITY
   rather than measurable Quantity
   MEANING rather than explanation.

   The OLD order change to
   Yielding place to new

3) School play.

4) Drama Group.   Guitry – Villa for Sale

5) Career – Choice – PARENTS –
   Apprenticeship

6) Army career – transfer to
   Entertainments – SINGAPORE
   meeting with more TEACHERS – influences
   Barker, Nichols, Schlesinger –
   introduction to writers – Gordon Craig
   Bernard Shaw, Gorchakov – (Staniss. S.(director))
   & Eric Bentley.
   Army Shows – what one did in them

②

7) Demob. Back to drawing office
            leaving   "   "
            Despair

8) Baxter

9) Rep — First one. Newquay.

10) Progression through various reps
    to Grand Swansea / Clifford Evans.
    Stanislavsky — v — Rhienhardt
    Illustration of production
    1) Murderers walk into crowded room
    2) Hugo shooting him — OUTSIDE CURTAIN.
    Lydia Sherwood — one of Komisarjevsky's
                          most brilliant pupils
    Rachel Roberts — now wife of Rex H.
    Richard Burton _____

11) next progression to Monthly rep.
Luxury – for Henry $\overline{VI}$ parts 1.2.3
Producers preamble – gang of thugs etc.
Why droops my Lord? etc. etc

12) London Production – FIRST.
ST JOAN. – Siobhan McKenna.
My role – in the play.

How it led to Hancocks Half Hour.
The man – Hancock – What if there is no god.
The idea of the comic (as opp. to Comedian)
As a Tragic figure – Tragedy meaning the
~~Setting of the Human~~ Man Overstepping certain
Natural LIMITS – there are all present
in Greek Drama Prometheus Oedipus – Orestes – etc.
the parallel in Adam + Eve – the lesson
of arrogance + the disregarding of a Sacred
Command – a refusal to obey – to recognise
a certain LIMIT and the awful consequences
that proceed from it —

④

$^{3}_{13}$)

13) Moby Dick — Orson Welles.
     Open Stage Production. First Experience
     Illustration of playing for a laugh — actor
     " originally playing Keni. told to play Elijah the prophet
     " What Exactly Do you want me to do?'

(Do?) ~~Stand~~ within 3 feet & do your damndest —

     Experience of working for an ACTOR —
     EMPLOYER — what it MEANT —
     One vision truly carried out / HE
     was there every night to see it

     Orsons description of the English
     ~~Middle~~ Classes vowel sound —
     pinched & snobbish. Lacking generosity
     Theory of American pronunciation
     Pilgrim Fathers — Plymouth
     —

     effect of environment on Speech.
     Heat on lips — Java, China etc
     Displaced European —   Australian
     affected by Climate + natives   S. African

(5)

14 Orson asked me to go America/ Elijah
Octavius / and fool in Lear
(he played it in a wheel chair)
My other offer to play "Buccaneer"

15
15 The musical. The fundamental ridiculousness
of it — to me — Singing the LINES — instead of
saying them — illustrate — ~~this they & Solo~~
Berlioz — Faust —   O! My lover he is coming
Thy Hand is frozen   Yes he's coming down the hill
                            O! he's coming yes hes coming

If you can say for certain sure
That you'll be true to me, then I'm your Pal
Just your pal
But remember that it
Must be purely spiritual —

———

The inability to DANCE
despair of the choreographer —

(16) Peter Grenville's production of   2 INCIDENTS
Hotel Paradiso — Difficulties
of STYLE — Lack of tradition
in England as opposed to the Comedie Francaise
Maxime — a part that has no real LOGIC
can only be played for STYLE + STYLE is
what is lamentably lacking

Distinguished actress — it BAFFLED her
why don't I get that Laugh?

Her: We must get out of here quickly —where's my hat?
Him: oh! dear! I left it on the landing!
Her: That's charming — you left it on the landing

Style — wrong for the playing etc.

___

Coming thro' the window
TROUSERS — etc.

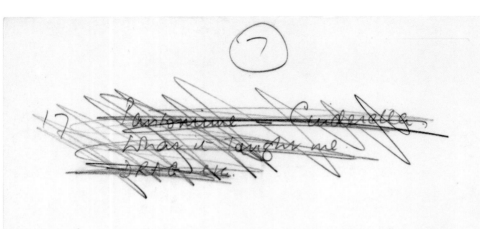

17 ~~Pantomime — Cinderella~~
~~What it taught me.~~
~~RADA etc.~~

───────────────

19 <u>Revue.</u>   <u>Share My Lettuce</u> /

Not a revue at all in the <u>WRITING</u>, / One
~~only in the~~ Nor in the playing — ONE AUTHOR.
essentially using one's own personality

Reflections of <u>ENGLISH ATTITUDES</u>

1)   Tea Party Sequence

2) \ The WHORE

3) √ The object — being asked IS MIND IT.

⑧

(18)   Pantomime Cinderella

Drag — all the problems it raises.

9

(19) Back to revue — But this time
more truly in the sense of a collection
of items — characterisation etc.
Authors — Harold Pinter
Sandy Wilson
Lionel Bart
Peter Cooke etc. etc

Two authors complained about my
interpretation.

1) Pinter — Coffee stall sketch. PAUSES.

2) Bart   Mardi Gras   Quality of writing

/o

(20) <u>Second revue</u>

why it was Bad.

---

(21) Shaffer Plays
Authors original idea / Dickensian
working with Maggie. (character)
Idea of IMMEDIACY in
playing on Sustained
melodic notes.

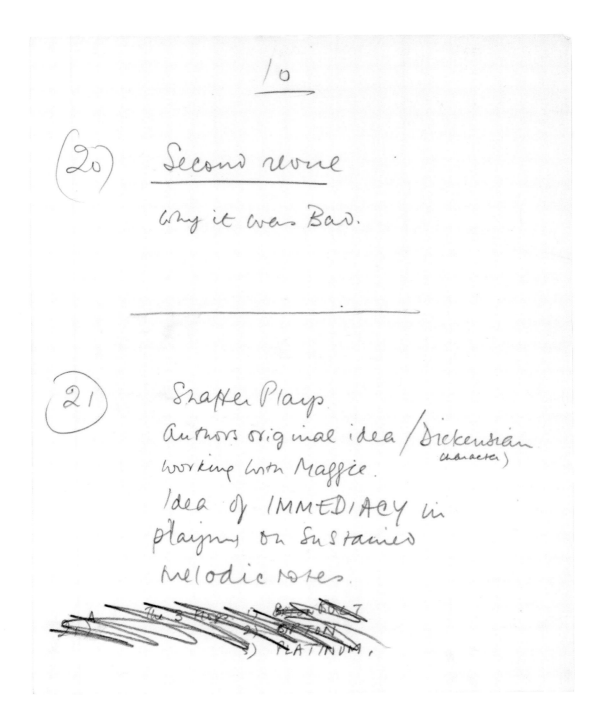

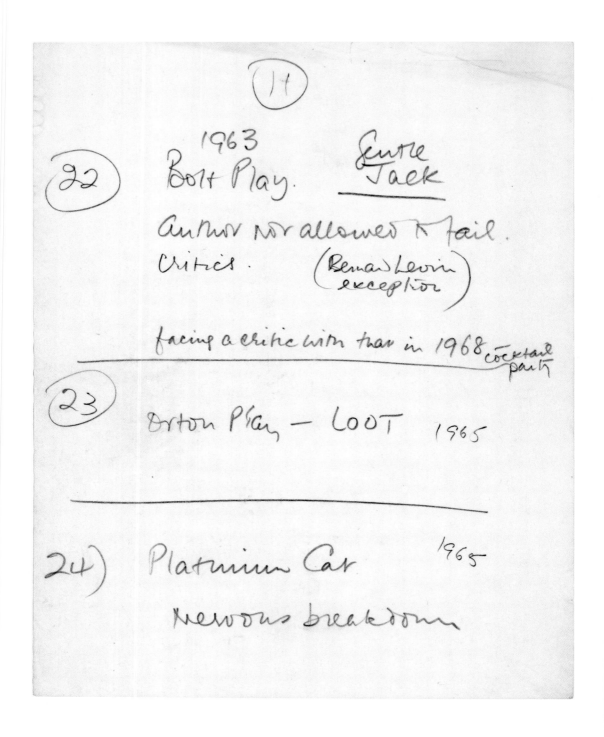

11

22

1963
Bolt Play.   Gentle
                Jack

Author not allowed to fail.
Critics.   (Bernard Levin
             exception)

facing a critic with than in 1968 cocktail
                                      party

23

Orton Play — LOOT   1965

24) Platinum Cat   1965

        nervous breakdown

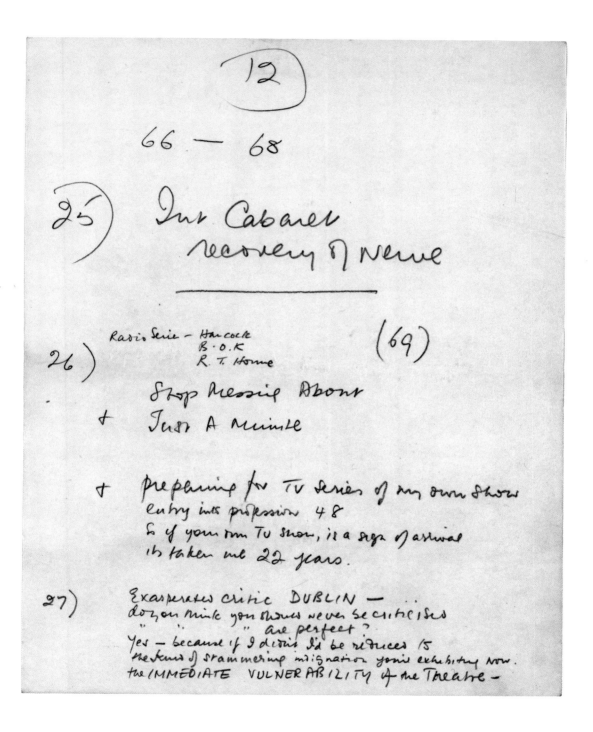

(12)

66 — 68

25) Int Cabaret
recovery of nerve

_____

26)   Radio Serie – Hancock   (69)
                    B · O · K
                    R. T. Home

      Stop Messing About

+   Just A Minute

+   preparing for TV series of my own show
      entry into profession 48
      So if your own TV show, is a sign of arrival
      its taken me 22 years.

27)   Exasperated critic DUBLIN — ..
      do you think you shows never be criticised
         "   "   " are perfect?
      Yes — because if I didn't I'd be reduced to
      the kind of stammering indignation your exhibiting now.
      the IMMEDIATE VULNERABILITY of the Theatre —

28) Irony of being led closer to Christianity thro the
theatre
by agnostics — SHAW starts serious
Enquiry (ST JOAN) — his religious irreligiousness,
the production of Family Portrait — the
Beethoven Hymn of Creation — the L.C.C.
County Hall. Lost.

Nor irony. Proper. Because theatre as we in
Europe know it — grows out of the first enactment
of the Morality Play which is born of the
Organised Church.

Dilemma of the inability to worship
in Community. Need to spread the WORD —
as Eliot says — "we learned many MORE WORDS
here
but LOST THE WORD

we must be forever rebuilding the Temple.
But are we perhaps WRONG to think of bricks & mortar
Perhaps if we accept — where two or
three are gathered Together in my name
there is a church . . . . — . in any
case thats another Subject for another
day — its only purpose here is to
let you know what side I'm on

KENNETH WILLIAMS

Personal Scripts

" PARTY LINE "

by Derek Collyer

THE CORNER OF A ROOM: SOUNDS OF A PARTY IN
PROGRESS. KEN STANDS ALONE FROM THE CROWD,
TENTATIVELY FINGERING HIS GLASS.
TWO GIRLS ARE IN CONVERSATION NEARBY.
ONE LEAVES. SEEING THE GIRL ALONE, KEN SQUARES
HIS SHOULDERS AND WALKS OVER TO HER, FIRMLY.

KEN: (SUDDENLY AGGRESSIVE) I've decided to
talk to you.

GIRL: (STARTLED) Pardon?

KEN: (EVEN MORE AGGRESSIVE) I said; I am
going to talk to you. Any objections?

GIRL: (CONFUSED) Well - er - no.

KEN: Don't turn away, don't look around -
I'm talking to you, right?

GIRL: Er .. yes.

KEN: Because I read about it in a magazine
article, see? To get yourself a woman you've
either got to be aggressive or submissive.

GIRL: Oh yes, I read that too....

KEN: Shut up. Aggressive or Submissive.
Well all my life up to now I've been submissive.
And what's it got me? Nothing worth having, I'll
tell you that. So I've decided to be Aggressive.

The Kenneth Williams Show, produced by Terry Hughes, 1976. The role of the girl
was played by Claire Neilson.

- 2 -

GIRL: But surely....

KEN: I said shut up woman and listen while I'm talking!! It said be Frank, Forthright and To the Point.

GIRL: So?

KEN: ~~So it's been a very nice day, hasn't it!~~ *So this is a lousy party isn't it*
~~Hasn't it!!.~~

GIRL: ~~Yes.~~ *Well I thought it was quite pleasant*

KEN: ~~And she looked lovely in white!~~ *They're all boring out there*

GIRL: ~~Who did?~~ *Oh? Do you think*

KEN: ~~The bride!~~ *Yes I do think ——*

GIRL: But it's not a wedding.

KEN: ~~Don't argue with me!~~ Frank, Forthright and To the Point. So I'll level with you. I don't drink a lot so when I've had a few of these I get ~~randy~~ *sexy*. And when I get ~~randy~~ *sexy* I need a woman. So you and me are going to get out of here, get in a taxi, go back to my place and have a right old ding-dong. Right? Right??

GIRL: If you say so.

KEN: Right!

- 3 -

GIRL: Don't go away, I'll go and get my
coat.

KEN: You just do that!

SHE LEAVES SHOT. KEN WATCHES HER GO, AND
SOFTENS.

KEN: (FALTERING) You - do - that. (SUBMISSIVE
SELF) Blimey it works! Works on the wife
anyway - next time, p'raps I'll try it on
some bird I don't even know.

. . . .

Tag?

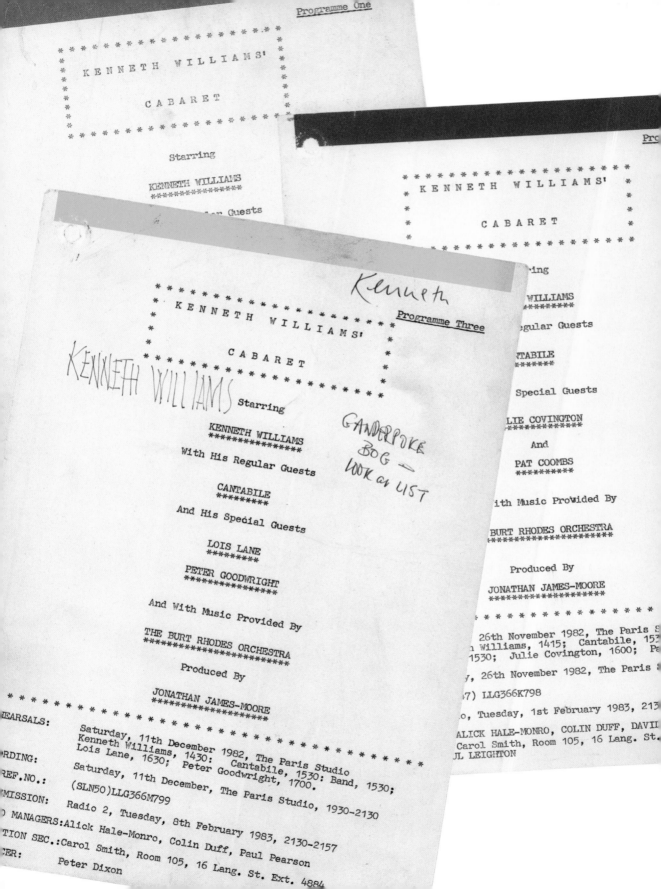

1.

1.	BAND:	<u>OPENING SIG.</u>

B.Rhodes=M/S=B.Rhodes

2.	ANNOUNCER:	Ladies and gentlemen, Kenneth Williams' Cabaret.

For the next twenty-seven minutes, starting now, without hesitation, repetition or deviation, but with interruption from star guests, you will be in the company of Mr. Kenneth Williams

3.	KENNETH:	Good evening and may I say what an honour it is for

you to have me. Since the last show, the BBC has been bombarded with calls! People crying out for more! We want sagacity and great wit, bring back the great wit! The producer said are you the great wit? I said me, the great wit? No, you great twit! I'm a cult. I am your actual cult figure, I'm the biggest cult going - in fact it's been given the wrong slant in some quarters - some listeners got the cult mixed up with the occult - they thought I was dabbling! 'Cos I'm a dab hand at the old ouiga board you see - one rap for no, two raps for yes and three for the bilinguals - Anyway, there was a flood of correspondence about the Astral Plane. They told me never to cross water when Mars is under Uranus - which I never would anyway - it wreaks havoc with the plumbing - never eat oysters when there's an R in the month, never eat a Swiss Roll on a Monday, I wouldn't eat a Swiss Roll any day, what's wrong with a British Roll - nothing!

CONT'D OVER/

Kenneth Williams' Cabaret (Programme One), produced by Jonathan James-Moore, 26 November 1982.

1.	BAND:	OPENING SIG.

2.   ANNOUNCER: Ladies and gentlemen, Kenneth Williams' Cabaret.
For the next twenty-seven minutes, starting now,
without hesitation, repetition or deviation, but
with interruption from star guests, you will be
in the company of Mr. Kenneth Williams.

3.   KENNETH: Good evening and welcome to half an hour of radio
fun, frippery and frolic - it was to have been an
hour actually but half the show got cut on account
of the script writer was half cut and the titular
heads didn't approve. I said you're quite right,
he shouldn't wear those high heels - it was a
disgrace - I mean, inebriated is one thing but he
was blowing on his birthday cake and lighting the
candles! And some of the ideas were ludicrous!
Wanted me to come on in the ~~doiva~~ slingbacks,
diamante bodice and singing - 'Light the lights,
clear the tracks, you've got nothing to do but
relax....' I said no thank you, it's not me -
I'm more your suave, butch compere with the dulcet
tones doing the good evening and welcome bit -
you notice how I do it trippingly on the tongue -
effortless isn't it? Good evening and welcome -
no strain. You must never strain your opening
announcement, your greens yes, but not your
opening announcement.

CON'T OVER/

Kenneth Williams' Cabaret (Programme Two), produced by Jonathan James-Moore,
26 November 1982.

HOWARD IMBER

_____

THE KENNETH WILLIAMS SHOW.

LINK TO SKETCH "VICE IN VERSE".

KEN: Here - I was having a bit of a moan
                        to the Producer this morning. I said "Look,
                        why can't we have a bit more culture on this
                        show?" I said "Just look at all those great
                        works of literature - they were all done in
                        verse. And they're still going strong". I said
                        "Shakespeare's in verse, Chaucer, Dylan Thomas,
                        Eskimo Nell". I said "We're so mundane. Let's
                        have some warmth - some feeling - let's have
                        some poetry. After all, who wants prose all the
                        time. I don't get any warmth and feeling
                        from prose". He said "You ought to try Eskimo
                        Nell".

                        Anyway, he agreed. He said "Get on
                        with it then. So I have. Mind you - it's
                        lucky I'm good at poetry. I've been writing
                        poetry for years - on and off - I write it
                        on and the attendant comes and wipes it off.
                        Anyway - I know you're all aching for a bit
                        of real culture - so here goes...........

CUT TO COURT SCENE.

Pages 254–258 'I remember chatting to him after the recording of this – a courtroom scene in limerick form. He loved it, dressing up in his ermine as the Judge! He altered the script a bit but I didn't mind.' **(Howard Imber)**

HOWARD IMBER

THE KENNETH WILLIAMS SHOW.
SKETCH. "VICE IN VERSE".

SET: A COURT SCENE. KEN AS THE JUDGE. VARIOUS SOLICITORS,
POLICEMEN, WITNESSES AND JURY. THE DEFENDANT IS NOT SEEN
UNTIL HE SPEAKS. GENERAL HUBBUB.
THE JUDGE BANGS HIS GAVEL. THE COURT IS QUIET.

1st POLICEMAN:	Call Algernon Marmaduke Sprout.
JUDGE:	Go steady, there's no need to shout.
SPROUT:	(UNCOUTH) I'm here, you great bum,
1st POLICEMAN:	Now just watch it chum,
JUDGE:	Oh, come on now - stop messing about.

CLERK STANDS TO READ CHARGE.

CLERK:	The accused, last Monday, did go Sir,
	In the Newmarket Ladies Enclosure.
	He lost his shirt and his pants,
	On a ten to one chance -
JUDGE:	Ooh - and the charge is indecent exposure.
JURY:	(SING) That was a cute little crime,
	Tell us another one,
	Just like the other one,
	Tell us another do.
JUDGE:	Now then, there's no need to be mucky,
	Let's hear our first witness - now duckie,
	Were you on the spot?
2nd POLICEMAN:	Yes - I saw the lot,
JUDGE:	Caw - stone me, aren't some people lucky.

HOWARD IMBER.

THE POLICEMAN READS SLOWLY FROM HIS NOTEBOOK.

2nd POLICEMAN: I was standing close by him throughout.

      He was starkers without any doubt.

      He hadn't a shred,

      So I went up and said,

JUDGE: (IMPATIENT) Oh, come on now, stop

      hanging it out.

THE DEFENCE SOLICITOR RISES.

DEFENCE: M'lud.....

JUDGE: Who are you?

DEFENCE: The defence.

JUDGE: ~~So~~ you are - ~~aren't I flippin'~~ dense. *So you are, 'course you are aint I dense*

DEFENCE: I submit it's unjust,

      To accuse him of lust,

JUDGE: Alright, don't get cross - no offence.

DEFENCE: There's a witness that I'd like to bring.

      She says she saw the whole thing.

WOMAN: It was ever so short (GIGGLES IN COURT)

JUDGE: ~~Silence in court~~ *a tree*

WOMAN: (RETIRING) Well, it were just like a

      ~~small piece of string.~~ *in that case you'd see, the whole thing from quite diff angle*

JUDGE: Well, I think it all sounds most improper.

      What did you do next, tell us Copper.

2nd POLICEMAN: I gave him my helmet,

JUDGE: What - to use as a pelmet?

2nd POLICEMAN: Yes - that's true......

JUDGE: Ooh - it sounds like a whopper.

HOWARD IMBER.

WOMAN:	I said to him "Mate, you are dirty".
	And, you know, he got ever so shirty.
	He streaked off down the course,
	Yes, just like an 'orse,
JUDGE:	Oh, so it was him who won the three-thirty.

Defence

PROSECUTION: A photo was called for M'lud

My Client's a quick thinking man
+ devised an ingenious plan

(HANDS JUDGE PHOTO AND POINTS)

He produced a blue pencil
and a kitchen utensil
with his face in a hood

That's him look, all covered in mud.

It's not all that clear,

JUDGE:	Oh, don't worry dear,
	'Cos the main parts are ever so good.

what you
might call a flash in the pan —
Well Sprout

JUDGE:	Well, Sprout, you can tell us your side.
SPROUT:	There's no need Sir, I've been fairly tried.
	And as my missus said
	Only last night in bed,
	She said "Sprout, you've got nothing to hide".
JUDGE:	Well, Jury, you've sat through this trial,
	Do you wish to retire for a while?
FOREMAN:	There's no need to go out
	(POINTS TO PHOTO)
	It's the end of young Sprout,
JUDGE:	Yes, that's obvious - it sticks out a mile.
FOREMAN:	*He's guilty - as red as his face is*
	Sir, a verdict of "Guilty" we bring,
JUDGE:	*in all of these cases*
	So, the sentence can be just one thing.
	It's quite clear to this court
	You've no means of support,
	So you'll obviously have to wear braces —
	So, I'm afraid - you'll just have to swing.
	Legal aid will supply you with braces

HOWARD IMBER

GENERAL UPROAR. THE JURY STAND TO SING:-

JURY: Oh, what a terrible crime,

Let's have another one,

Just like the other one,

Let's have another one do.

KENNETH WILLIAMS

Wit & Wisdom

The nice thing about quotes is that they give us a nodding acquaintance with the originator which is often socially impressive.

> **Caesar:** *Bilious — what are you doing with your thing?*
> **Bilius:** *I'm sorry Sir, but for the good of Rome you must die!*
> **Caeser:** *But you're my personal bodyguard and champion gladiator, I don't want to die! Treachery! Infamy! Infamy! ... They've all got it in for me!*

On falling in love: *'I don't think it's possible with someone like me. I'm a complete egotist, you see. My world revolves about myself — first thing in the morning I look in the mirror and think "Ooooh, ooooh, what a dish!" This wonderful figure, you know? And this hair? Spun gold — it's been described as spun gold!'*

I heard this man say to another man in this club in St James', 'I've just come from Evita.' And the other one said, 'Oooh, you don't look very brown.'

'Mr Horne, how bona to varda your dolly old eek!'

There was a young man called Clyde
Who once at a funeral was spied
When asked who was dead
He smilingly said,
'I don't know I've just come for the ride.'

Critics are like eunuchs in the harem: they're there every night, they see it done every night, but they can't do it themselves.

'Aphrodisiacs – like oysters – if you don't swallow them quickly your neck goes stiff'

On his autobiography: *I was going to call it* A Cult Chronicle *or* Chronicle of a Cult. *Because I am a cult figure, I'm an enormous cult … I am! I'm one of the biggest cults you'll get round here, I can tell you!*

‘Matron, take them away!’

Doctor: *You may not realize it, but I was once a weak man*
Matron: *Once a week's enough for any man!*

How lovely to see you all and may I say,
what an honour it is for you to have me here tonight

‘Stop messin' about!’

‘I've got a viper in this box, it's not an asp’

Sandy: *Oh, Mr Horne this great wave came! Oh, terrible great wave Mr Horne! Washed us over board! I was clinging to the deck Mr Horne! Clinging for dear life!*
Horne: *Did you manage to drag yourself up?*
Sandy: *No, we wore casuals.*

This lady said 'Emma Chessit' so she put down, 'Best wishes to Emma Chessit'. Then this woman said, 'What you written in 'ere?' She said, 'Your name — Emma Chessit.' 'I said how much is it!'

'Hello me deerios. Well, tonight I shall have great pleasure … But first of all …'

It's ridiculous, isn't it! I've come all the way from Great Portland Street to be treated like a load of rubbish! I mean, just kick me as you pass, I say!

The Khasi of Kalabar: *They will die the death of a thousand cuts!*
Princess Jelhi: *Oh, but that's horrible!*
The Khasi of Kalabar: *Not at all my little desert flower, the British are used to cuts!*

'Frying tonight!'

On being an actor: *There has to be a degree of arrogance because I don't think anyone could walk onto a stage and ask a whole mass of people — be it 500 or 2000 — to look at him without his saying, 'I am worth looking at.'*

During a heated debate on Parkinson: *His inference is the man who's sticking the doorknobs on has got a job that is monotonous and dreary … What do you think about doing something night after night — I've done this play now at The Globe, I mean I've said it so many times, I'm beginning to wonder what it means!*

❝Mr Williams, you have … a spastic colon!❞

Most of the time, last thing at night, I am praying and I am asking for the sins to be forgiven and the trespasses to be forgiven.

❝Go on Kenny, show us your diction!❞

I'm asexual. I should've been a monk. I'm only interested in myself and I would regard any kind of relationship as deeply intrusive and anything which invaded that would be a threat, so consequently I live a life of celibacy … I'm not interested in the other. The whole idea of other people's adventures in that sphere, I must say well good luck to them! It seems to me a very messy business.

Afterword

by Wes Butters

' I wonder if anyone will ever stand in a room that
I have lived in, and touch the things that were once
a part of my life, and wonder about me, and ask
themselves what manner of man I was '

Diary, 22 April 1963

It was January 2006 and fate was to strike, again. As I thumbed through my well-worn copy of his diaries, the introspective entry Kenneth had written forty-three years previous stopped me in my tracks. It was prophetic to say the least: there I was, surrounded by 'things that were once a part of [his] life', and the words were speaking about *me*.

Some weeks prior to this, a casual surf of the auction website eBay had led me to a pair of framed photographs of Stanley Baxter and John Vere, buried deep amongst 'Oooh Matron!' key rings and *Carry On* novelty mugs. The description

simply stated, 'Once belonged to the late great Kenneth Williams'. The starting bid was £9.99. There were no bidders.

Thinking about it, Williams has shown up in my life quite a few times. Aged ten, I can vividly recall begging my mum to buy me *What A Carry On – The Official Story of the Carry On Film Series*. I adored the series because, for me, *Carry On* land was an ideal place to live: a happy, cartoon-like world, where everything, and everyone, was colourful and funny. Funny voices and funny people – exactly how I saw myself: the joker of the class, the one who did impersonations of the teachers. Then there were the times I spent watching *Willo the Wisp* and *Galloping Galaxies* after school, entranced with the vocal ability of the 'funny man out of the *Carry Ons*' who I'd also seen on *Wogan*, telling silly stories about how he'd wear a jockstrap when he'd next guest present the programme, and bragging to the audience about being the biggest 'cult' in the business.

I scrolled back up the page to find out if the seller was reputable, moreover that the inscribed pictures I had stumbled upon were genuine. His name was vaguely recognizable. But was it a coincidence or could it be the same person? I clicked on 'Email the seller' and punched out: 'Dear Mr Chidell, you're not by any chance Kenneth Williams's godson are you?' His response arrived the next morning: 'Yes, and I've got more stuff to put on eBay in the coming weeks.' I have never typed an email as fast: 'No, please don't do that. How much would you want for ALL of it?' He replied with a rough list of what he had, named his price and offered to personally deliver it all.

My fears that it was a hoax were allayed when the afternoon of our meeting arrived and a car pulled up outside my flat. Robert Chidell emerged, accompanied by his mother Angela. When her then 12-year-old son was named a beneficiary in Kenneth's will, her reaction was splashed across the media: 'Kenneth left Robert a lot of personal effects which we will treasure', she said, unaware that her following line would be the reason for him eventually selling the bulk of it. 'He enjoys skate boarding a lot – but only after he's finished his school work of course.'

Nearly two decades later, in need of money for a snowboarding holiday, Kenneth's godson was unloading those same personal effects onto my doorstep.

'I remember going round to his flat and my mum saying, "Just take what you want"' he told me. 'There were a few things in his desk that I was told I could choose. I think being a kid my mum wanted to keep things quite simple for me. She said, "Ok, let's have a look. What would you like?" And then my mum said, "We may as well take his clothes because they're of no use to anyone anymore."'

It intrigued me that Robert appeared unaware of Kenneth's continued fame, yet there was, I sensed, a genuine love, even though he'd only met him a couple of times: 'When I was about 8 or 9, I was at my granny's, and he turned up. He was making us all laugh so much. It's one of the few occasions, being that young, I keeled over, laughing. My stomach was curling in! I can't remember what he was saying but it was something to do with space. He had me in fits of laughter. I've never really seen it as a claim to fame but I used to tell everyone Kenneth Williams was my godfather. It wasn't showing off, I was just very proud of it. I never wanted to make anything to my advantage of him, his death, or my connection with him. I wanted to do the best that I could with his possessions which is why I'm glad I met you.'

There was one question that I just *had* to ask. For no matter how many hours spent on the web or ploughing through the twenty or so books that deal with Kenneth's life or career, there has been no conclusive answer: whatever happened to his diaries? (I was once shocked to read that they'd been burnt by a friend of Kenneth's terrified of the sexual secrets they would reveal if ever released unabridged.) 'I had them all in my bedroom. Loads of boxes. His whole life, under my bed at my mum's. I dipped into them here and there, wanting to have a look at what he'd written and how he felt. I did try and search through them looking for the last diary entry but because there were so many it was impossible. They weren't insured – how can you insure them? – so I guarded them with my life. But then I had to sell my half of them to Paul Richardson because I owed him for some legal bills. I don't know where they are now.' (Locked away in a London bank vault, I've since discovered.)

For nearly two hours, Robert guided me through the treasure trove. I admit I was desperately trying not to get too over-excited should he then decide to double the price or, worse still, have second thoughts about selling them. Finally he opened the last bag and began to take out Kenneth's clothes. Shock prevented any verbal reaction, I just sat and observed this rather morbid fashion show: a camel-coloured full length coat, a dinner jacket (from, one imagines, Kenneth's time hosting *International Cabaret*), a silk scarf, another coat from Marks and Spencer's (bought from his favourite branch on Oxford Street perhaps?) and a tweed coat that I recognised instantly as the one immortalized on the front cover of Michael Freedland's 1990 biography. (Stanley Baxter thinks Oxfam is the answer, but surely they belong in a museum?)

Soon after, through my friend David Benson (the actor who plays Kenneth in his acclaimed one-man show *Think No Evil of Us*), I was introduced to Michael Whittaker, Kenneth's closest and most loyal friend, a high-powered businessman renowned for his vow of silence when it comes to his most famous chum. David had shrewdly used my purchase as a way to meet him and within 24 hours we were gathered at Michael's Chelsea flat carefully examining the collection. Over the lunch that followed Michael volunteered countless unheard anecdotes and was encouraging when I said it would make a great book.

Quite suddenly I had found myself, for want of a better phrase, deep within Kenneth's inner-circle. In time I was introduced to the other important Michael in Kenneth's life, Michael Anderson. Then, Paul Richardson, who is now the sole owner of the diaries. Gradually, by mixing with those that truly knew Kenneth, the promise of a new biography – the first in over fifteen years – with their exclusive interviews, and my unseen material, looked ever more possible.

By April 2007, I learned that the epicentre of so many of Williams's myths and legends, Marlborough House, was to be demolished. The toilet he forbade anybody to use, the barren four walls of his living room, the kitchen with the stove covered in cellophane and a cabinet bursting with his 'capsules of poison' and, of course, the lone bedroom where they ended his life – gone forever. A diary entry four months before he died has Kenneth make reference to the reason behind this: 'I've got reliable assets of about 180 thousand, but *that* is earmarked for a home when this flat proves invalid. The lease is up in 2000 and whatever happens I mustn't bank on staying here.' Even though residents and Kenneth fans had protested since the Millennium's expiration, the land was indeed sold and the entire block of flats was making way for a new office development.

'Coming over on the bus the bulldozers had reached his flat. They might have finished it off by now,' announced David Benson to Michael Whittaker and I as he arrived at another of our lunches. It seemed likely that the opportunity of a final look at the apartment had been missed, even so, a pilgrimage to see the mound of rubble seemed appropriate. As fate would have it, the workmen had called it a day, leaving the wrecking ball to swing gently in the breeze next to Kenneth's flat that perched precariously on the edge. And then it entered my mind.

'We could get in there, take some pictures?' I said to David, half serious, half hoping he'd say no – but he was thinking along the same lines.

We assessed the situation, agreeing on a midnight break-in, wearing nothing but black, and working out how best to scale the scaffolding that encaged the building.

Over the next few hours, we went about our separate lives before reconvening. I began to have serious worries about getting caught and, rather than lose face, was hoping David would be the one to call it off. Potential newspaper headlines raced through my mind as I tried to take a nap, praying for him to have a change of heart: 'Ex-Radio 1 DJ and Kenneth Williams impersonator arrested in condemned building' or 'Carry On Don't Break Your Leg'. But the phone rang and the voice said, 'Ok, come and pick me up.'

We arrived at Marlborough House at midnight. The busy junction it overlooked was still bustling with traffic and revellers making their way home after a Saturday night on the town. It would be three hours before we could attempt our daring venture. David described his own futile effort in his online blog:

Miraculously, work had ground to a halt at the wall to Kenneth's bedroom (second bay window down).

'Appalled at my own bravery I found myself heaving my carcass up onto the wooden base of the scaffolding and reaching up to the first bar. Got it! Next part was to reach up to the bar above that and somehow pull myself up onto the planks of wood that constituted the lowest walkway. This was where the weakness in Wes' plan immediately became apparent. I soon realized that to achieve this stage of the journey would require me to belabour my entire body weight above where my head now was, with no purchase for my feet other than the slippery scaffolding pole. It was like being in a P.E. lesson all over again. I felt a surge of inadequacy flow through my body and, just like at school, I gave up. At once. No point in trying to pretend I could do it – just quit and admit defeat.'

We reversed roles: David was now on lookout and I was waiting for his green light. The adrenaline took over the moment it came. Without looking back I flew up the scaffolding some thirty feet to the second floor. I passed the blue plaque that read, 'Kenneth Williams 1926–1988 Comedy Actor Lived Here 1972–1988' (which was, in fact, put outside the window a floor below because the new owners refused to have it outside theirs), and grabbed the ledge of

Kenneth's bay window, thankfully left open a few inches. Unceremoniously hauling myself through it, I gingerly dabbed my hands and feet on the cold concrete floor, tapping my way through the darkness, convinced that this would end in tears, that it was only a matter of time before I'd shuffle into a gaping hole and plunge back to the ground. As my eyesight adjusted I could see the place had been totally gutted: an old sofa and a bathtub lying incongruously side by side, a cooker standing in the hallway, the missing front door exposing the communal stairwell and lift, and slabs of concrete and debris strewn everywhere. In the hallway, on the right, a small bathroom with broken tiles and Royal Doulton sanitary ware – the very toilet Kenneth Williams had fussed over religiously for sixteen years, now shattered into a million pieces. The next door led to the galley kitchen, where his hob was always protected by cling film and the cupboards would overflow with medicines instead of food. Then the final door through to the living room, ironically just as empty as he had kept it, and the walls still painted a cold white. Which meant the room I had entered was the bedroom – his single bed and writing desk only visible now using one's imagination.

His haunting diary entry of 22 August 1963 came back into my mind: 'I wonder if anyone will ever stand in a room that I have lived in, and touch the things that were once a part of my life, and wonder about me, and ask themselves what manner of man I was.'

In the shadows, I stood in his bedroom and wondered.

Since this all began I have found myself asking 'what if?' – What if I hadn't logged onto eBay that night? What if I hadn't have searched Kenneth Williams? What if the seller wasn't his godson? What if Robert Chidell had insisted on selling every bit of the collection piece by piece on eBay? What if Michael Whittaker had, as with every other request, refused to speak to me about his enigmatic friendship with Kenneth? What if I'd have arrived at the flat too late to see it one last time?

And, what if Kenneth hasn't asked himself questions in August 1963?

I think that this book will, after many years, provide the answers, by allowing us *all* to touch the things that were once a part of his life, and to each ask ourselves what manner of man he truly was.

I certainly would like, I suppose, to be thought of as someone that enlivened people's moments, diverted them from troubles for a little bit of the time, anyway. I would like them to say that he had a serious side. I would like them to say that he had another dimension. I think when my time comes I'll disappear in a flurry of talcum powder.

affectionately

Kenneth

Sources

Russell Davis (ed.), *The Kenneth Williams Diaries* (HarperCollins, 1993)

—— (ed.), *The Kenneth Williams Letters* (HarperCollins, 1994)

Kenneth Eastlaugh, *The Carry-On Book* (David & Charles Publishers, 1978)

Michael Freedland, *Kenneth Williams: A Biography* (Weidenfeld & Nicolson, 1990)

Sally and Nina Hibbin, *What a Carry On* (Hamlyn, 1988)

Brian McFarlene, *The Encyclopedia of British Film* (Methuen, 2003)

Robert Ross, *The Carry On Companion* (B.T. Batsford, 1996)

Joan Sims, *High Spirits* (Transworld Publishers, 2000)

Kenneth Williams, *Acid Drops* (Dent, 1980)

—— *Back Drops* (Dent, 1983)

—— *Just Williams* (Dent, 1985)

Credits

Photographic

Pages 10–11 © Hayden Productions, Page 12 © LWT, Page 27 © Terrence Donovan, Pages 44 and 46 © Top Foto, Page 85 © BBC, Page 88 © Helen Craig, Page 99 © BBC, Page 111 © Granada Television, Pages 118–119 and 121 © John Schlesinger, Pages 147, 152 and 156 © BBC, Page 181 © BBC, Page 182 © John Bratby Archive, Pages 185 and 186 © BBC, Page 206 © Ian Jeayes, Pages 220, 221 and 225 © Ian Jeayes, Page 229 © BBC, Page 264 © Lewis Morley Archive/ArenaPAL, Page 273 © Lewis Morley Archive/ArenaPAL

Scripts and Songs

Pages 93–94 © Peter Nichols, Pages 165–167 © Barry Took and Marty Feldman, Pages 248–250 © Derek Collyer, Pages 251–253 © Kenneth Williams, Pages 254–258 © Howard Imber.

Index

Carry on Kenneth dies after op scare

Kenneth Williams in Season

DESCRIPTION² SIGNALEMENT

Bearer Titulaire   ★Wife Femme

Profession } ACTOR
Profession }
Place and d
of birth
Lieu et d
de naissa
Count
Resi

MR. K.C. WILL

BRITISH PASSPO

DECCA
AUDIO ENTERPRISE LTD.

45 rpm

KENNETH WILLIAMS

"Hawkin' Me Greens Abaht"

THEATRE . . . by JOHN MORTIMER

So much fun when Williams is around

REVUE is a notoriously tricky thing to create. For at least half of the evening the two members of the company who can act must be provided with material of breathtaking wit.

The audience can then be plunged, every four minutes into total darkness

lying cockney